Chess Training Pocket Book

300 Most Important Positions and Ideas

Grandmaster Lev Alburt

Second, Revised Edition

Published by:

Chess Information and Research Center
P.O. Box 534
Gracie Station
New York, NY 10028

For ordering information, see page 188.

Distribution to the book trade in North America by:
W.W. Norton, 500 Fifth Avenue, New York, NY

Editing Services: ***OutExcel!*** Corp., Al Lawrence, President
Technical Editor: Mark Ishee
Proofreaders: Peter Kurzdorfer, Virginia Roberson
Typography: JM Press
Photos: Nigel Eddis; on the cover Olga Zoueva and GM Lev Alburt

ISBN 1-889323-14-4

Library of Congress Catalog Card Number: 99-066851

10 9 8 7 6 5 4 3 2 1

Printed in the United States of America

Foreword

You want an approach to learning that gives you the maximum results in the minimum amount of time. The idea of the *Chess Training Pocket Book: 300 Most Important Positions and Ideas* is just that simple. When you study any one of these positions, you can be sure that you are acquiring an important, practical piece of chess knowledge. Indeed, the major portion of all practical chess knowledge is represented in this little book of 188 pages. It's a small book, but its construction has taken me a lifetime!

I've devoted my teaching life to getting the quickest possible results for my students. Each position here is distilled from thousands I've shown to aspiring players both in Russia and the U.S. over the decades. Each diagram holds something special and important for you.

Not surprisingly, this most time-efficient approach is also the approach that leads my students to both the deepest understanding and the most enjoyment of chess. Wasting time has nothing to recommend itself!

This is a pocket book —a *vade mecum*—, meant to be carried with you in many contexts. It can be productively studied in almost any situation. Even a few minutes with a single position often pay dividends, and revisiting the same position frequently will make sure it becomes a part of your "active" playing knowledge.

So skip around, open the book to any page, and have fun. For, besides practical knowledge, there is beauty—and even humor— in these positions! It's not so important that you solve a position the first time you see it. It is important that it becomes a part of your knowledge, and a kind of helpful friend for life.

Chess is an enriching exercise, especially for your brain. It will keep you sharp and creative. Enjoy yourself—and let me know your comments and suggestions!

Grandmaster Lev Alburt
Former European Champion
Three-time U.S. Chess Champion
New York City, 1997

Contents

International Grandmaster Lev Alburt

Grandmaster Lev Alburt was born in Orenburg, Russia, on August 21, 1945. For many years, he lived in Odessa, a Ukrainian city located on the Black Sea. A three-time champion of the Ukraine (1972-74), he became European Cup champion in 1976. In 1979, while in West Germany for a chess competition, he defected and came to the US, making his home in New York City.

Mentored by three-time World Champion and eminent teacher Mikhail Botvinnik, Grandmaster Alburt first taught chess in the Soviet Union. He is now in the forefront of the innovative movement known as "the new chess pedagogy," which seeks new ways to teach chess to both beginners and more advanced players, regardless of their ages or backgrounds. GM Alburt's *Comprehensive Chess Course* is one of the most important works of this movement.

GM Alburt has won the U.S. Championship an impressive three times—in 1984, 1985, and 1990. He is known as the "Grandmaster of chess teachers." He is the only top-echelon GM to devote his career to teaching those below master strength.

Currently, GM Alburt is a popular columnist for *Chess Life*, a best-selling chess author, and a renowned teacher. He provides lessons through-the-mail, over-the-telephone, and face-to-face. Write to GM Alburt at P.O. Box 534, Gracie Station, New York, NY 10028, or call him at (212) 794-8706.

Chapter One: Making the Most Out of this Book

Making Your Time Count!

This book is written specifically for the non-master who wants to become a strong tournament player in the shortest period of time possible. Of course, it's also a great book for masters to use to review and retain the knowledge that earned them their rank.

Finding what's important is most of the battle; remembering it is the rest! We hold this truth to be self-evident: Not all chess knowledge is created equal. A chess player must sift the gold nuggets from the silt. Otherwise, he can waste hundreds or even thousands of hours of life, acquiring knowledge that is of little practical value. And because it's impractical, it can't be often used or even remembered for very long anyway!

The simple truth is this: To become a strong tournament player, you must indelibly carve into your chess memory a certain *limited* number of *essential* positions and concepts. As similar situations arise in your own chess games, these memories stir and come to your conscious mind, alerting you to the best course of action. Naturally, increasing levels of skill require an increasing number of essential positions and concepts. Experts have a greater storehouse than the average club player.

The purpose of this book is to provide you with the 300 positions essential to becoming a strong tournament player.

Chess Positions as "Zipped" Files

Those familiar with computers know that, to send information quickly and to store it in the smallest possible space, electronic files are "zipped" or compacted dramatically by

special programs. On retrieval, they can be quickly "unzipped" to burst into their full detail. The 300 positions in this book are very much "zipped files." Engaged with the "special programs" of your own problem-solving skills, each position will expand and make connections that provide volumes of chess-playing knowledge.

> Here's a promise: To be a strong player, you do not need to know hundreds of King and Pawn endgame positions—but only 12 *key* positions. Of course they have to be the right positions—and they're in this book! To be a master you do *not* need to know thousands of King and Pawn endings. You need to know 50 key positions.

As an example, let me introduce you to a specific position that will become an old and trusted friend, one you'll see again as position #133 on page 92.

White to move

This position alone contains perhaps a full 50% of the knowledge needed by a tournament player to play King and Pawn endgames well! So the right positions, effectively explained, can be more helpful than volumes and volumes of off-target "instruction."

Water under the Bridge—You're Supposed to Forget Things!

Let's be honest about our common human failings. I've been a world-class GM for decades, and I forget things about chess. A chess player's knowledge of the fundamental patterns and concepts can be compared to a city's water reservoir. We always want to add to the pool to increase our resources, but, at the same time, we realize that water—like some of our chess knowledge— is sure to evaporate. It's a law of nature. Here the analogy ends, because water is water, but chess knowledge can be divided into a hierarchy of importance. I make it a point to review and remember the crucial things.

While we can afford to let relatively unimportant information "evaporate," we should conserve the essential knowledge, to remember the most important, useful information. There are a number of ways to make sure that this essential knowledge is never forgotten and remains immediately available when a situation calls for it.

Each week, you can make diagrams of several positions that you feel are important to remember. You can put them in a conspicuous place, such as on the refrigerator door, or bedroom or bathroom mirror, or taped to your computer monitor, where you can glance at them every day. You can use a file card system. Or, if you use a computer, you can set up a special database to store positions for daily review. At the end of the week, you can move these positions to a file for review on a less frequent basis, e.g., once a week or once a month, replacing the old examples with new ones for your daily review.

One of the simplest and best ways to retain the critical knowledge is simply to carry this conveniently pocket-sized book with you in all sorts of different contexts—traveling, taking a break from work, having a quiet moment with your coffee in the morning. By revisiting these 300 positions frequently, in a variety of contexts, you'll make them never-to-be-forgotten, old friends who will come to your aid on many occasions.

And, like the friends they will become, there's no order that's best to meet them in. Group them, take them in page order, or simply open the book randomly, it's all the same.

Building a Personal Theory

To become a strong player, you will find it very helpful to begin to compile your own personalized chess theory. The greatest chess minds, such as World Champion Wilhelm Steinitz and Dr. Siegbert Tarrasch, developed their theories, of course, and as they did, they became world-dominating players.

These legendary players developed their own theories by studying how different kinds of moves and plans affected the nature and outcome of games—both their own and others'. You should begin to compile archives of positions that mean the most to you. The 300 positions in this book provide you with a foundation to build, revise, and expand your own "personal

theory" of the game. As you continue your chess growth, add to your archive those positions that communicate essential ideas in ways that are especially meaningful *to you*. And relocate or delete positions that become redundant or not as useful. Let them evaporate. Remember, isolating what's truly important is most of the battle!

In compiling your personal theory, you may find that you can profitably reorganize the material by themes. For this purpose you can photocopy the pages for your own exclusive use. Of course, it may be cheaper or more convenient to buy an extra copy and cut out the diagrams for this reorganization. Since the same position may embody several themes, e.g., decoy, Queen sacrifice, back-rank mate, etc., you may even find it useful to copy a position as many times as it takes to file it under all the themes it contains. One of my students who jogs several miles a day carries a few, torn-out pages from second copies of earlier volumes of my *Comprehensive Chess Course* so he can continue his studies and train his visualization abilities—in this case, literally "on the run."

Archiving your own games will confirm that you are moving to the highest level of learning! "Learning" is a single word that has a lot of different meanings. Educators speak of a "hierarchy of learning" that is best followed in sequence to learn a concept in depth. What we call "knowledge" is sometimes really just the first rung on the ladder of learning.

As chess players, we first learn to identify—to name— a back-rank mate, then to recognize when others use this idea effectively, then to identify situations that hold potential for such a mate, to find these mates in problems, and then finally, to synthesize our knowledge and create back-rank mate threats in our own games. This last step is the highest level of learning, and the one most chess players seek. For without it, we're forever restricted to the ranks of the "appreciator"; with it, we join the ranks of the creators.

> It's extremely effective for you to archive positions from your own games. Record positions in which you faced problems and made errors in tournament play or other important encounters.

Include brief annotations containing the concrete lines of play that would have resulted in a more desirable conclusion. Also include notes on how to avoid any mental lapses that may have led to the errors.

Among the 300 positions that represent the knowledge necessary to becoming a strong tournament player, some positions do need to be memorized (e.g., Philidor's key Rook and Pawn endgame). But the exact positions that best convey broader conceptual ideas may differ a bit from player to player. That's why compiling your "personal theory" is so important. For instance, different examples can be used to demonstrate the theme of back-rank mate. My favorite example is #1, Bernstein-Capablanca, on page 26. I find that it sticks with me and reminds me of the important characteristics of such positions. But you may find another position more meaningful to you.

Whether you use a three-ring notebook, a card index, or a computer, the positions that represent your own theory can be effectively organized into opening, middle game, and endgame positions. Each of these categories could be divided further, if you wish, into types—for example, Sicilians separated from Queen's Gambits, middlegames with open files separated from those with pawn barricades, endgames with passed pawns separated from those without them. And each of these subcategories can be again subdivided by tactical devices or strategic themes.

> The 300 Positions selected for this book will be useful to everyone, and will alert you to the kinds of positions and ideas that are essential to the development of your own theory.

To be a Good Player, Did I Have to be Born with Special Skills?

No one is born with special skills. Some of us are born with special potential, but no one can even know this potential exists until we develop it into skills or abilities. The great world champion Emanuel Lasker said that anyone of reasonable intelligence could become a chess master—with the right training.

> So the simple answer is that you were probably born with the potential to become a very strong chess player, a force to be reckoned with by even titled players like myself.

One important way that this book is different from other puzzle books or books on tactics is that solving these specially selected positions will combine the learning of essential knowledge with the training of all these essential *abilities* or *skills*.

Use This Book to Develop Both Your Analytical Skills and Your Intuition!

Following the process we're describing in this chapter will take you naturally to the point of developing your skills. One particularly valuable chess playing skill is keeping positions clearly in mind. We call this skill *visualization*. Visualization is an important tool in *concrete analysis*, in which you work your way through the important lines by visualizing the sequences of moves, and in this way divining the future of a position.

But another important ability is to study the elements of a position and—without visualizing many variations or perhaps even any at all—have an idea (some players call it a "feeling") of what the right move or plan may be. Using highly developed intuition, great masters can play five-minute games that are marvels of chess art. This *intuitive skill* is often compared to "inspiration," and is sometimes seen, incorrectly, as simply a gift from God. But we all have the potential to develop our chess intuition, because it is really the result of developing our knowledge to the highest levels of learning.

To train *intuition*, give yourself just one or two minutes per position. When you first begin intuition training, you may be able to solve only one or two positions out of eight correctly, being confident that you are correct and seeing the reasons why. You may also solve another one or two by guessing without really knowing why you are correct. This is a perfectly acceptable score for the kinds of positions that I have chosen for this book, even for an expert!

To train your *analytic* ability, however, you must build up to giving yourself a much longer time period, for example, 20 minutes per position. Imagine yourself having reached a critical juncture in a tournament game, where it is important to calculate very carefully. Under real conditions you must check and recheck to make sure you have calculated correctly, and you must be sure you have accurately visualized the positions that result at the end of each variation.

Under analytic training conditions, your goal is to score at least 75% correct. You should do lots of double checking!

Combine intuition and analysis in probing the same position. Try combining the two approaches. Choose a position you want to study. Apply your intuition for one or two minutes, and make a written note of your choice of moves. Then use the position for analytic training, spending about 20 minutes for a complete analysis—without moving the pieces. When you finish, record your lines. You can work from diagrams or from the position set up on a board. (Most players profit a little more by taking the time to set up the position, and then studying it on the board; this process more closely approaches real playing conditions.) Take care that you are accurately visualizing the end of each line. Then move the pieces as you might in an adjourned game to verify and expand the depth of your analysis.

The Sequence of this Combined Intuitive-analytical Exercise Could Be:

- Studying the position for two minutes applying intuition;
- Analyzing in your mind for up to 20 minutes (or even longer in very complex positions);
- Setting up the position on a board and moving the pieces to check your analysis.

Try out these different approaches. Invent your own. Have fun! Whatever training technique results in pouring the essential chess positions and concepts that are contained in this book into your pool of chess knowledge is the right one for you.

Training with Groups of Positions

There are several ways in which groups of positions can be used. Two of the most effective that I use with my students include one that was developed by the famous trainer IM Mark Dvoretsky for his grandmaster candidates.

Dvoretsky's training method. Dvoretsky has his students set their clocks for twenty minutes, and then gives them four positions to solve, one at a time. In this exercise, you are thus faced with balancing your desire to verify your analysis of each position carefully against the need to make a decision. After all, you have to complete all four positions within the time limit. In a real game, if you move too quickly, without having thought deeply enough, you may choose a "safe" move, but, by not choosing the best move, you may find your position deteriorating. On the other hand if you think deeply and make a fine move, you may find yourself in time trouble, and be forced into making bad decisions later.

> Finding the right balance between intuition, analysis, and time management skills is the object. And this is a practical, game-winning skill indeed!

After each position in this Dvoretsky exercise, you stop the clock and check your answer. If correct, you start your clock and go on. If incorrect, you deduct up to eight minutes from your remaining time before going on. Vary the penalty depending on how far off your solution is from the correct one—is it simply not the best move, or is it an outright blunder? You can also vary the time allowed for this kind of exercise, giving yourself more or less time depending on your strength, or on whether you want to concentrate on developing analytic or intuitional skills. For instance, if you solve everything correctly in just 12 minutes, reduce the time to 10 minutes. Or, if necessary, you can increase the time until your skills improve.

Alburt's antidote to tunnel vision. Once years ago, I had a student who, in spite of his considerable experience, had a habit of sticking with a single line of analysis at critical junctures, even when there were actually several attractive candidate moves. He did this even when his chosen line became unclear. I realized that this habit is common to many players. So I invented an exercise to get him to pay attention to all logical candidates, given the time constraints he would face in practical play. I now use it to great advantage with all of my students.

Once again, choose four positions. Your task is to solve just one or two of the four in 10 to 20 minutes, depending on your strength. You may even consider solving one out of four as a draw, and two as a win.

How to Think!

Aaron Nimzovich, the great theoretician and one of the original grandmasters crowned by Czar Nicholas at the St. Petersburg tournament of 1914, used to stand on his head in the corner of the hall before a tournament game. I suppose he wanted to increase the blood available to his brain, hoping this would help him think more clearly. But you're expecting some advice that's a bit more practical, and you deserve to get it.

Use candidate moves. When you tackle any position, whether here in this book or in your own games, first make a mental note of all the moves that suggest themselves—the candidate moves. Sometimes the very best move leaps to mind immediately—that's your chess intuition at work! But usually two, three, or even four come to mind. If one candidate move seems much better than the others,

begin analyzing it immediately, and continue until you see either that you can reach a successful conclusion, or that the line becomes murky. Or you may even find a flaw.

> **Go Forward in Reverse!**
> A useful rule of thumb:
> Reversing the move order often works!
> (For example, look at position #21 on page 36.)

Since time is always a factor, the moment you find a move for your opponent that makes the outcome uncertain, you should try another candidate move. Make a mental note of what you've discovered so far, and go on.

How to Think about a Position

- Intuitively choose the candidate moves.
- Start with the most appealing candidate move and analyze it. If it leads to a desired outcome, make it. (If you have enough time, take a brief look at the other candidate moves to see if any of them promise something better.) If its outcome is unsatisfactory or unclear, begin to analyze the next-most-appealing candidate move.
- Keep mental notes on your discoveries as you go along. The "tricks" in one line will often recur in other lines—and may sometimes suggest a new candidate move to consider.
- When your intuition tells you that there should be a forcing combination in the position, but your concrete analysis can't make it work, try the brainstorming technique of reversing the move order.
- In a timely fashion, make a decision. Write your choice on your score sheet, and then—before actually moving the piece on the board—verify it with a fresh look at your selected move. If it holds up, make it!

The 300 Most Important Chess Positions are Next!—What Should You Expect?

You'll find that the diagrams in this book are arranged four to a left-hand page. Their solutions are given on the facing, right-hand page. Every four-position group lends itself to the various training techniques I have suggested in this chapter. In addition, each position can be taken by itself and studied in any way you choose. One way to determine which approaches work best for you is to take a few positions and work on them, one at a time. See how long it takes for you to decide on your preferred first move, and how long it takes to work out any variations to their endpoints.

As we've seen, I have chosen only those positions that I consider to be most important for becoming a strong tournament player. Some positions illustrate essential concepts. Others, in their solutions, depict in a concrete way the most desirable placement of pieces in similar positions. You must be able to visualize these final positions in advance; for example, certain typical mating patterns—and you must know how to arrive at them from different starting points; for example, see #22, Menchick - Thomas.

You'll learn from 300 realistic positions. In serious games, no one will announce that you now have a position that you can win by use of a pin or some other specific tactical device! You need to learn when situations arise that suggest the possibility of one or more of any number of winning tactics. You need to learn how to entice your opponent into creating such opportunities for you. Sometimes we don't know if a combination is in the offing. Indeed, sometimes it is wrong to go for one. And sometimes strategic issues, not tactical ones, are important.

This book is designed to help you train for actual tournament play. That's why the book is not organized by themes.

The positions given in the main part of this book are carefully arranged, but not in a way that will give you clues on what theme or tactical device is used—or on how difficult your task may be.

And, unlike other books, but exactly like actual chess games, in some positions there is no win involved. In fact, sometimes the position is lost and the task is to find the course of action that makes it most difficult for your opponent to win. Even on the highest levels, many players in "lost" games have saved the draw, or even turned their games around completely by putting up the stiffest possible resistance. You want to find ways to set up a trap, to offer chances for your opponent to make an error, or to create complications that will force your opponent to use too much time and to get into error-producing time pressure.

On the right-hand pages, before the full solutions are given, all of the exercises have titles, and many have helpful comments that appear in *italics*. You can allow yourself to glance at these before formulating a line of play for the position if logical candidate moves don't immediately suggest themselves to you. Remember, your main purpose is not just to test yourself, but to develop your skills of intuition and analysis!

And have fun!

Key to Symbols Used in This Book

#	checkmate
+	check
++	double check
!	an excellent move
!!	an outstanding move
?	a weak move
??	a blunder
!?	an interesting move
?!	a dubious move
=	an equal position
±	White is better.
∓	Black is better.
+-	White is winning.
-+	Black is winning.
corr.	correspondence game

Chapter Two:
The 300 Most Important Chess Positions

1.

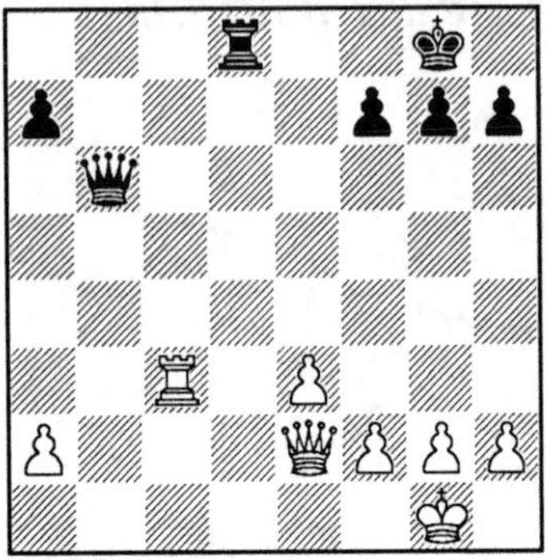

Black to move

2.

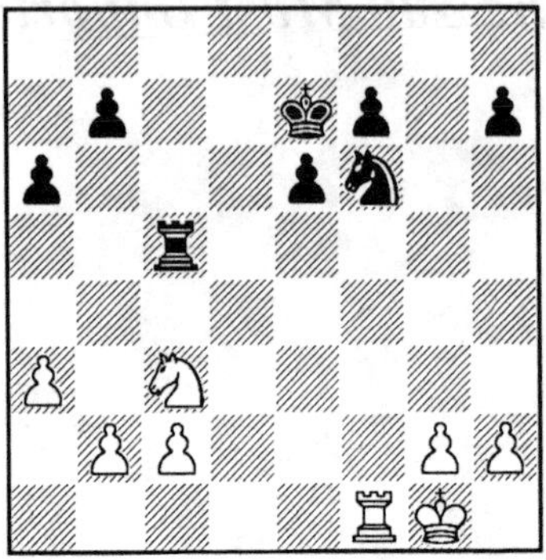

White to move

3.

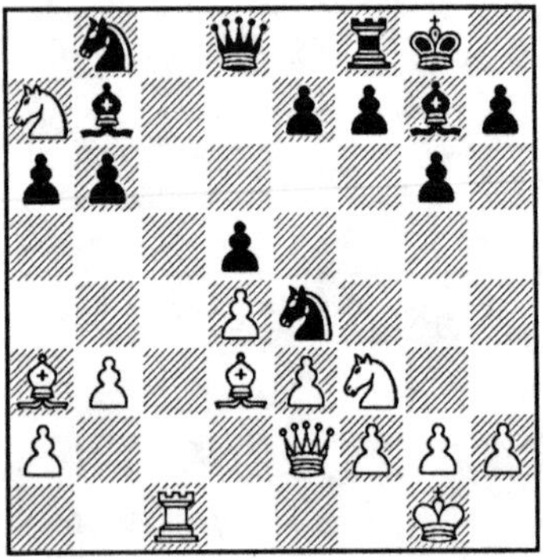

White to move

4.

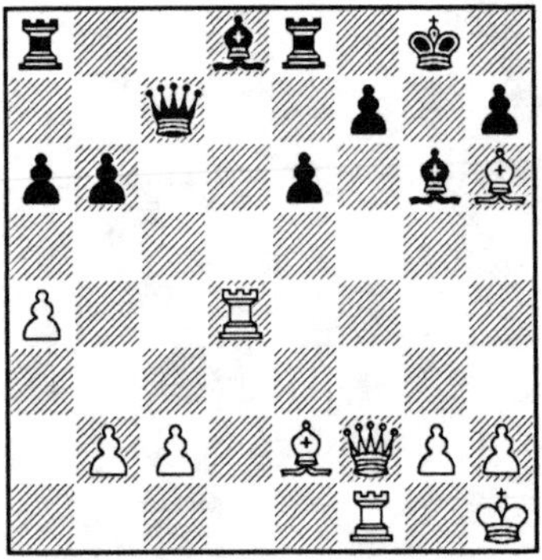

White to move

1. The Classic Deflection

Black can get a better game after 1. ... Qb1+ 2. Qf1 Qxa2 (not 2. ... Rd1? 3. Rc8+) due to his outside passed pawn. But with White's first rank so weak, let's look for more.

1. ... Qb2! (In the actual game, White resigned here.) **2. Rc8!?** (2. Rc2 Qb1+ 3. Qf1 Qxc2; 2. Qe1 Qxc3 3. Qxc3 Rd1+ 4. Qe1 Rxe1#) **2. ... Qb1+ 3. Qf1 Qxf1+ 4. Kxf1 Rxc8 0-1**. (Bernstein - Capablanca, 1914)

2. Go for the Pawn Ending

Doesn't 1. Rxf6 Kxf6 2. Ne4+ win a piece?

It does not — Black has an in-between capture with **1. ... Rxc3**. Still, after his own in-between move, **2. Rxf7+ Kxf7 3. bxc3**, White should win — not because of his extra but weak queenside pawn, but thanks to his potential outside passed pawn on the g-file. The game might continue **3. ... b5 4. Kf2 Kf6 5. Kf3 Kf5 6. g4+ Ke5 7. h4 h6 8. Ke3**. White will create a passed g-pawn, and then exchange it for Black's passed e-pawn. At that point, White's King will be much closer to the queenside pawns than Black's, so White will win.

3. Seize the File & Penetrate

Doubling to dominate the c-file leads to penetration on the 7th.

1. Qc2! Qd7 2. Qc7, with overwhelming advantage. White won after **2. ... Ba8** (defending against 3. Qxd7 and 4. Rc7) **3. Nc8!! Bf6 4. Qxb8 Bc6 5. Bxa6**. (Seirawan - Rivas, 1980)

4. Dark Square Struggle

1. Rxd8! Qxd8 2. Rd1 Qe7 3. Rd7! (deflection!) **3. ... Qxd7 4. Qf6 1-0**. (Klovan-Ruban, 1986)

5.

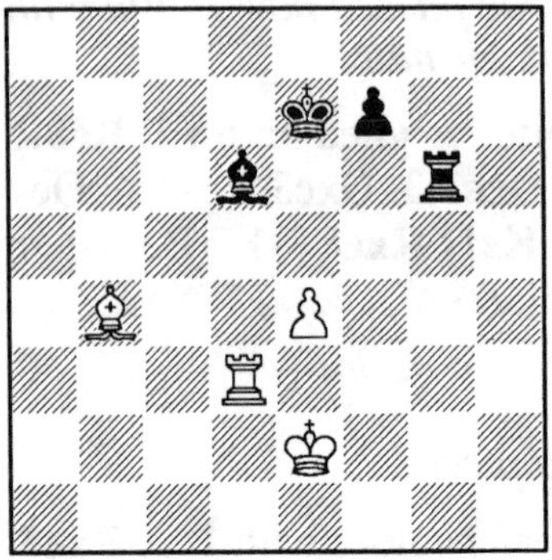

White to move

6.

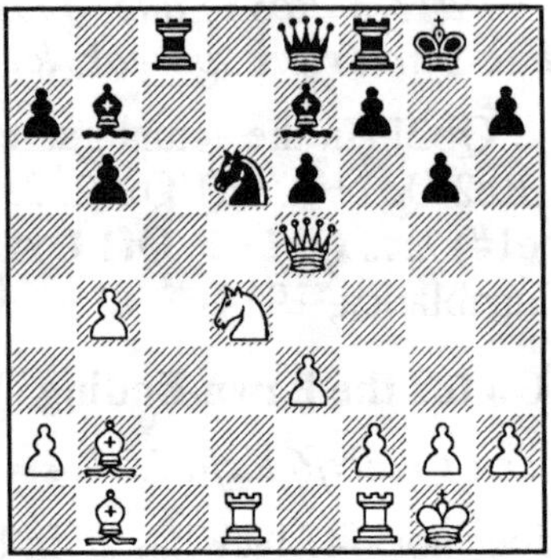

Black to move

7.

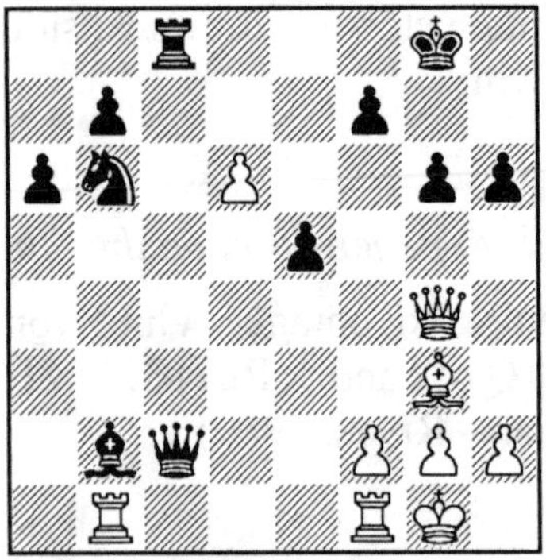

White to move

8.

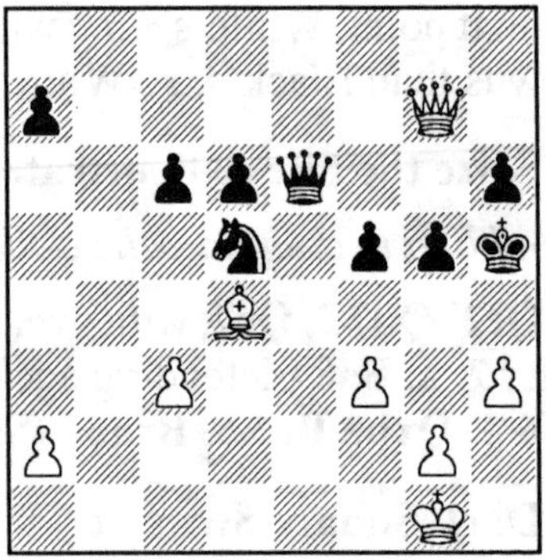

White to move

5. Absolutely Pinning & Winning

1. Rxd6 Rxd6 2. e5 1-0.

6. The Long Diagonal

If you are attracted by 1. ... Nc4, forking the Queen and Bishop, forget it! Black here played 1. ... f6, giving up a pawn. Why?

White has a terrible threat that works against **1. ... Nc4**, as well as against most other moves. **2. Qg7+! Kxg7 3. Nf5++ Kg8 4. Nh6#** — a typical Bishop-plus-Knight mate. Clearly 1. ... f6 was the lesser evil. (Simagin - Polugaevsky, 1961)

7. Two Are Too Many

When a pawn coming to the 7th rank attacks a piece, the pawn has two squares to use for promotion — it can take the piece or move straight ahead. This extra option often makes the pawn unstoppable.

1. Rxb2! (first deflecting the Queen from protecting the Rook) **1. ... Qxb2 2. Qxc8+ Nxc8 3. d7 1-0**. (Engels - Maroczy, 1936)

8. Minimum Force

Consider driving the Black King even further into White's position.

1. g4+! fxg4 2. hxg4+ Kh4. (You should have foreseen this position and your next move before playing 1. g4+.) **3. Qxh6+** (deflection) **3. ... Qxh6 4. Kh2**, followed by **Bf2#**. (Schlechter - Meitner, 1899)

9.

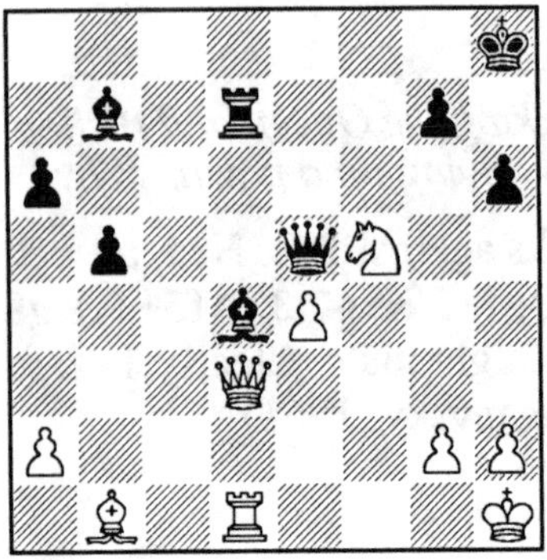

Black to move

10.

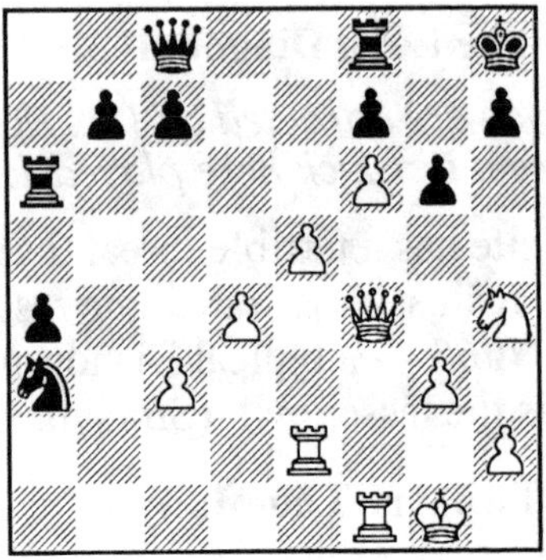

White to move

11.

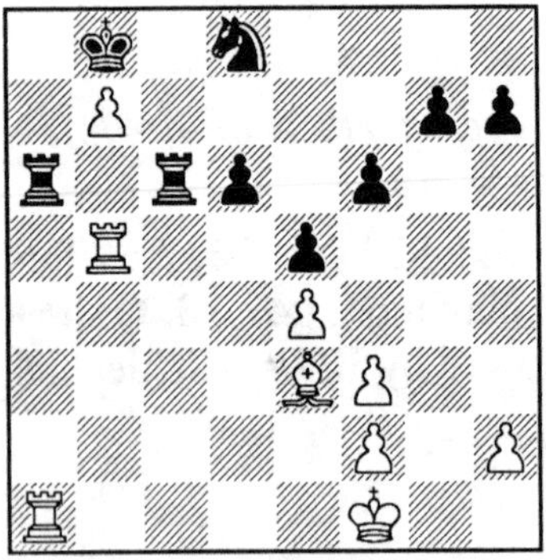

White to move

12.

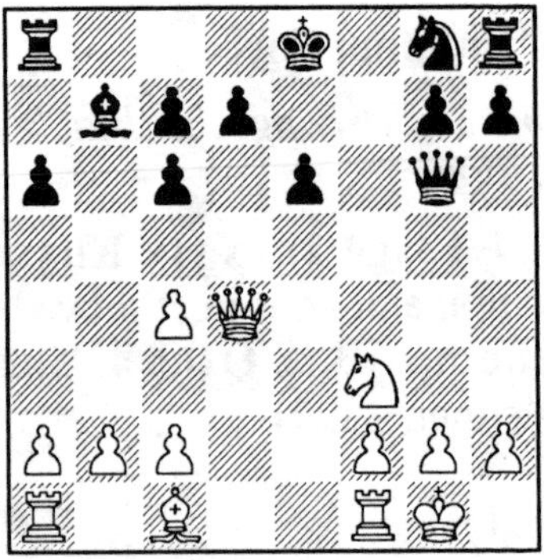

White to move

9. No One Wins by Resigning

Black thought he could not save his Bishop on d4, and so he resigned. But can you make a threat that takes precedence over White's?

1. ... Bg1!!. This powerful double attack wins for Black! Indeed, desperate circumstances require desperate remedies. (A kamikaze piece such as Black's Bishop is called a "desparado.") Black should have exploited the weakness of the h2-square, already in the sights of the Black Queen. Ideas here include discovered attack, double attack, relative pin, and the not-so-usual Queen plus Bishop mating pattern. (Popil - Marco, 1902)

10. The Queen Can Hang!

You probably chose **1. Qh6**. If you simply decided to make this move and to think more after the forced **1. ... Rg8**, that's okay. It's even better if you foresaw that **2. Nf3** (threatening 3. Ng5) **2. ... Qf8 3. Ng5!** works anyway, because if **3. ... Qxh6**, then **4. Nxf7#**. (Kolvic - Koch, 1959)

11. Promote the Pawn!

1. Ba7+ Rxa7 2. Rxa7 1-0. (Chigorin - Yankovic, 1889)

12. White to Play and ...

Be very careful! The tempting **1. Ne5** loses to **1. ... Qxg2+** (the only defense — but what a defense!) **2. Kxg2 c5+**, and White is a pawn down in a bad position. Any normal move is better, e.g., 1. Qd3, or even the daring 1. c5, sacrificing the pawn to keep the b7-Bishop locked out.

13.

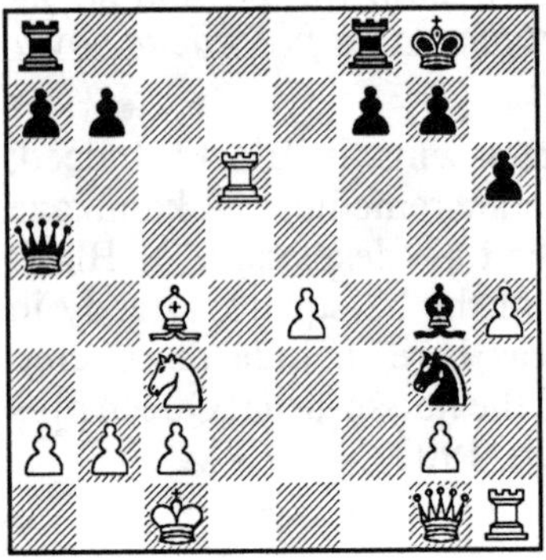

White to move

14.

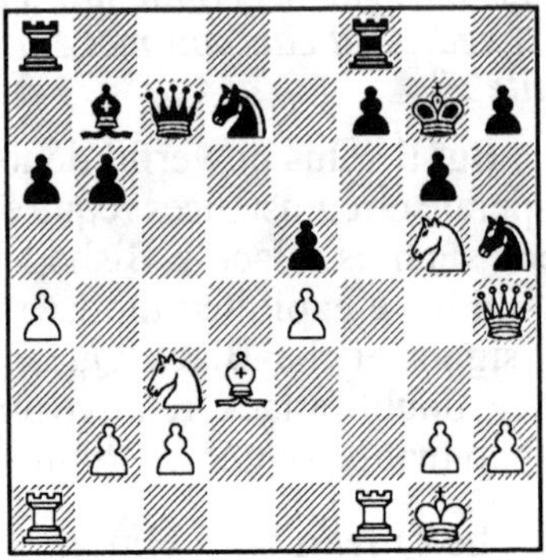

White to move

15.

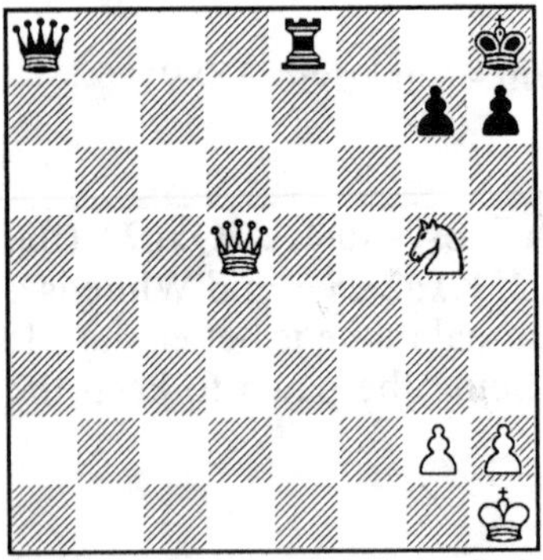

White to move

16.

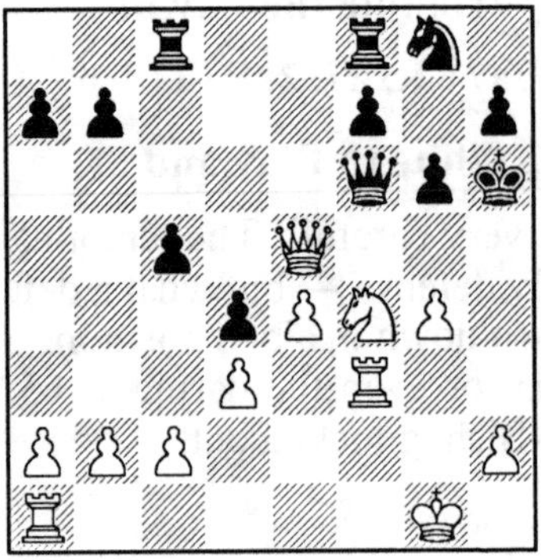

White to move

13. **Too Ugly to Play**

Think hard before putting your Rook on a boxed-in square like h2!

1. Qd4!, and White, up a pawn, is much better, with his h1-Rook ready to go to the good square e1. Of course, White should have foreseen that 1. ... Nxh1? loses to 2. Rg6. (Pachman - Barcza, 1952)

14. **Killer Fork on e6**

1. Rxf7+! Kg8 (1. ... Rxf7 2. Ne6+) **2. Rg7+!**. Here you may want to relax and make an "easy" move, say 2. Rxf8+ or 2. Ne6. But an extra pawn doesn't always win! Why not be precise to the end, and win convincingly and quickly? (Of course there was no need to think about what to do *after* 1. ... Kg8 when considering Rxf7+.) **2. ... Kh8 3. Rxh7+ Kg8 4. Rg7+ Kh8 5. Rxg6**, and the game is over. (Kupper - Olafsson, 1959)

15. **Classic Smothered Mate**

White is down material and must think attack.

1. Nf7+ Kg8 2. Nh6++ (2. Nd6+?? Qxd5) **2. ... Kh8** (2. ... Kf8 3. Qf7#) **3. Qg8+ Rxg8 4. Nf7#**.

16. **Hang It All!**

If, after 1. g5+, the reply 1. ... Qxg5+ were not check, then White could win with 2. Rh3+. Still, the Black King is in a very dangerous spot ...

1. Ne6!. This brilliant move combines the creation of a mating net (1. ... Qxe5 2. Rh3+ Qh5 3. g5#) with a discovered attack on Black's Queen. (Antoshin - Rabar, 1964)

17.

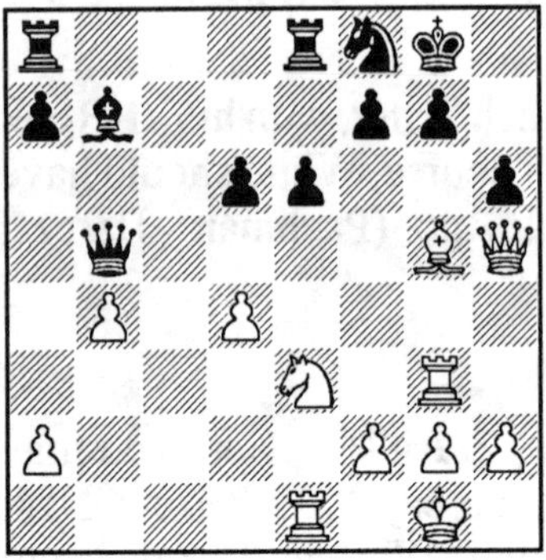

White to move

18.

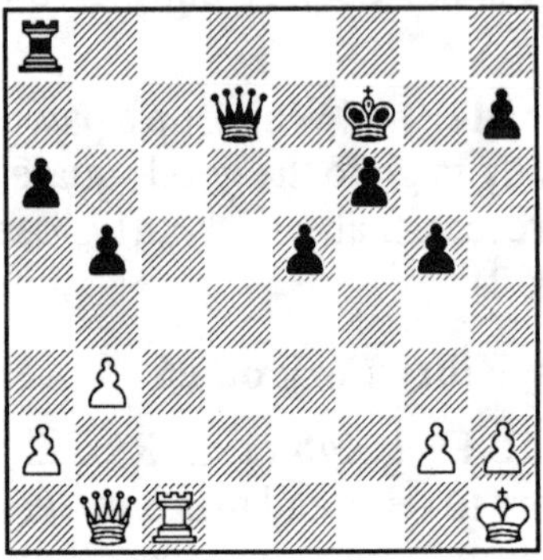

White to move

19.

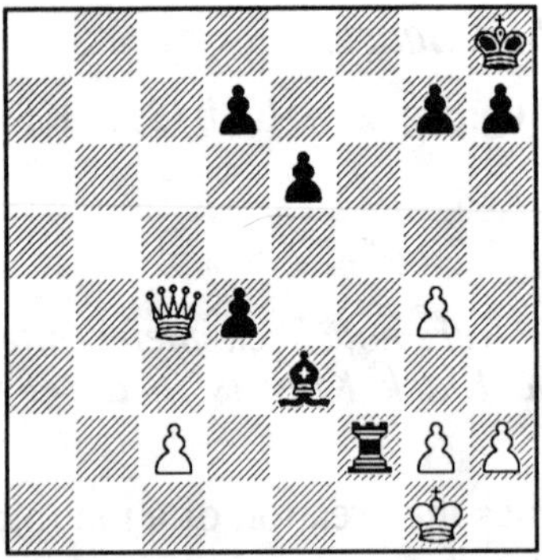

White to move

20.

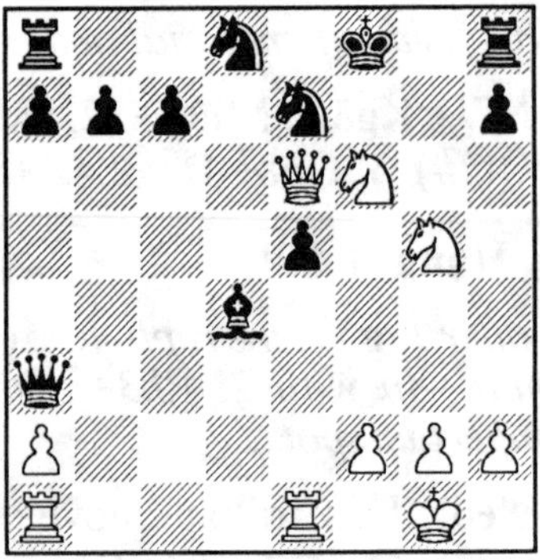

White to move

17. The Windmill

This famous "windmill" combination was first played in the game between Mexican Champion Carlos Torre and by then former World Champion Emanuel Lasker (Black) in the Moscow International, 1925. White's Bishop on g5 is pinned against his Queen, but such a "relative" pin (rather than the "absolute" pin on the King) can be broken if the price is right!

1. Bf6! Qxh5 2. Rxg7+ Kh8 3. Rxf7+ Kg8 4. Rg7+ Kh8 5. Rxb7+ Kg8 6. Rg7+. (The Rook slides back and forth, snatching material.) **6. ... Kh8 7. Rg5+ Kh7 8. Rxh5 Kg6**. (Lasker fights on ingeniously — this double attack by the King wins back a piece.) **9. Rh3 Kxf6 10. Rxh6+**, with a decisive material advantage. (Torre - Lasker, Em., 1925)

18. Create a Winning Skewer

After 1. Qxh7+? Ke6, Black's King protects his Queen. So ...

1. Rc7! (decoys the Queen farther away from her King, but still along the same rank) **1. ... Qxc7 2. Qxh7+ 1-0**.

19. Not So Quick!

Should you play 1. Qc8+ in this position?

1. Qc8+? is a bad idea because of 1. ... Rf8+ (discovered check), winning for Black. **1. Kh1** is a must.

20. Four-Knights' Mate!

1. Qf7+ Nxf7 2. Ne6#. (Clemenz - Eisenschmidt, 1862)

21.

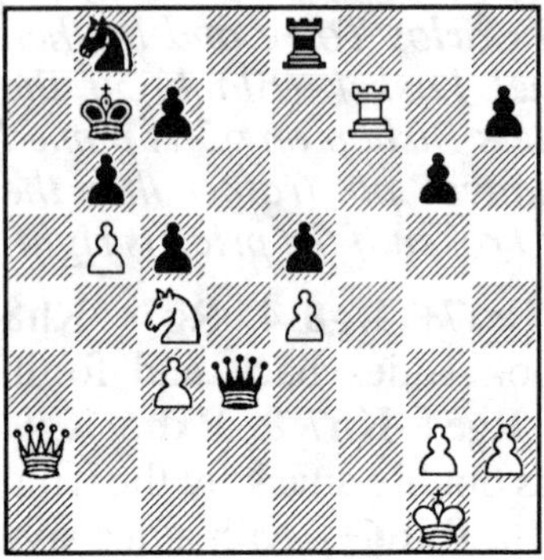

White to move

22.

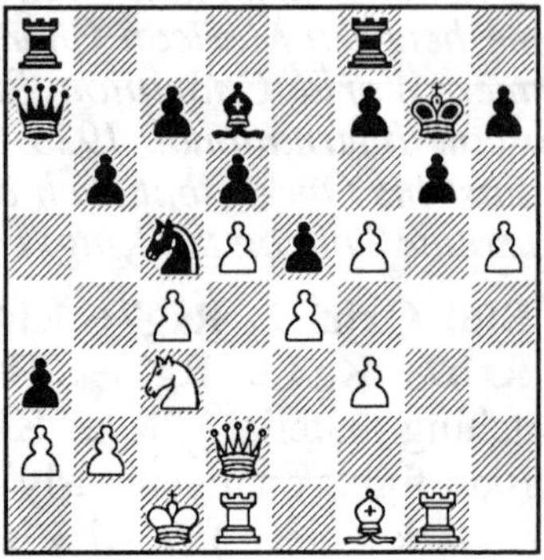

White to move

23.

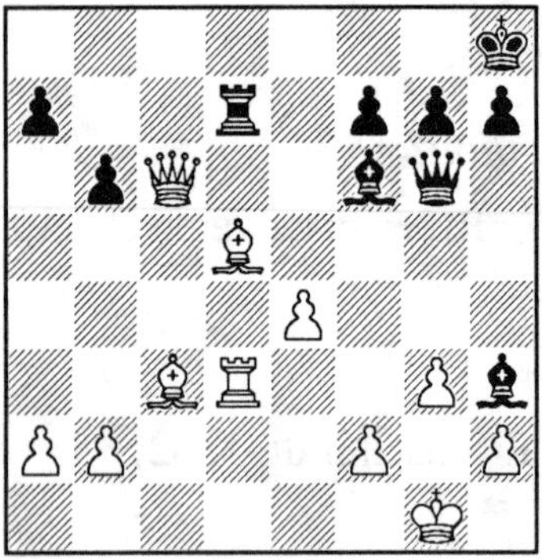

White to move

24.

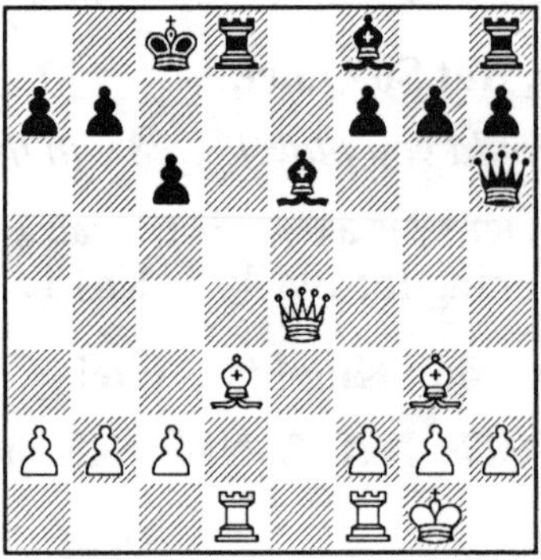

White to move

21. Reversing the Move Order

Yes, you may start by analyzing 1. Rxc7+ Kxc7 2. Qa7+ Kd8 3. Qxb8+, or 2. ... Kc8 3. Nb6+ Kd8 4. Qxb8+. Maybe White's winning. But as lines grow longer and murkier, it's time to stop, make mental notes of your discoveries, and move ahead — or rather, move back. Return to the original position and look for other candidate moves. What about reversing the move order? This means sacrificing the Queen. Still, it might be worth looking at for a few seconds ... .

1. Qa7+! Kxa7 2. Rxc7+ Ka8 3. Nb6#. (Shiyanovsky - Pogrebissky, 1955)

22. Mate on a Long Corridor

White should consider opening the g-file, but preliminary analysis (sample lines) is not very promising. Don't be stubborn — look for another way to attack.

1. f6+ Kh8 (1. ... Kxf6 2. Qg5+ Kg7 3. h6+ Kg8 4. Qf6) **2. Qh6 Rg8** (defending against mate on g7) **3. hxg6 fxg6**. (All Black's replies are forced. An in-between ... axb2+ wouldn't help after White's calm Kb1.) To find her combination, the first Women's World Champion, Vera Menchik, relied on her knowledge of a typical mating pattern: **4. Qxh7+ Kxh7 5. Rh1#**. An important Rook and pawn mate. Remember it! (Menchik - Thomas, 1932)

23. Open the File

1. Be6!, and Black resigned here because of **1. ... Bxe6** (1. ... Rxd3 2. Qe8#) **2. Qc8+ Bd8 3. Qxd8+!** (x-ray action of the Rook) and mate next move. (Keres - Levenfish, 1947)

24. Crisscrossing Bishop Mate

1. Qxc6+ bxc6 2. Ba6#.

25.

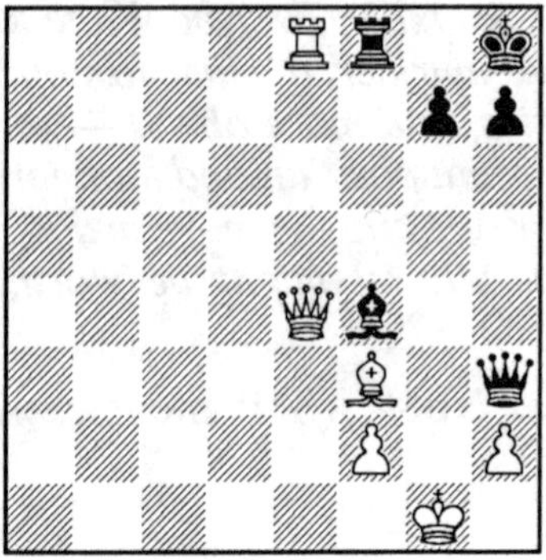

Black to move

26.

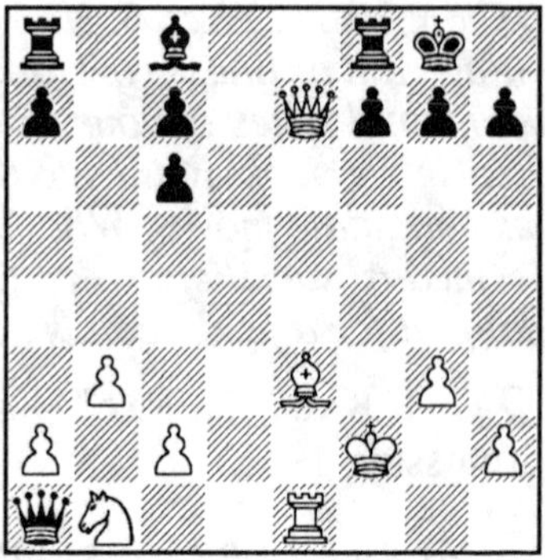

White to move

27.

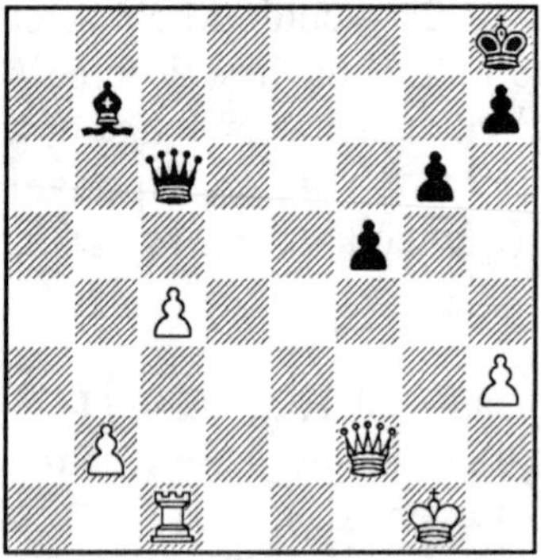

White to move

28.

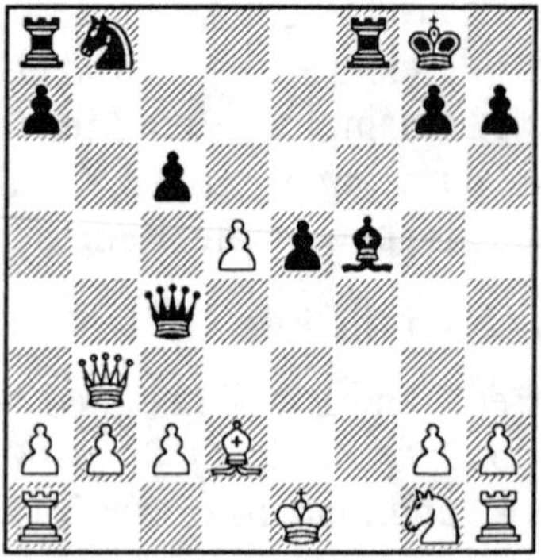

Black to move

25. Model Queen & Bishop Mate

Black wins by a typical maneuver, one you should memorize: 1. ... Bxh2+ 2. Kh1 Bg3+ 3. Kg1 Qh2+ 4. Kf1 Qxf2#. Now imagine that the f2-square is protected (add, for example, a White Knight on d1). Can Black achieve more than a draw?

Yes, he wins by playing **1. ... Bh2+ 2. Kh1**, and now another discovered check, **2. ... Be5+**, wins the undefended Rook on e8. Black will be up an Exchange and a pawn, and should win.

26. Force the Back-Rank Mate

Here's another example of using knowledge of a basic pattern (back-rank mate) to solve a complicated position brilliantly!

1. Qxf8+! Kxf8 2. Bc5+ Kg8 3. Re8#. (Boatner - Patterson, 1958)

27. Transposing to a Win

Black's threats on the long diagonal are annoying and dangerous. White would welcome the exchange of Queens.

1. Qd4+! Kg8 2. Qd5+ Qxd5 3. cxd5 Bxd5. White gives back a pawn to achieve the exchange of Queens. He's up the Exchange for a pawn, and (most important) has an outside passed pawn. This is as far as you needed to calculate, because this position is obviously better than taking a draw, after, for example, 1. Kh2 Qd6+ 2. Kg1 Qc6. In fact. the ending is easily won by White: **4. b4 Kf7 5. b5 Ke8 6. b6 Be4** (6. ... Kd7 7. Rd1) **7. Rc7 Kd8 8. Rxh7** + -.

28. Double Trouble

Visualize the final mate and find a tool (double check) to reach it.

1. ... Qf1+ (decoy) **2. Kxf1 Bd3+ 3. Ke1 Rf1#.** (Schulten - Gorwitz, 1846)

29.

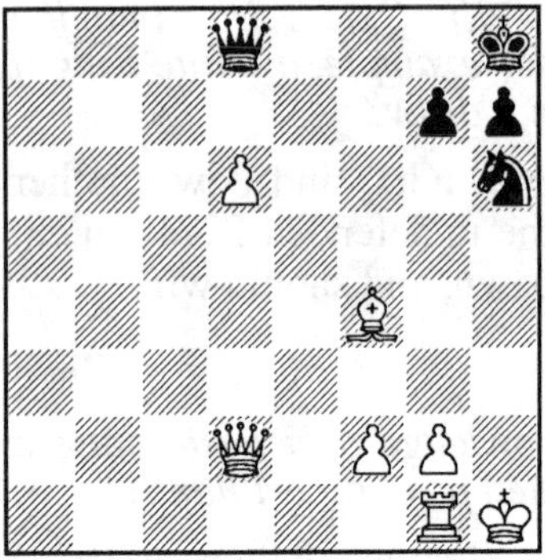

Black to move

30.

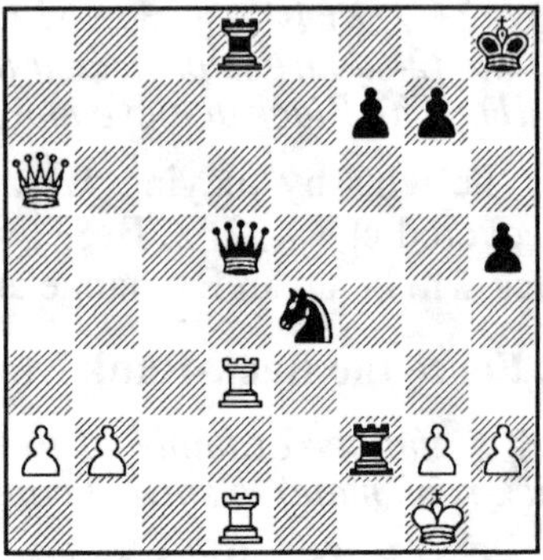

Black to move

31.

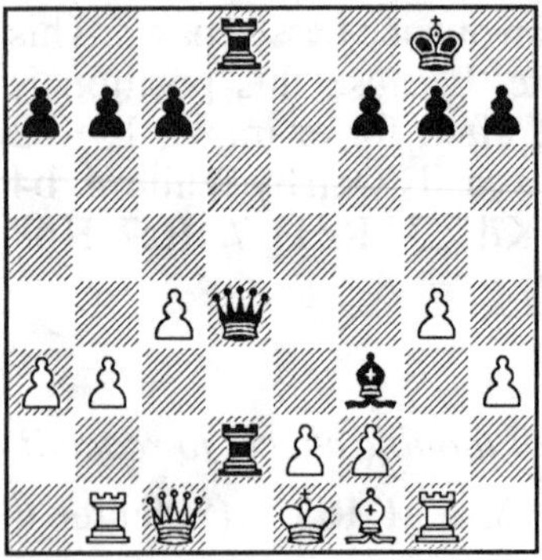

Black to move

32.

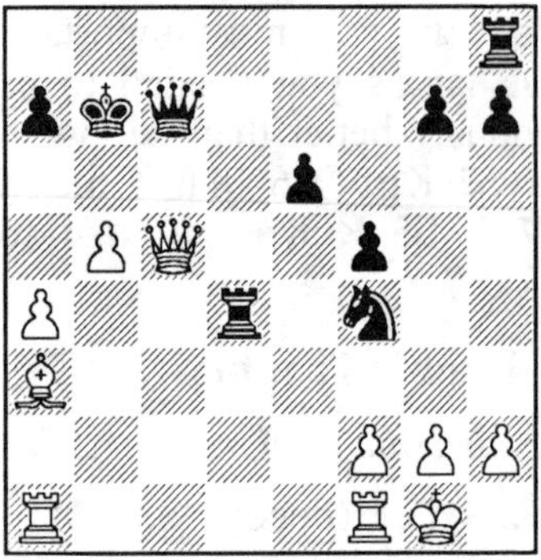

Black to move

29. Saved by the Last Knight

*Black is down a Rook and a pawn, so the first moves are virtually forced: **1. ... Qh4+ 2. Bh2 Ng4 3. Qf4**, and now Black can win a Queen for a Knight with 3. ... Nxf2+. If you've seen this much, that's great; if you decided pragmatically to play the only reasonable first move (1. ... Qh4+), that's very good too. Now practice visualization: Try to see the position after 3. Qf4 very clearly. First evaluate (lightly) the consequences of 3. ... Nxf2+ 4. Qxf2 Qxf2. Then consider whether Black has anything better. Hint: Changing the move order often helps.*

Of course! **3. ... Qxh2+! 4. Qxh2 Nxf2#**. He's smothered!

30. Rook Sac & Smothered Mate

Yet another complex position that boils down to the basic smothered mate.

1. ... Rf1+! 2. Rxf1 (2. Kxf1 Qf5+ 3. Ke2 [3. Kg1 Qc5+] 3. ... Qf2#) **2. ... Qc5+ 3. Kh1 Nf2+ 4. Kg1** (4. Rxf2 Qc1+ with a back-rank mate) **4. ... Nh3++ 5. Kh1 Qg1+ 6. Rxg1 Nf2#.** (Evans - Larsen, 1957)

31. The Simplest Win

1. ... Rd1+ 2. Qxd1 Qc3+! and mate next move. (Makarczyk - Sliva, 1952)

32. On Edge

A Rook & Knight, corridor mate

1. ... Ne2+ 2. Kh1 Qxh2+! 3. Kxh2 Rh4#. (Meo - Guistolizzi, 1959)

33.

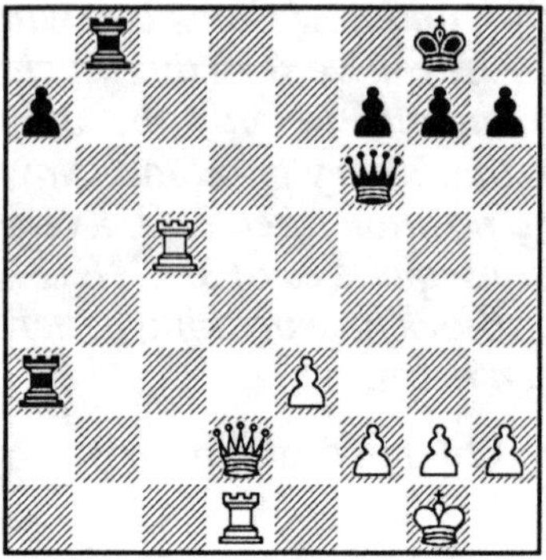

White to move

34.

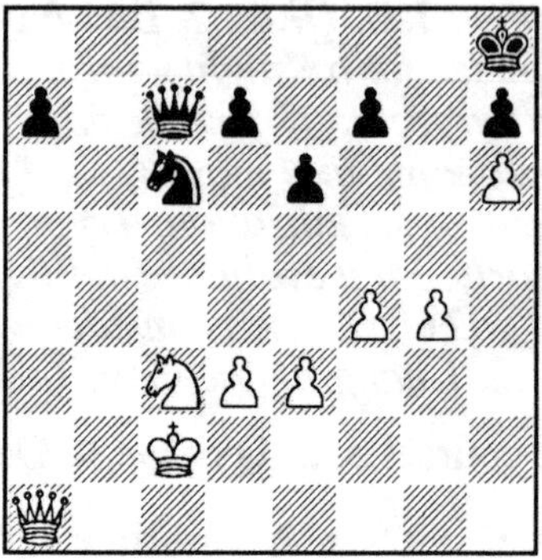

White to move

35.

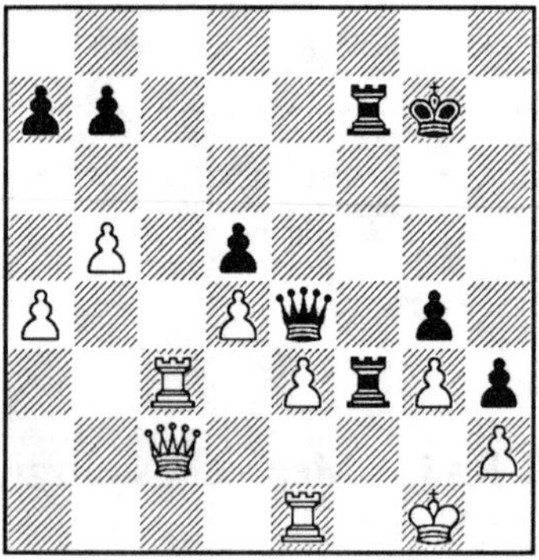

Black to move

36.

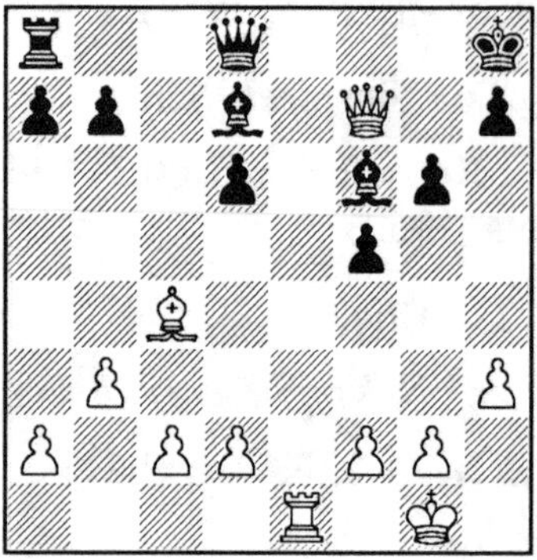

White to move

33. Double-Attack Deflection

1. Qb4! Rd8!. (The only move to stay in the game. Otherwise, White snatches the a3-Rook. If 1. ... Rb3, then 2. Qxb3.) Did you foresee this defense? Even if you didn't, consider the position correctly solved — there is nothing wrong with playing **1. Qb4**, even if you haven't seen all the lines leading to the forced win.

2. Rcd5! Rd3. (Not 2. ... Rxd5 3. Qb8+ Qd8 4. Qxd8+, with a winning x-ray attack; after 2. ... Ra1 White wins with 3. Rxd8+ Qxd8 4. Rxa1.) **3. R5xd3!**. (Black hoped for 3. R1xd3?? Qa1+!, turning it around —4. Rd1 Qxd1+ 5. Rxd1 Rxd1+.) **3. ... Rxd3 4. Qb8+**, winning. (Guldin - Bagdatiev, 1963)

34. One Discovered Check Deserves Another

1. Nd5+? (Or 1. Nb5+?), hoping to win the Queen, fails miserably to double check: **1. ... Nd4+**, and mate in two. Any normal move would suffice as a correct one. My pick would be 1. Kd2.

35. Mate in the Corner

Black has a promising line: 1. ... Rf2 2. Qxe4 (2. Qxf2 Rxf2 3. Kxf2 Qg2#) 2. ... dxe4, with the idea of ... Rg2+ and ... R7f2, and mate with two Rooks and the h3 wedge pawn. But Black's position may offer an even more forceful line than this.

1. ... Rf1+! 2. Rxf1 Qh1+! (the Rook sacrifice 2. ... Rxf1+ doesn't work, but as often happens, reversing the move order is effective) **3. Kxh1 Rxf1#**. (Borsyak - Kizilov, 1962)

36. Overburdened Queen

1. Re8+! Bxe8 (1. ... Qxe8 2. Qxf6#) **2. Qg8#**. (Nezhmetdinov - Kotkov, 1957)

37.

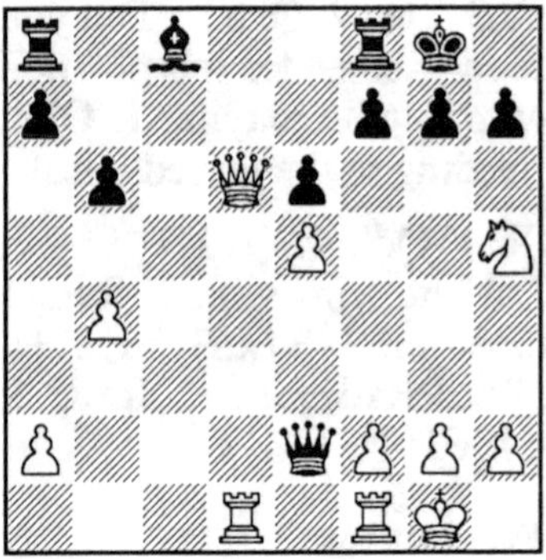

White to move

38.

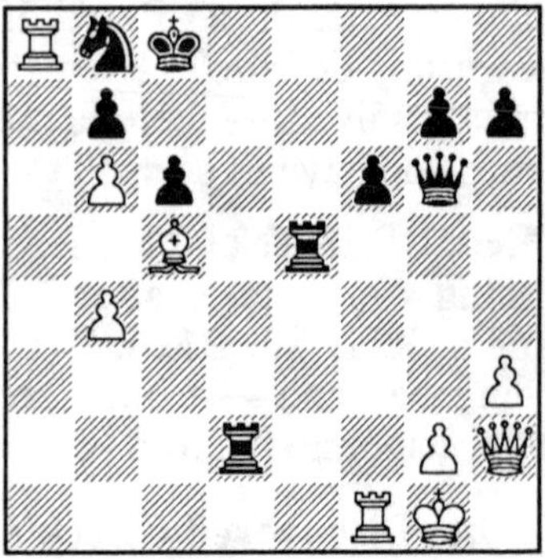

White to move

39.

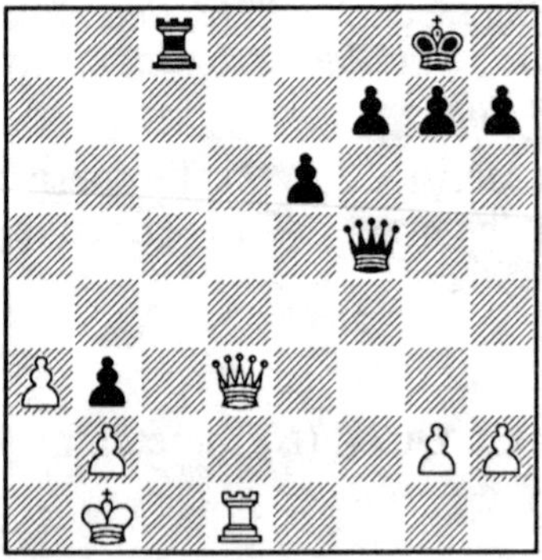

Black to move

40.

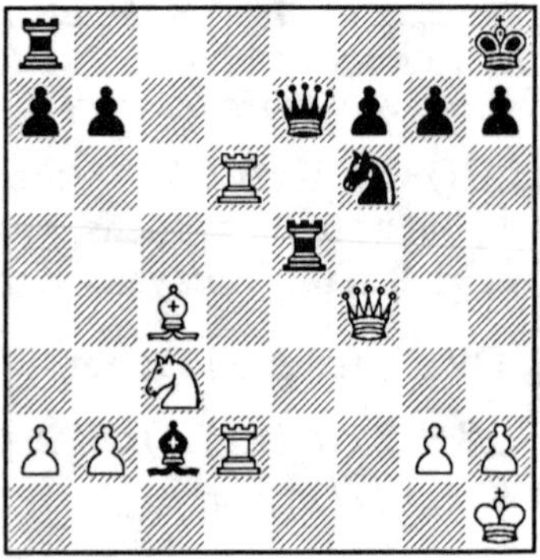

Black to move

37. Good Knight!

In this position, Grandmaster Gregory Levenfish played 1.Ng3. Could he have done better?

Yes! **1. Nf6+! gxf6 2. exf6** would have won. White now has two threats: 3. Qg3+ and 3. Qxf8+, both followed by mate. Motifs—potential back-rank weakness, opportunity to obtain a wedge pawn while opening a path to the Black King. (Levenfish - Rumin, 1936)

38. Double Sac & Mate!

While other plans are promising, too — for example, 1. Be3 and 2. Bf4 — White's best is **1. Rxb8+!** (decoy) **1. ... Kxb8 2. Qxe5+!** (deflection/opening a file) **2. ... fxe5 3. Rf8+**, with the now familiar back-row mate. (Alekhine - Reshevsky, 1937)

39. Double Pin & Mate!

Because of Black's pawn on b3, back-rank mate suggests itself...

1. ... Rd8! 0-1. (Mikenas - Aronin 1957)

40. Medal of Honor for Interference

Black should consider the "normal" 1. ... Re1+ 2. Bf1, and now, from this support position, look for ways to deflect the White Queen. But if this idea doesn't pan out, look for others on move one — try interference. And remember, your pieces are always ready to follow your orders, no matter how dangerous the assignment!

Black played **1. ... Bd3!**, putting his Bishop into a blistering triple attack. White resigned because he loses the Exchange (he's already down a pawn) after 2. Bxd3 Qxd6. If, after 1. ... Bd3!, either Rook takes the Bishop, the White Bishop will be cut off from the f1-square, and 2. ... Re1+ will lead to mate. Motifs: weak back rank, underprotected d6-Rook. (Fuchs - Korchnoi, 1965)

41.

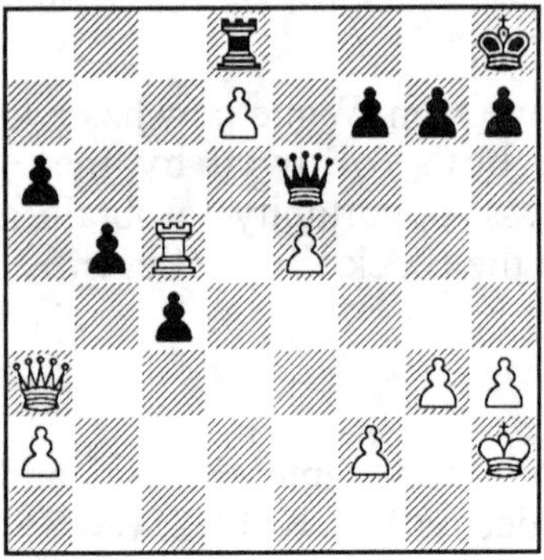

White to move

42.

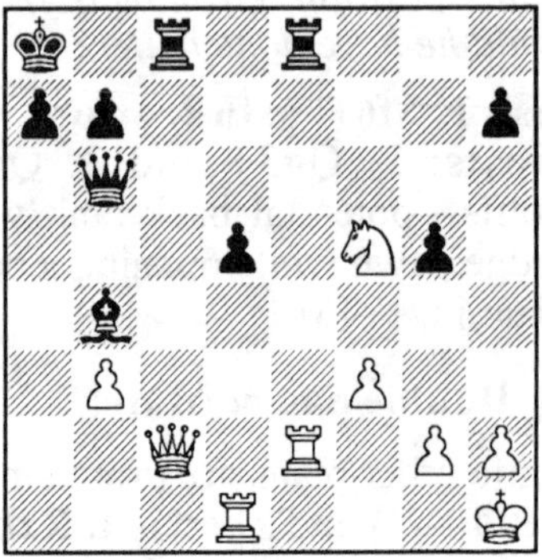

White to move

43.

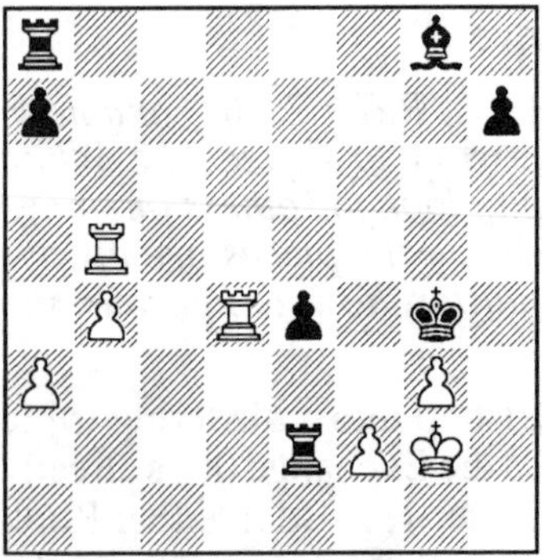

White to move

44.

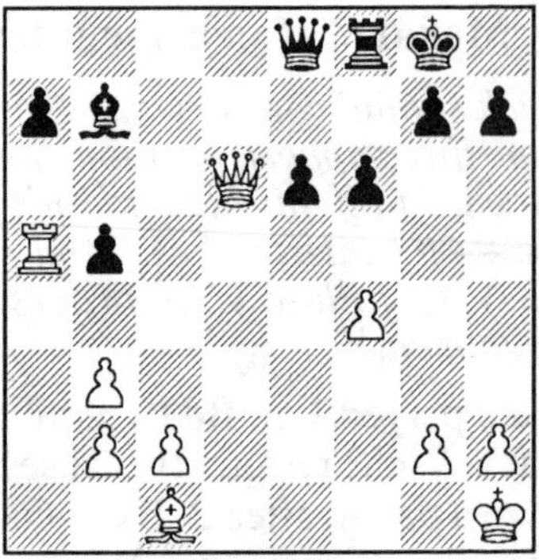

Black to move

41. One Good Queen Deserves Another

Normal is 1. Rc7, and if 1. ... h6, then 2. Qd6. But a sample line — 2. ... Qxd6 3. exd6 Kh7 (to prevent 4. Rc8, pinning and winning) seems drawish. Can White achieve more?

Playing against an amateur in 1939, Alekhine dashed in with **1. Rc8!**. After the forced **1. ... Rxc8** (1. ... Qxd7 2.Qxf8+), he unleashed the prepared and not so obvious **2.Qe7!!**, winning. Motifs: very bad back rank weakness; White pawn on 7th rank. Ideas: decoy, deflection, pawn promotion. (Alekhine - NN, 1939)

42. Pawn Pilfering & Punishment

Should White play 1. Rxd5 here? Examine 1. ... Qf2 or 1. ... Qa6, trying to exploit White's first rank.

After **1. Rxd5?** Qa6? 2. Ng3, White maintains equality. Instead, **1. ... Qf2!** wins. Thus, White should reject 1. Rxd5 and consider other candidate moves, such as 1. Qd3 or 1. Rxe8 Rxe8, and now, for example, 2. Ng7. (Teschner - Portish, 1969)

43. Pawn Mate

If White could play f2-f3, it would be mate. Hmm.

1. Rxe4+ (deflection, annihilation of a defender) **1. ... Rxe4 2. f3#.** (Lombardy - Medina, 1973)

44. Seize the File!

1 . ... Qd8! 2. Qxe6+ (Or 2. Qd2 Qxd2 3. Bxd2 Rd8 4. Be3 Rd1+ 5. Bg1 Rd2, and Black should win.) **2. ... Rf7!**. (Black sets up a Queen + Rook battery, recognizing that the pin is temporary.) **3. Qe1 Re7 0-1**. What makes 1. ... Qd8! difficult to find is that Black offers a pawn to be taken with check! Motifs: back-rank weakness, unprotected Bishop on c1. Themes: double-attack, challenging the file. (Neikirch - Botvinnik, 1960)

45.

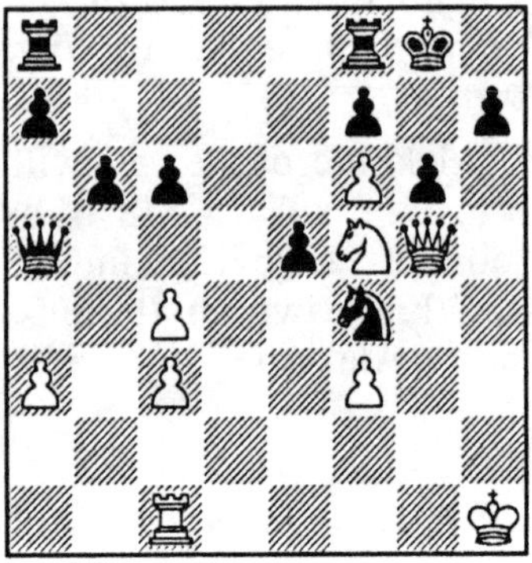

White to move

46.

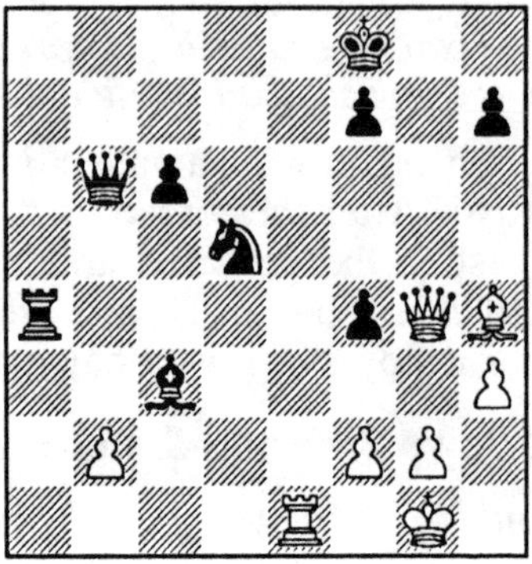

White to move

47.

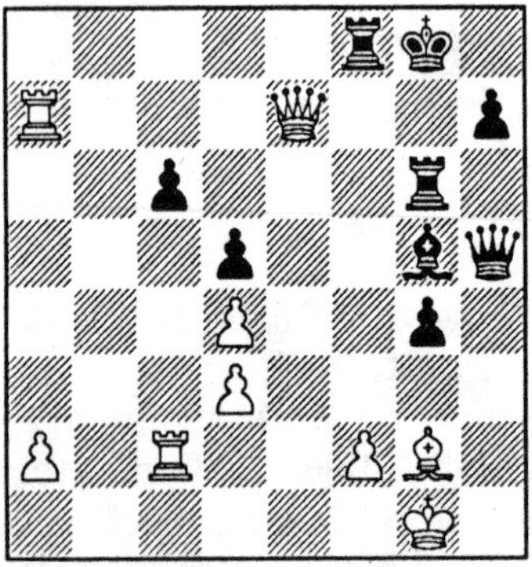

White to move

48.

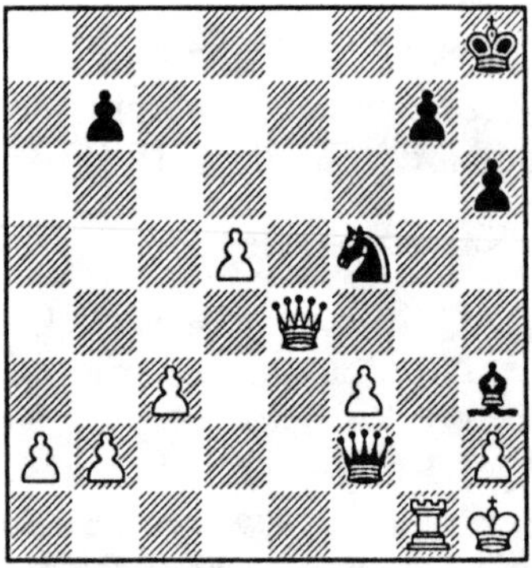

Black to move

45. Family Feud

White is down a Rook against his brother, and his only chance is to attack. He has several attractive options —for instance, 1. Rc2, 1. Ne7+, or 1. Qh6. You could rely primarily on your intuition, but there is a real risk of going wrong! Try to figure out the consequences of your favorite move. If it wins, do it. But if it "only" draws or is unclear, consider the next-most-appealing move, and if necessary a third one too. Then compare outcomes.

1. Qh6!. (1. Rc2 is met with 1. ... Qxa3, ready for check, and on 1. Ne7+ Kh8 2. Qh6, Black defends with 2. ... Nh5. So the immediate 1. Qh6 is most flexible — and strongest.) **1. ... Nh5** (1. ... Ne6 2. Ne7+ Kh8 3. Rc2, threatening 4. Qxh7+ and 5. Rh2#; if 3. ... e4, then 4. Rh2) **2. Qxh5!! gxh5** (2. ... Kh8 3. Qh6 Rg8 4. Rc2 gxf5 — defending against Qxh7+ — 5.Rh2, winning) **3. Rg1+ Kh8 4. Nh6**, and now there is no defense against **5. Rg8+** and **6. Nxf7#**. Do you see how knowing the basic patterns — such as smothered mate — makes more complex positions easier to understand? (Romanovsky, P. - Romanovsky, A., 1907)

46. Decoying the King

1. Qc8+ allows escape to g7, so ...

1. Re8+! (decoy) **Kxe8 2. Qc8+ Qd8 3. Qxd8#**. (Evert - Hotcel, 1969)

47. The Linear Mate

1. Bxd5+! (deflection, opening of the file) **1. ... cxd5 2. Qxf8+** (elimination of the defender) **2. ... Kxf8 3. Rc8+**, and mate next move. (Budrich - Gumprich, 1950)

48. Royal Asphyxiation

1. ... Bg2+ 2. Rxg2 Qf1+ 3. Rg1 Ng3+ 4. hxg3 Qh3#. (NN - Anderssen, 1872)

49.

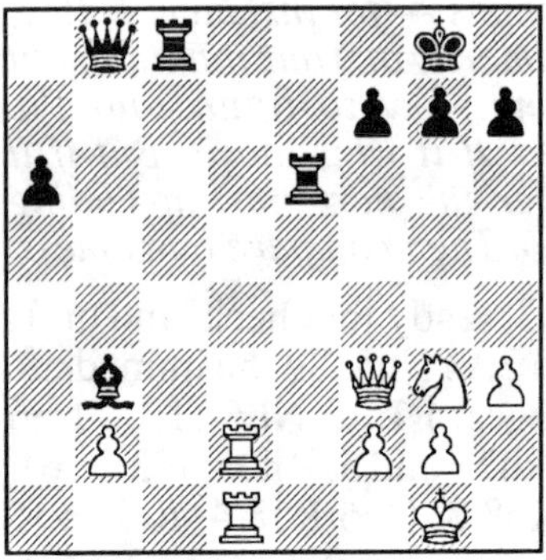

White to move

50.

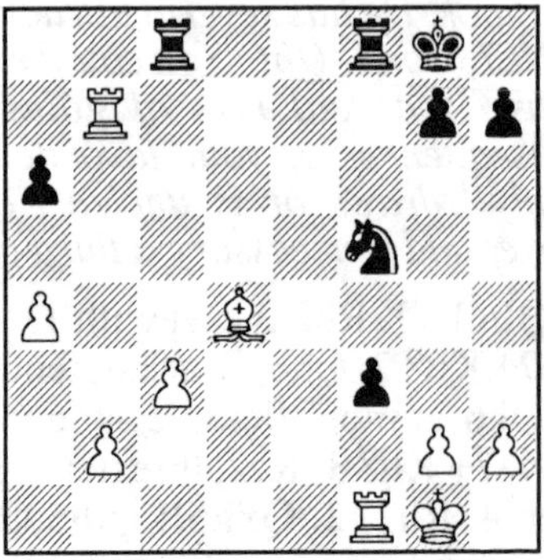

Black to move

51.

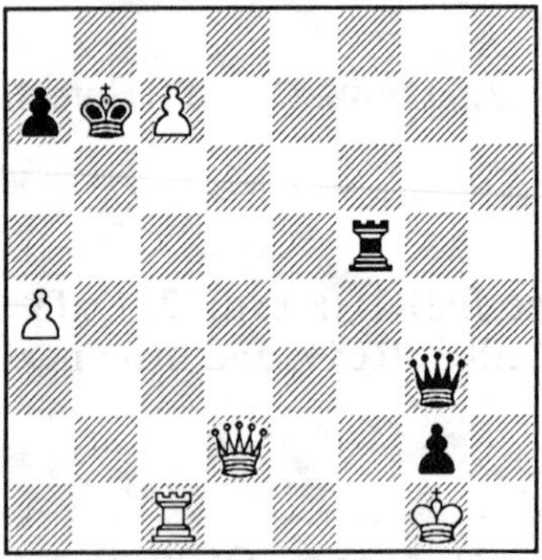

Black to move

52.

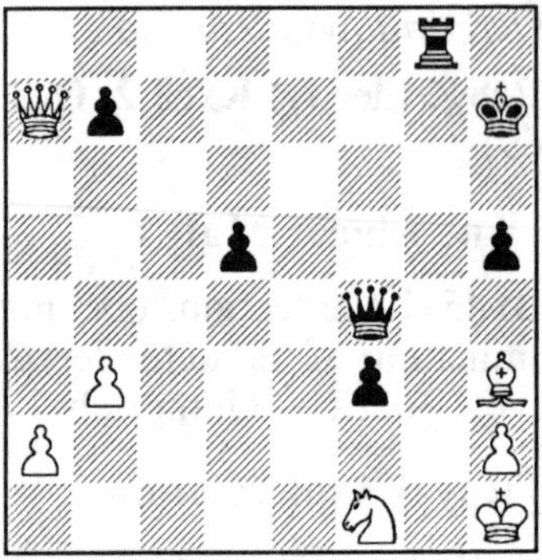

Black to move

49. Don't Fall for a Trap, Set One!

Double-check the tempting 1. Qxb3? Qxb3 2. Rd8+, and you'll find an easy defense for Black, 2. ... Re8, winning.

Any non-blundering move may be considered a passing grade. The best move, however, is **1. Rd7**. It takes control of the 7th rank, and creates potential threats (Qxf7+, Rb7), while setting up various pitfalls for Black, such as 1. ... Rf6? (or 1. ... Rec6?) 2. Qxb3, etc. So 1. Rd7 is the strongest move, and also sets deadly traps.

50. The Pawn's the Thing That Will Catch a King!

1. ... fxg2 doesn't promise much, as even the simple (and simplifying) 2. Rxf5 Rxf5 3. Rxg7+ should be at least equal for White. What about 1. ... Nxd4, opening the c-file?

Indeed, **1. ... Nxd4! 2. cxd4 f2+!**. The far advanced pawn helps create back-rank mate possibilities. **3. Kh1** (3. Rxf2 Rc1+) **3. ... Rc1! 0-1**. Motifs: far-advanced pawn with a Rook behind it, potentially open file for Black's c8-Rook, promotion, back-rank mate. Themes: opening the file/deflection (of c3-pawn), decoy. (Nedekovic - Siladi, 1957)

51. Underpromotion

1. ... Rf1+ (decoy) **2. Rxf1 Qh2+** (another decoy) **3. Kxh2 gxf1(N)+**, and Black wins.

52. Cornering the King

Material is even, but Black can create dangerous threats—and follow up to final victory.

1. ... f2 (threatening ... Rg1#) **2. Bg2** (2. Qxb7+ Rg7; 2. Ng3 Qf3+ 3. Bg2 f1(Q)+, winning — pin, deflection) **2. ... Qf3! 0-1**. If 3. Qxb7+, then 3. ... Kh8!. (Stoltz - Kotov, 1952)

53.

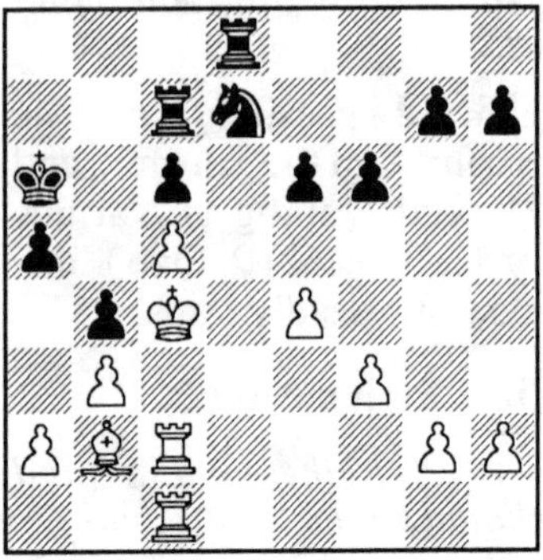

White to move

54.

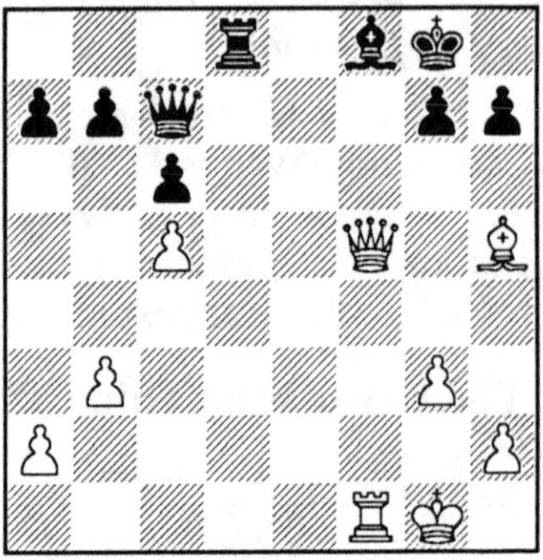

White to move

55.

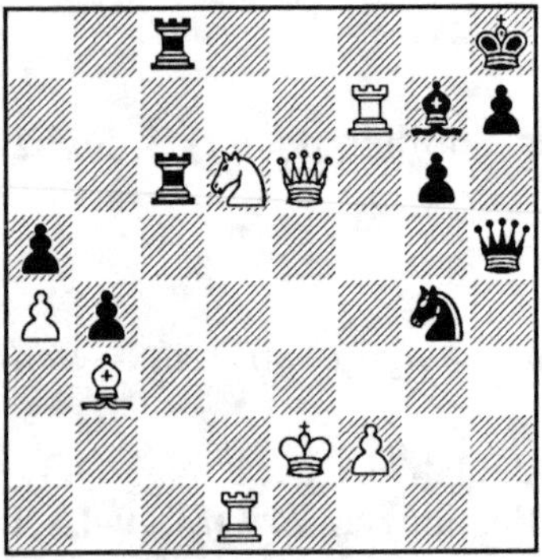

White to move

56.

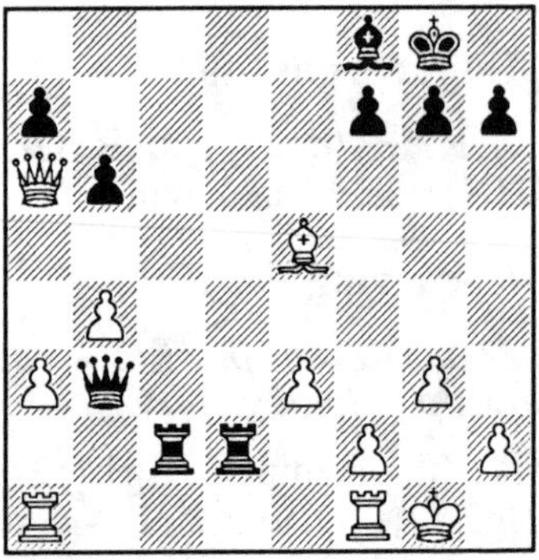

Black to move

53. King in the Middle

Pinning the Knight is attractive, but did you consider the reply 1. ... Ne5+?

After **1. Rd1?**, Black (a master) trusted his grandmaster opponent, following with the weak 1. ... Kb7??. Instead **1. ... Ne5+!** would have won for Black after **2. Bxe5 Rxd1 3. Bxc7** (both players thought White would be winning material here) **3. ... e5!**, and the trap springs shut. There is no defense to the coming mate on d4. (Such a mate in the middle of the board is unusual in the late ending.) A good rule of thumb is that after the smoke of a forced variation clears — perhaps after the final capture — visualize the position very clearly and think for at least one more move ahead. Best was 1. f4 or even 1.Kd3, fighting for equality. (Gligoric - Commons, 1972)

54. Stirring Up a Combination

Direct assault with 1. Qe6+ Kh8 2. Rf7 stalls after 2. ... Bxc5+ 3. Kh1 Qd6. In this famous game, Czech Grandmaster Reti first created, then exploited, back-rank vulnerability.

1. Bf7+ Kh8 2. Be8! (interference) **1-0**. (Reti - Bogolyubov, 1926)

55. Clear, Then Smother

1. Rf8+! (freeing the diagonal and the f7-square) **1. ... Rxf8** (or 1. ... Bxf8 [interference] 2. Qg8#) **2. Qg8+ Rxg8** (blocking) **3. Nf7#**. (Nicolov - Slavchev, corr.)

56. Clear the Way for the Blind Pigs

Doubled rooks on your opponent's second rank always terrify him, and often devastate his position. Nimzovich himself called them "Blind Pigs." They devour all they touch.

1. ... Qxe3! 1-0. If 2. fxe3 Rg2+, and mate in two; or if 2. Bf4 Rxf2. (Nimzovich - Capablanca, 1927)

57.

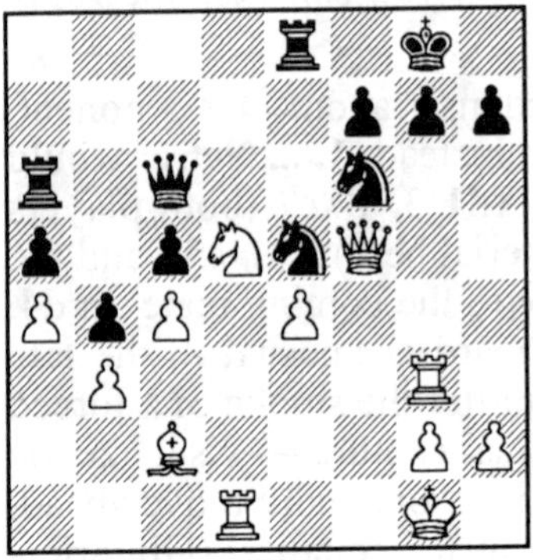

White to move

58.

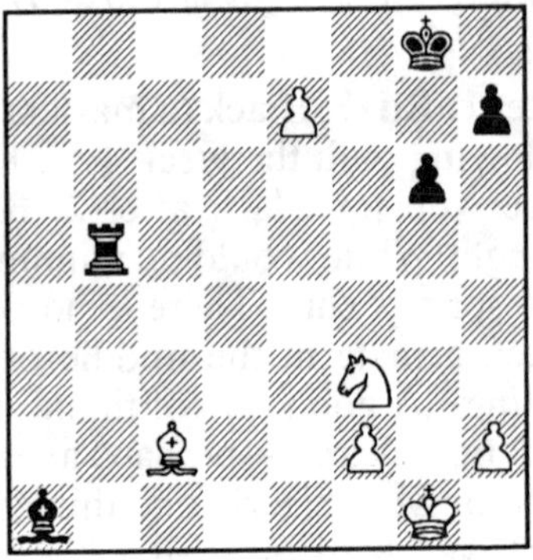

Black to move

59.

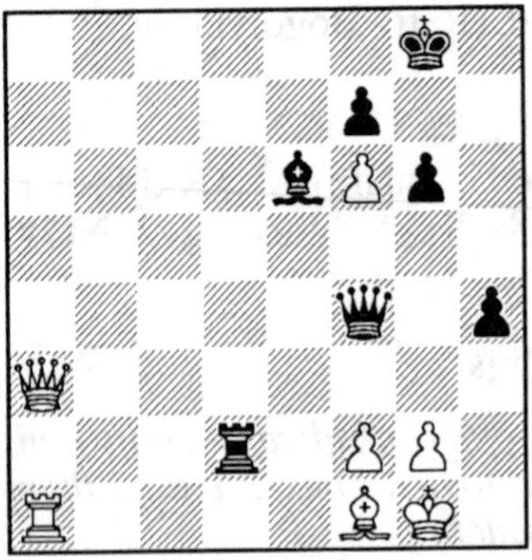

White to move

60.

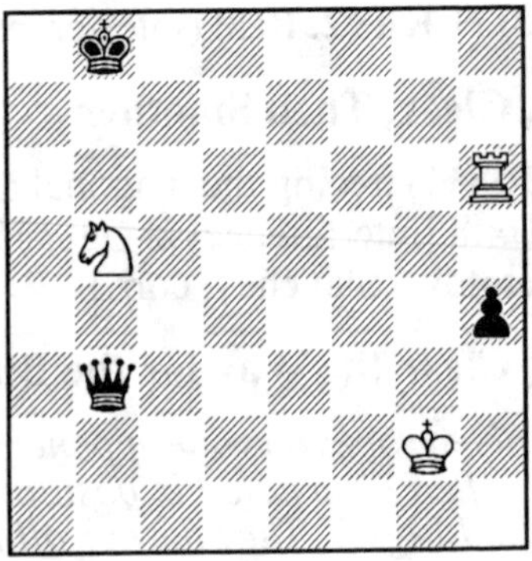

White to move

57. Deflect, Deflect, Mate!

This one took me some time and several false starts. Back-rank weakness, deflection, fork, pin, and blocking all may be at work!

1. Ne7+!. The only winning move. It deflects the Black Rook from the back rank and simultaneously opens the d-file for the White Rook. Still, after **1. ... Rxe7**, the e8-square is protected by the Queen, so you should have foreseen **2. Qxf6!**, when White's threats (Qxg7#, Qxe7, etc.) are too numerous and powerful, while 2. ... Qxf6 3. Rd8+ leads to forced mate. (Gragger - Dorn, 1959)

58. Don't Flip a Coin!

Black must first stop the e7-pawn from queening — either by 1. ... Kf7 or 1. ... Rb8. Does it matter? (Hint: Watch the a4-e8 diagonal.)

Black can draw if he chooses the right line. Correct is **1. ... Rb8! 2. Ba4 Kf7 3. e8(Q)+ Rxe8 4. Ng5+ Kf6!** (the easiest draw will be in the Bishops-of-opposite-color ending) **5. Nxh7+ Kg7 6. Bxe8 Kxh7, draw**. The natural 1. ... Kf7? (forgetting about the a4-e8 diagonal) loses to 2. e8(Q)+! Kxe8 3. Ba4, and the pin wins the Rook and the game. (Ragozin - Boleslavsky, 1945)

59. Queen Sacs Can Be Moving!

The wedge pawn on f6 creates mating motifs, especially if His Majesty can be forced to move to f8.

1. Qf8+ Kxf8 (1. ... Kh7 2. Qg7#) **2. Ra8+**, and mate in three.

60. Check & Discovered Attack

1. Rb6+! Ka8 (1. ... Kc8 2. Na7+ or 2. Nd6+) **2. Nc7+**, winning Black's Queen. Note that if it weren't for Black's pawn on h4, the game would end in a draw by stalemate!

61.

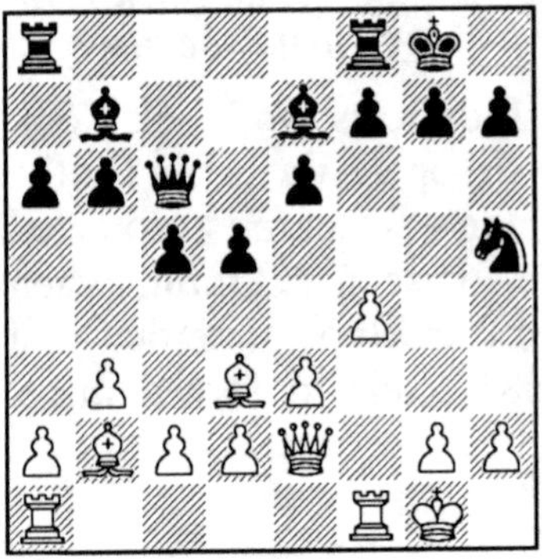

White to move

62.

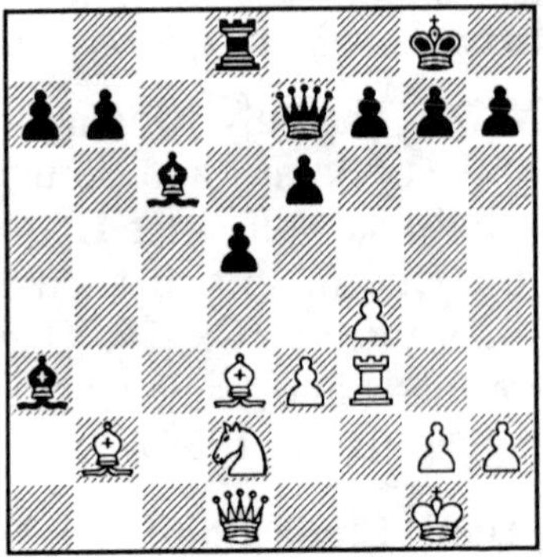

White to move

63.

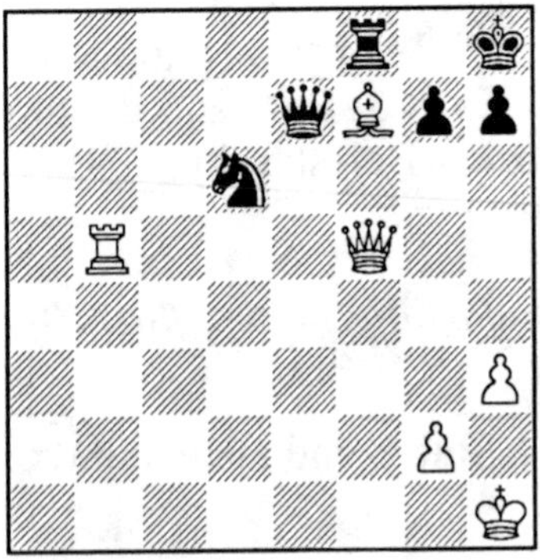

White to move

64.

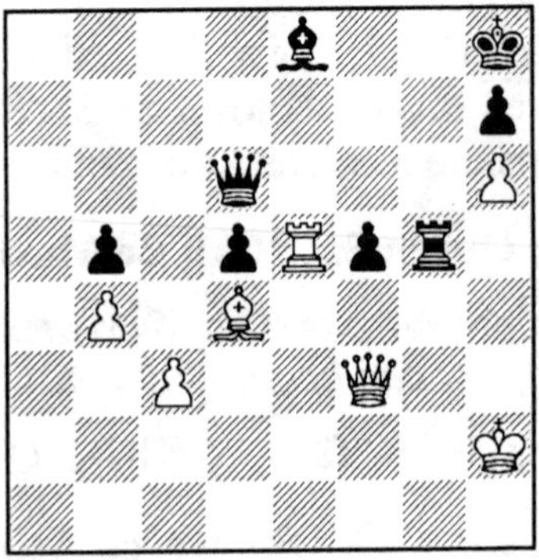

White to move

61. Classic Two-Bishop Sacrifice

Black just played ... Nf6xh5, taking the Knight. He expects, after a "normal" Qxh5, to play ... f7-f5, with a good game. Instead Lasker creates a beautiful and important-to-know combination.

1. Bxh7+! Kxh7 2. Qxh5+ Kg8 3. Bxg7! Kxg7 (3. ... f5 4. Be5 Rf6 5. Rf3 Kf8 6. Rg3, and 3. ... f6 4. Bh6! both lead to White's decisive advantage) **4. Qg4+ Kh7 5. Rf3 e5 6. Rh3+ Qh6 7. Rxh6+ Kxh6 8. Qd7**, and White won. (Lasker, Em. - Bauer, 1889)

62. Lasker's Sacrifice

Materially, the game is approximately equal. White has a piece for three pawns. But in the opening and middlegame, the piece is often just a bit better. The typical way an extra piece can prove its usefulness is by attacking.

1. Bxh7+! Kxh7 2. Rh3+ Kg8 3. Bxg7! (the so-called "Lasker sacrifice" of both Bishops, from his famous game against Bauer, above.) **3. ... Kxg7?** (3. ... f5 4. Be5 is an easy win for White, but Black can resist more staunchly with 3. ... f6, although 4. Bh6 Qh7 5. Qh5 Bf8 6. Qg4+ still wins.) **4. Qg4+ 1-0**. Should you see all these lines before you play 1. Bxh7+ to begin? No, but you should see as far as 3. Bxg7 — and at least a few sample lines thereafter, showing that your attack will most likely succeed. (Alekhine - Drewitt, 1923)

63. Model Rook & Bishop Mate on the Rook file

1. Qxh7+! Kxh7 2. Rh5#.

64. Anything to Unpin!

1. Qg3! (bad is 1. Kh1? Qxh6+) **1. ... Rxg3**. (Black is lost, for example, 1. ... Rh5+ 2. Kg2 or 1. ... Qxh6+ 2. Qh3 Qd6 3. Kh1.) **2. Rxe8#**. (Duras - Spielmann, 1912)

65.

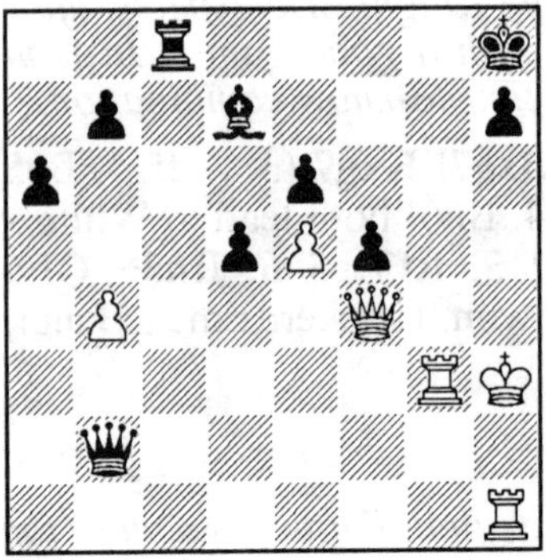

White to move

66.

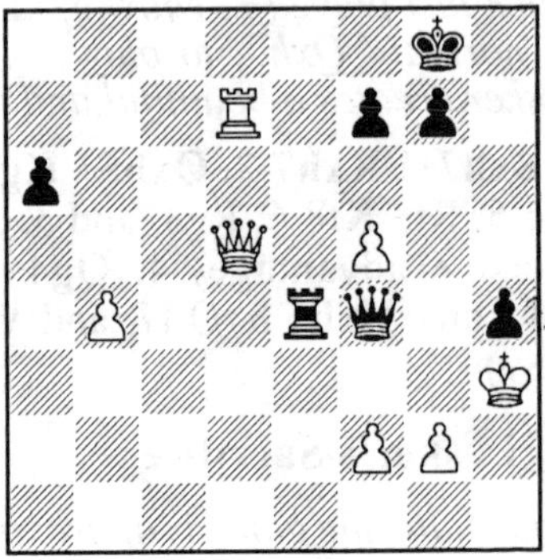

Black to move

67.

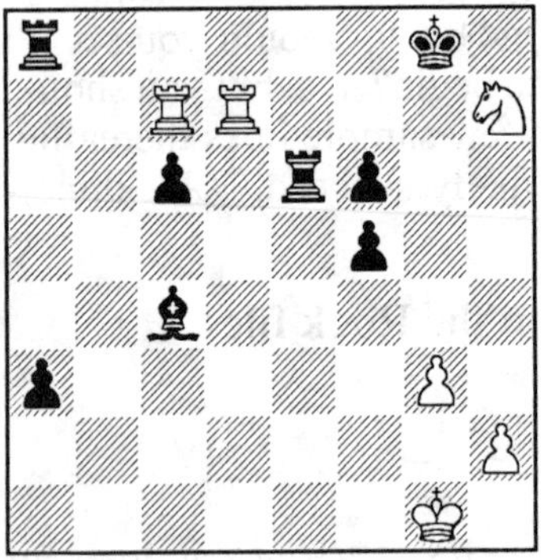

White to move

68.

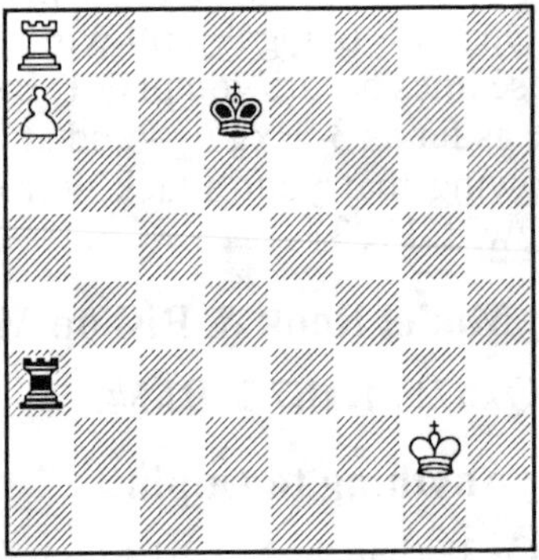

White to move

65. His Majesty Steps Aside

White is down in material. He's ahead in the attack, but his own King is in the way of his h1-Rook. In a famous game, American Grandmaster Harry Nelson Pillsbury played a move you probably considered: 1. Qh6, threatening mate via f6 and g7. But what to do after 1. ... Qxe5, Black's only reply?

1. Qh6! Qxe5 2. Qxh7+!! Kxh7 3. Kg2#. The White King slides demurely out of the way of his own Rook and, in doing so, delivers checkmate! (Pillsbury - Maroczy, 1900)

66. Removing the Defender

1. ... Re3+! 0-1. (Tarjan - Karpov, 1976)

67. Blocking the Royal Retreat

1. Rg7+ Kh8 2. Nf8. The threat of Ng6, mate, decoys Black's Rook to f8, where it blocks the King's escape. **2. ... Rxf8 3. Rh7+ Kg8 4. Rcg7#**. (Morphy - Morian, 1866)

68. Rook Ending: Skewer 101

White to move wins with **1. Rh8 Rxa7 2. Rh7+**, skewering the Black pieces (a geometrical motif with King and Rook on the same rank). Black to move draws by moving toward the pawn: **1. ... Kc7!** (or 1. ... Kc6!) **2. Rh8 Rxa7 3. Rh7+ Kb6**.

Now make a small change: Put the Black King on e7. White wins no matter who is to move. As in the original position, 1. Rh8 wins, while Black on move can now neither bring his King close enough to the pawn (1. ... Kd7 2. Rh7+) nor to g7. (The only safe squares on the kingside to avoid the decisive skewer or check are g7 and h7.)

69.

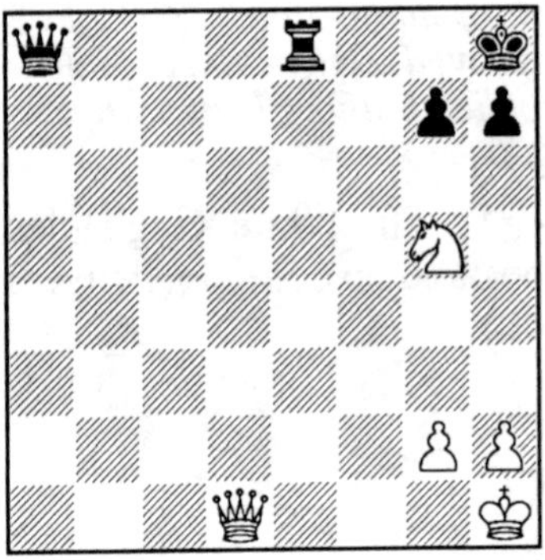

Black to move

70.

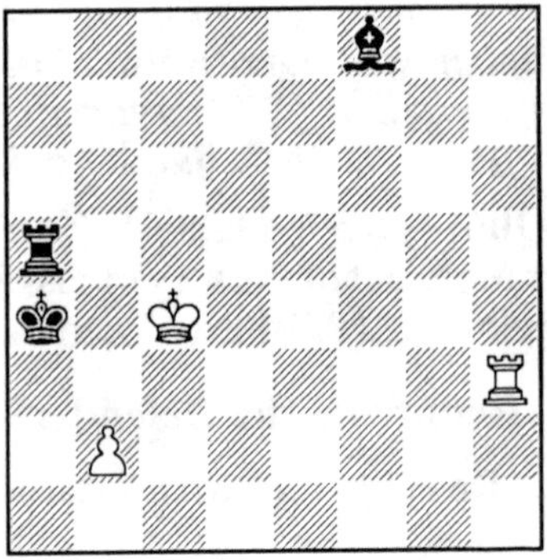

White to move

71.

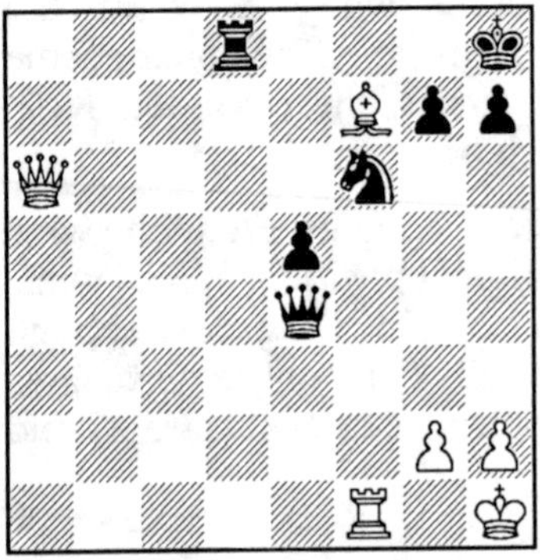

White to move

72.

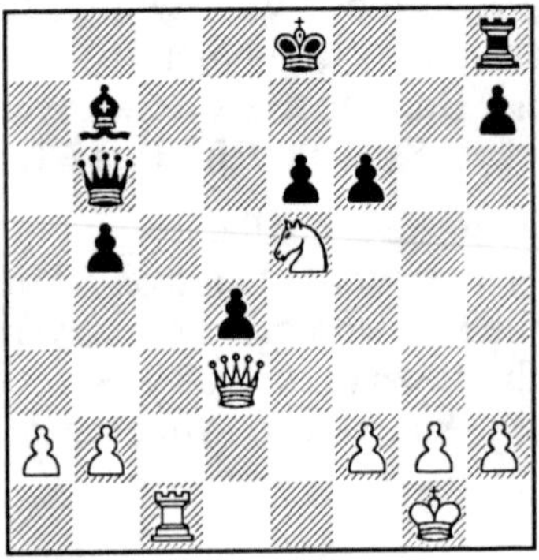

White to move

69. Exploiting the Back Rank

Of course Black can try — and achieve — the exchange of Queens. In the resulting R + 2 pawns vs. N + 2 pawns ending (with all pawns on the same side, aiding the short-moving Knight), Black will have some winning chances (say 60%). But White's first rank is vulnerable — his Queen must defend it against mate. And White's g5-Knight is undefended. These weaknesses should encourage Black to look for more — NOW!

1. ... Qd5!. A powerful double attack. (Tempting is 1. ... Re2, but White still holds on with 2. Nf3 Ra2! 3. Qd4!.) **2. Qc1** (2. Qxd5 Re1#) **2. ... Qxg5** (deflection), and Black wins.

70. Mate with the Last Man

1. b3+ Ka3 2. b4+ Ka4 3. bxa5 Kxa5 leads to a drawish Rook vs. Bishop position. Look for more.

1. Ra3+! Bxa3 2. b3#.

71. Watch out for Traps!

You probably see that 1. Rxf6 gxf6 leads to mate in one, and that 1. ... Rd1+ (or 1. ... Qe1+) fails because of the defense 2. Rf1. Now follow the routine — double-check your analysis.

Otherwise, it's easy to overlook **1. Rxf6 Qc6!!**, winning an Exchange and eventually the game. From various candidate moves, I'd prefer 1. h3, making luft and setting up a trap: 1. h3 Qd3??. (This *seems* to win a tempo, or to lead to a pawn-up ending—the bait in a trap must be attractive to be effective!) 2. Rxf6, winning.

72. Take the Seventh!

1. Qg3! fxe5 2. Qg7 Rf8 3. Rc7 Qxc7, and Black soon resigned. Equally hopeless was 3. ... Qd6 4. Rxb7 d3 5. Ra7 Qd8 6. Qxh7, with mate coming soon. (Botvinnik - Euwe, 1948)

73.

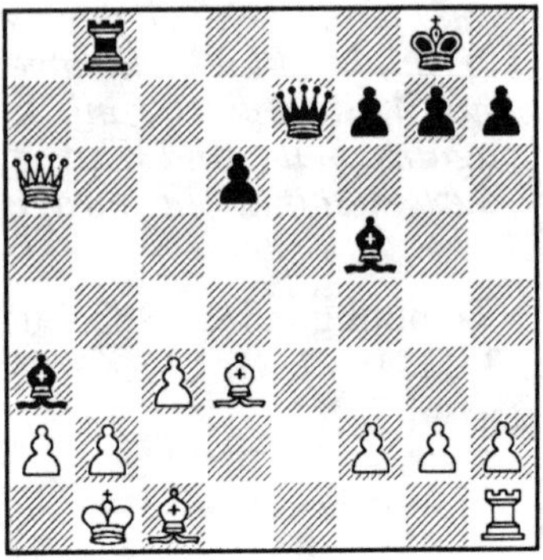

Black to move

74.

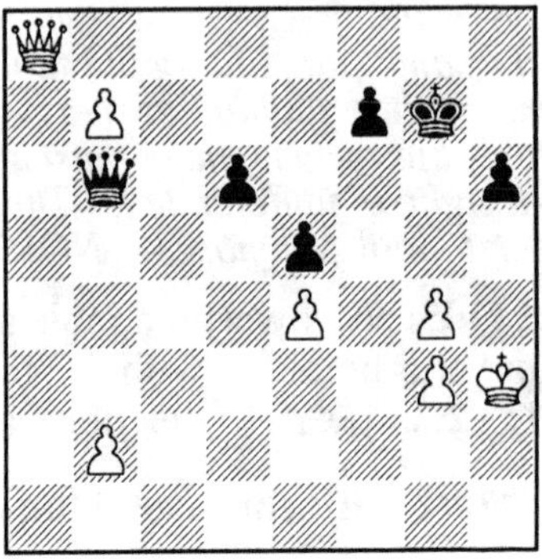

Black to move

75.

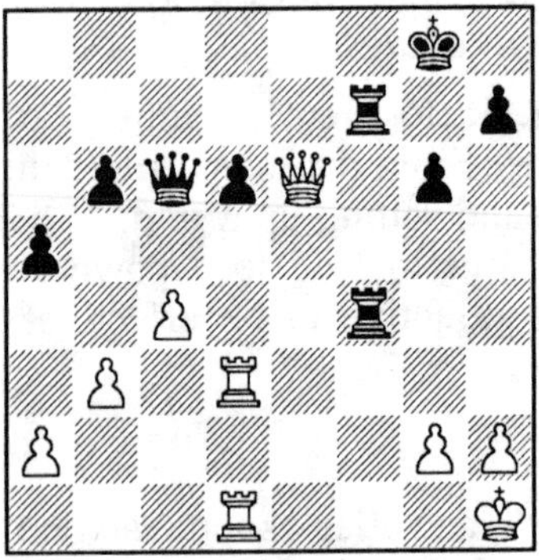

Black to move

76.

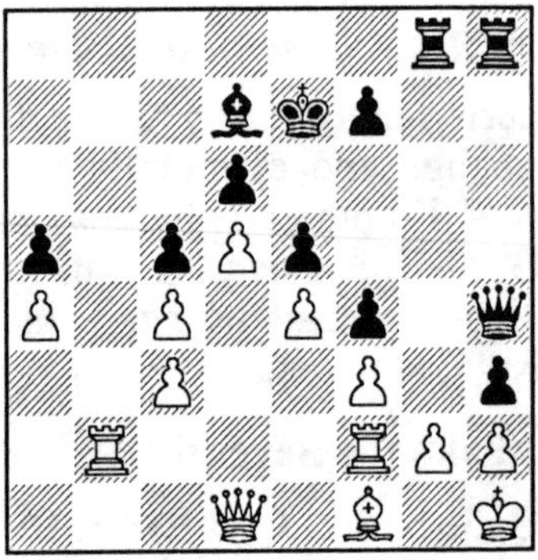

Black to move

<u>73.</u> Pin Again!

Black is down two pawns, but he's attacking and pins are everywhere. Slam White to the mat with a cross-pin!

1. ... Qe2!. Cross-pin — it's a double pin, and here also a double attack on d3 and b2! Did you see how to continue after **2. Rd1!**, White's most natural and best defense (if 2. Qxa3 Qxd3+ 3. Ka1 Qb1#)? The tempting 2. ... Rxb2+? (hoping for 3. Bxb2?? Qxb2#), is answered by the simple 3. Ka1, when Black has a draw by perpetual check, but that's all. Also wrong is 2. ... Bxb2? 3. Qxd6, and things are getting murky, if not outright bad for Black. Stay calm and find the easy and convincing **2. ... Qxd1 - +**. Remember: Sometimes it's not enough to find *one* brilliant move! (Poshauko - Kholosar, 1941)

<u>74.</u> Queen at His Back!

1. ... Qg1 (threatens 2. ... Qh1#) **2. g5 h5! 3. g4 h4!**, and mate is inevitable. (Federov - Vasiliev, 1974)

<u>75.</u> The Battery Gets a Boost

If only the f7-Rook wasn't pinned, Black's powerful Rook battery would mate on f1.

1. ... Qe4, deflecting the Queen, **0-1**. An unusual oversight by one of the world's greatest tacticians, who was too immersed in his own plans to consider carefully his opponent's threats. (Geller - Ostoic, 1969)

<u>76.</u> Decoy the h-pawn

1. ... Qg3!. Threatening 2. ... Qxh2+ 3. Kxh2 hxg2+ 4. Kg1, and Black's Rook will come to h1 with decisive effect. **2. hxg3 hxg2+ 3. Kg1** (3. Kg2 Rxg3#) **3. ... Rh1+ 4. Kxg2 R8h8 5. gxf4 gxf4 0-1**. (Bleule - Wegener, 1956)

77.

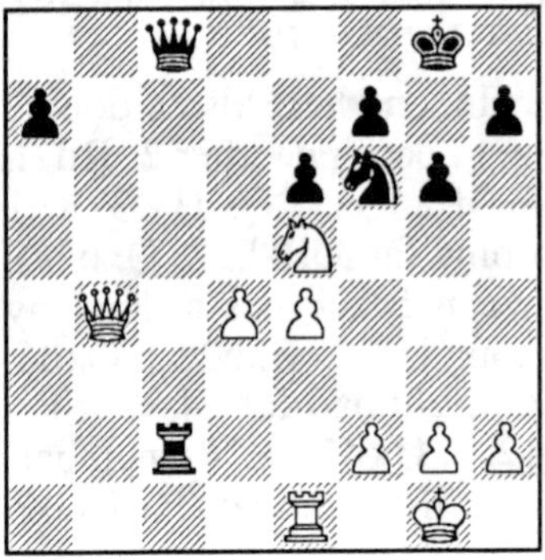

Black to move

78.

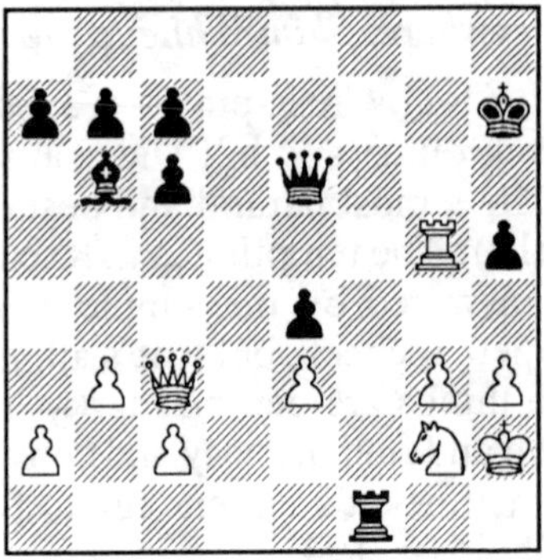

Black to move

79.

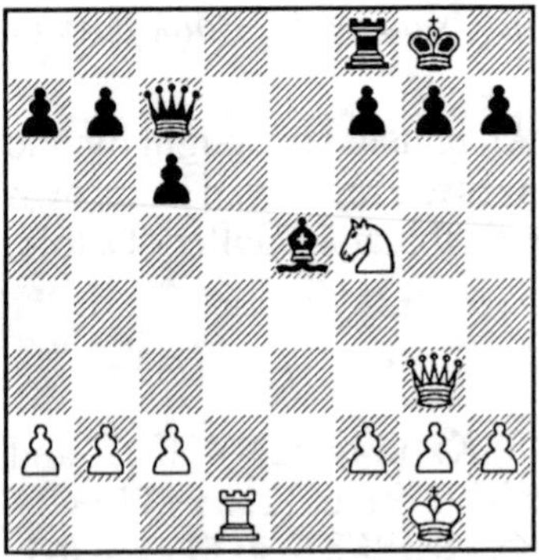

White to move

80.

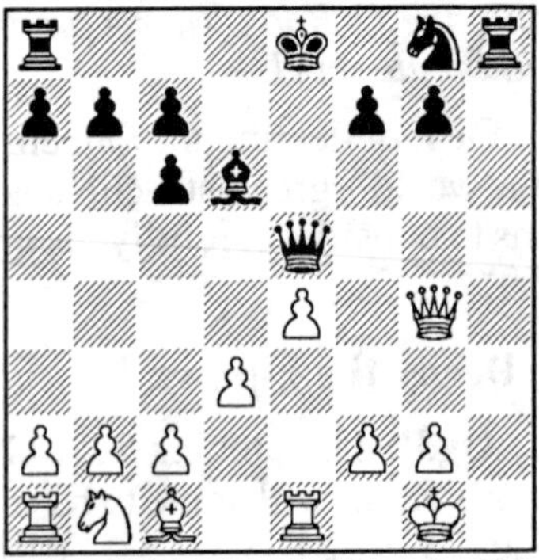

Black to move

77. Double Deflection & Back-Rank Mate

Let's try to deflect the White Rook from the first rank with 1. ... Nxe4 2. Rxe4. Now 2. ... Rc1+ can be defended with 3. Re1. But don't give up! You've deflected the Rook. Now deflect the Queen from supporting her back rank.

1. ... Nxe4! 2. Rxe4. (If you could have imagined this position in your mind very clearly while considering 1. ... Nxe4, you'd probably have found the following double attack.) **2. ... Qb7!**, winning for Black. If **3. Qe1**, then **3. ... Qxe4** (final deflection). Motifs: back-rank weakness; underprotected e4 pawn; overworked Rook and Queen. (Novichkov - Luzganov, 1963)

78. Mate by Matricide

The "typical" Rook sacrifice doesn't work: 1. ... Rh1+ 2. Kxh1 Qh3+ 3. Kg1, and White's e3-pawn shields the King from Black's Bishop. But as is so often true, reversing the move order helps: **1. ... Qxh3+** (decoy) **2. Kxh3 Rh1#**. Motif: White's King cramped by his own men. (Lupanov - Gusev, 1922)

79. Checks Take Precedence!

Look for checks, forks, deflections — and an eventual back-rank mate.

1. Nh6+ Kh8 2. Qxe5 Qxe5 3. Nxf7+ 1-0. After 3. ... Kg8 4. Nxe5, White is a piece and a pawn ahead, while 3. ... Rxf7 4. Rd8+ leads to a forced mate. Motifs for the combination: back-rank weakness (no *luft*, German for air), pinned g7-pawn; e5 and h8 squares reachable by Knight fork. (Capablanca - Foxcroft, 1918)

80. Charge Your Battery (Classic Decoy Mate)

1. ... Rh1+ 2. Kxh1 Qh2#. (Maderna - Villegas, 1943)

81.

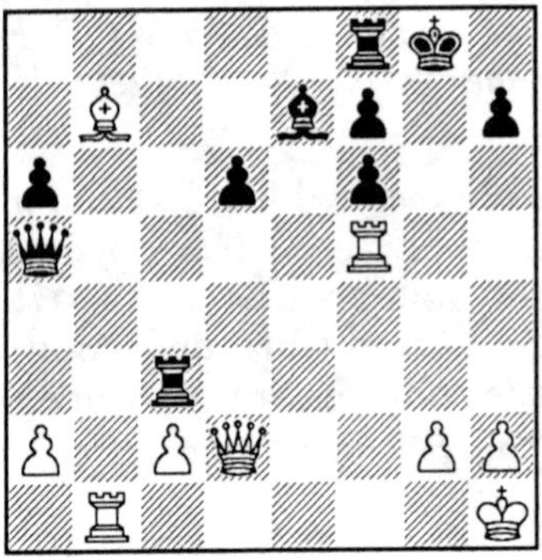

Black to move

82.

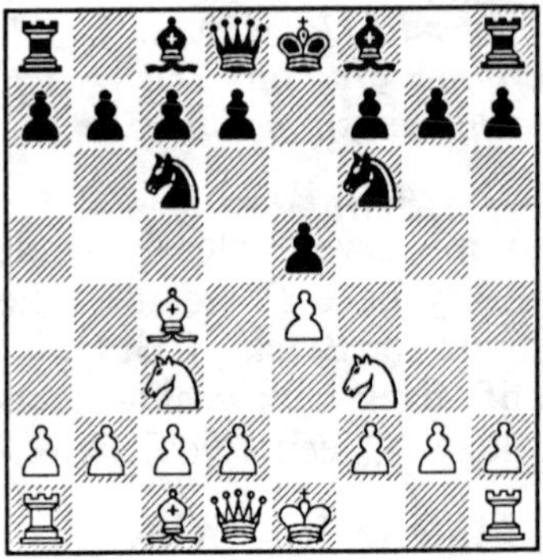

Black to move

83.

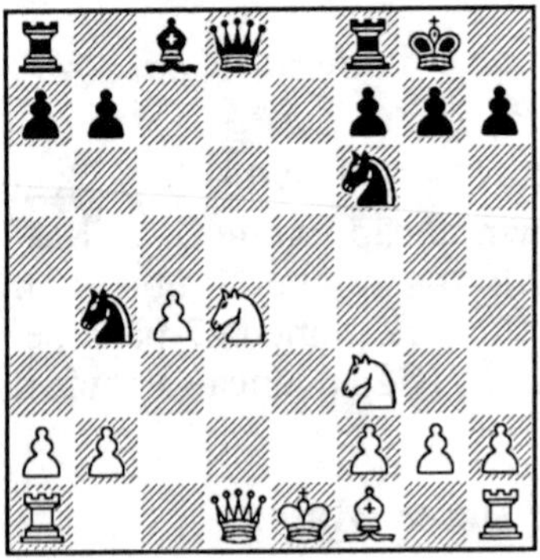

Black to move

84.

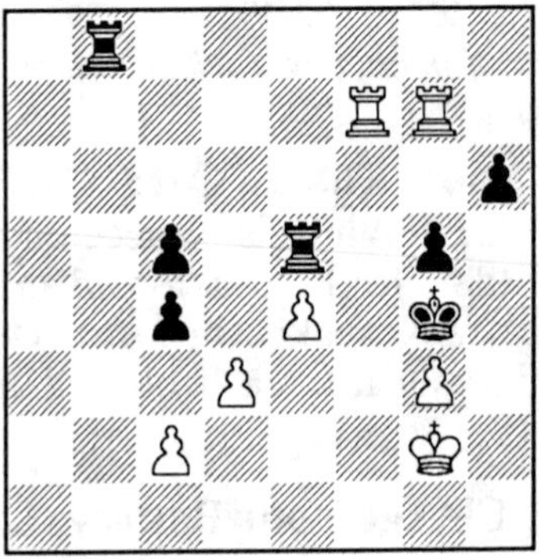

White to move

81. Pinned? Unpin and Win!

Yes, you should consider moves like 1. ... Qxf5 (exchanging Rooks) and 1. ... Qxa2. But note the lack of moves available to the White King. So look for more — say, for back-rank mate.

1. ... Rb3! (discovered attack, in-between move), and White resigns in light of **2. Qd1 Rxb1 3. Qxb1 Qxf5**. (Maric - Gligoric, 1964)

82. Opening Fork Trick

After the opening moves of the Vienna Game, 1.e4 e5 2. Nc3 Nf6 3. Bc4 Nc6, why is the natural 4. Nf3 considered toothless? (The same position can be reached by different move orders, e.g. 1. e4 e5 2. Nf3 Nc6 3. Bc4 Nf6 4. Nc3.)

Black equalizes with the "fork trick," a temporary or "sham" Knight-for-pawn sacrifice: **4. ... Nxe4 5. Nxe4** (after 5. Bxf7+ Kxf7 6. Nxe4 d5, Black has two strong Bishops and a better pawn center, which together more than compensate for the temporary exposure of the Black King) **5. ... d5**, winning back the material with a good game.

83. Buried with His Own Cavalry

White is up a pawn but behind in development. Still, he is ready to finish deploying if allowed to play Be2. So ...

1. ... Qa5! 2. Nd2 (2. Qd2 Ne4 3. Nb3 Nxd2 4. Nxa5 Nxf3+ is winning for Black too) **2. ... Qe5+! 3. Ne2** (leads to smothered mate in one, but White is lost anyway) **3. ... Nd3#**. (Lasker, Ed. - Horowitz, 1946)

84. Blocking the Royal Retreat

1. Rf4+ Kh5 2. Rh4+! gh4 3. g4#. Black's own pawn on h4 prevents his King's escape. (Durao - Katoci, 1957)

85.

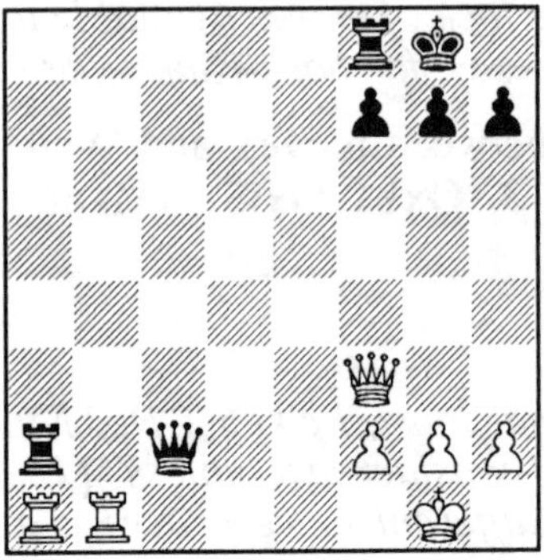

Black to move

86.

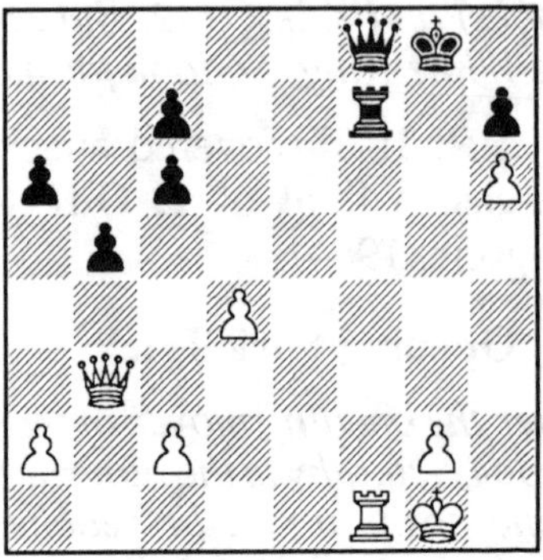

White to move

87.

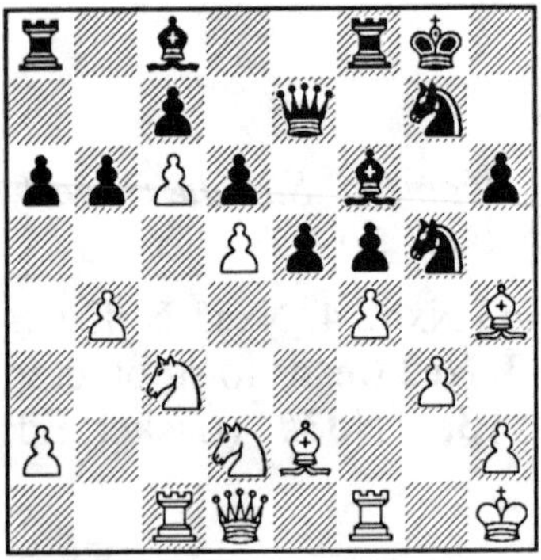

White to move

88.

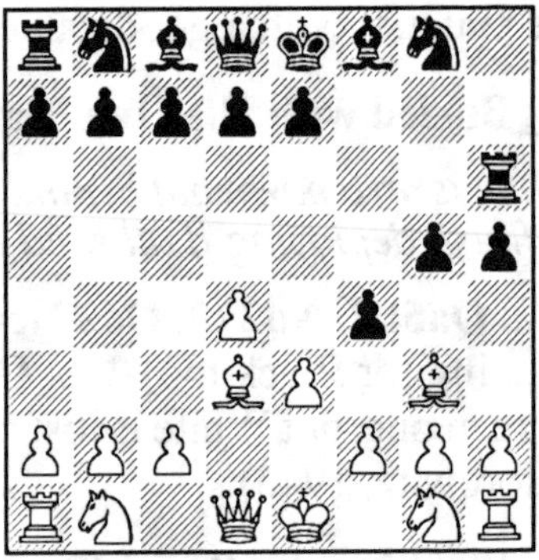

White to move

85. Attack the a-Rook Again — But Be Careful!

Black must do something decisive NOW, before White makes luft with 1. g3 or 1. h3.

1. ... Qb2! wins, as the White Queen can't leave her defense of the f2-square, and there is no other defense against the coming ... Rxa1. Wrong is 1. ... Rfa8?, permitting White to deliver a back-row mate of his own with 2. Qxa8+!.

86. Traveler's Checks

White wins by first improving the position of his Queen, then by driving the Black King into the corner, where he'll be smothered — and mated.

1. Qg3+ Kh8 2. Qe5+ Kg8 3. Qg5+ Kh8 4. Rxf7 Qxf7 5. Qd8+ Qg8 6. Qf6+, and mate next. In the actual game, White erred with 1. Qe6?, eventually drawing. (Damjanovic - Lutikov, 1969)

87. Cutting Off Reinforcements

1. a4!. Now the Black Queen's Rook and Bishop will be cut off from the rest of his forces for a long time. Otherwise, Black could play 1. ... b5 and later, at the proper moment, ... a5. Now on **1. ... b5**, White has **2. a5**, and on **1. ... a5**, he has **2. b5** — in both cases sealing the queenside. (Petrosian, T. - Gligoric, 1959)

88. The Queen Clears the Way

This position arises after 1. d4 f5 2. Bg5 h6 3. Bh4 g5 4. Bg3 f4? 5. e3 h5 6. Bd3. Black has just played the suicidal 6. ... Rh6??. He was clearly too greedy to begin with, but after 6. ... e5!, he could still keep fighting. In fact, Black would have won a piece, albeit for two pawns and the disadvantage of his King being stuck on e7. He would be worse, but not completely lost.

7. Qxh5+! (deflection) **7. ... Rxh5 8. Bg6#.**

89.

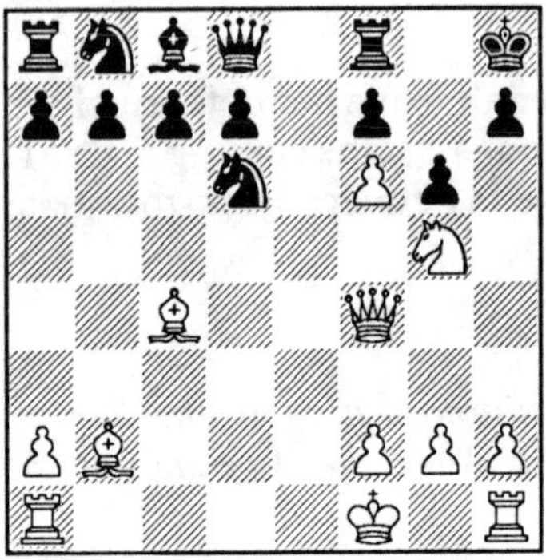

White to move

90.

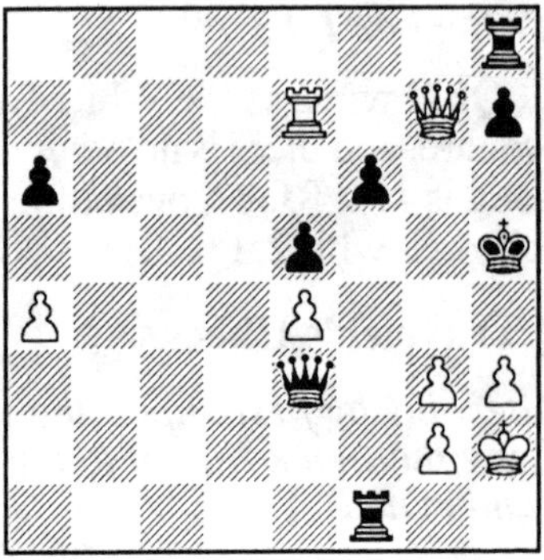

White to move

91.

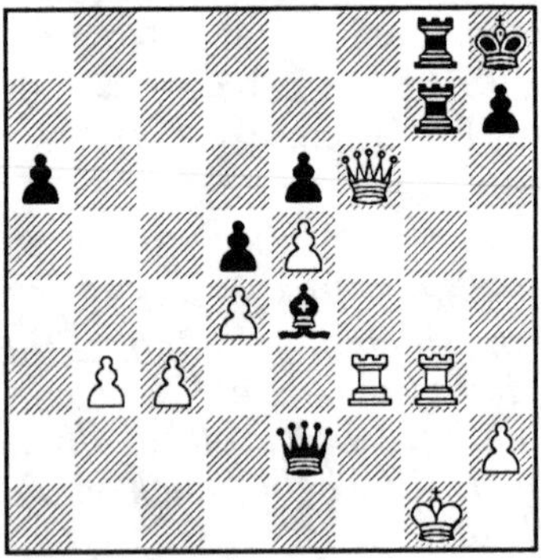

White to move

92.

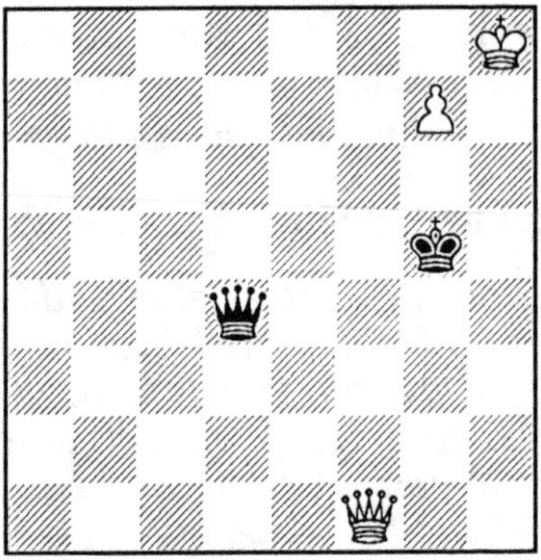

White to move

89. Overwhelming Attackers

White has at least five men attacking the vulnerable Black King. Note also the hole on g7 and Black's lack of development. White's Queen, Knight, and f6-pawn are especially menacing, so there is little surprise that White, just two pawns down in return for this great position, has more than one path leading to victory. If you preferred 1. Nxh7! — great! White wins after 1. ... Kxh7 2. Qh4+ Kg8 3. Qh6 Nf5 4. Qxg6+. But now please think about how the game will continue after 1. Nxf7+.

1. Nxf7+ Nxf7. (1. ... Rxf7 is no better — 2. Bxf7 Nxf7 3. Qh6 Qg8 [3. ... Nxh6 leads to mate after 4. f7+] 4. Re1 Nxh6 5. f7+ Qg7 6. Re8+) **2. Qh6!! Nxh6**. (After 2. ... Rg8 3. Bxf7 White's threats are decisive.) **3. f7+** and mate next move. (Denker - Gonzales, 1945)

90. Missed Pawn Mate

Women's World Champion Nona Gaprindashvili here missed a rare chance to mate with her pawns, choosing a perpetual check — 1. Qg4+ Kh6 2. Qg7+, etc. Instead, White should play:

1. Rxe5+! fxe5 2. g4+ Kh4 3. Qe7+! Qg5 4. g3 mate! (Gaprindashvili - Vereczy, 1974)

91. Cutting the Defenders in Half

When mate is in the offing, only the forces defending the King count!

1. Qxg7+! Rxg7 2. Rf8+. (Marshall - Treybal, 1930)

92. Decoy & Skewer

1. Qg1+ Qxg1 2. g8(Q)+ 1-0. Black lost so easily because his King was misplaced. White's task would be much more difficult with Black's King on a2 or a3, far away from the main action.

93.

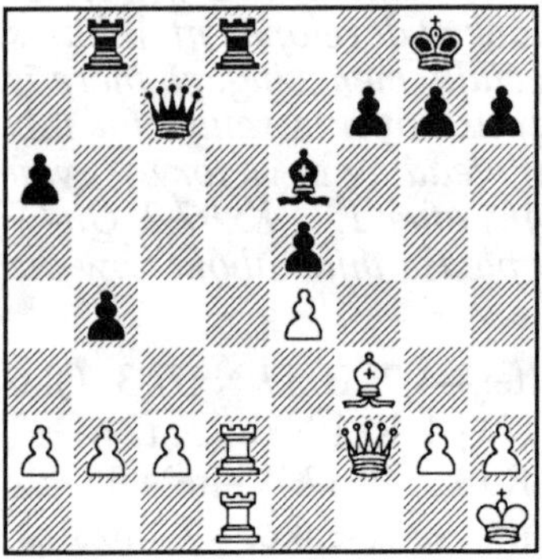

White to move

94.

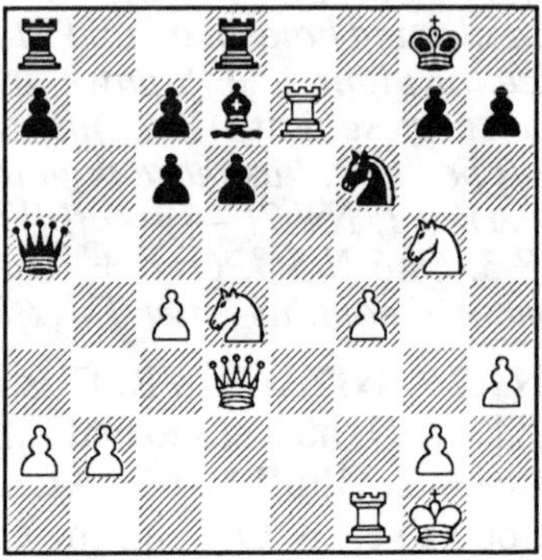

White to move

95.

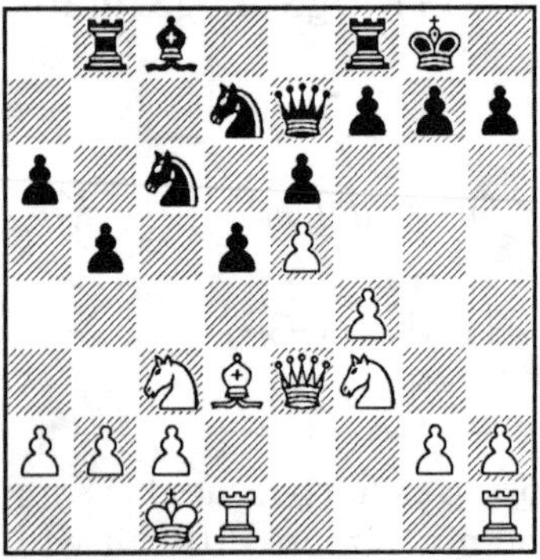

White to move

96.

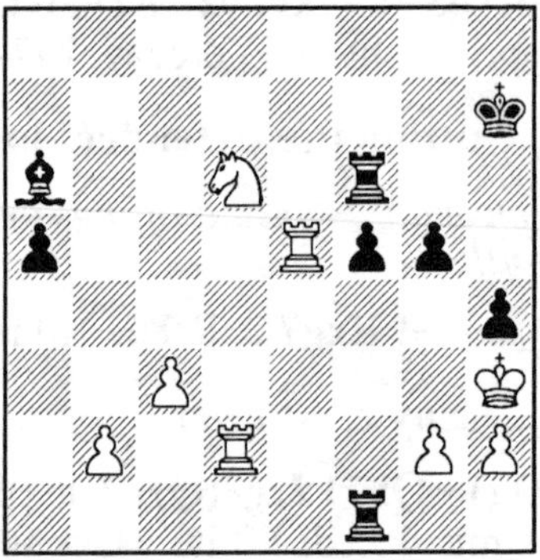

Black to move

93. Deflection Detection

White is worse strategically (e.g., he has a bad Bishop on f3), but his Rook battery on the d-file, combined with Black's lack of luft, should provide White with some hope — and make him think hard.

1. Qa7! Qa5 2. Qxa6 Qc7 3. Qa7! 1-0. Motifs: weak back rank, underprotected d8-Rook. (Rovner - Kamishov, 1946)

94. Making It Safe for Her Majesty

The g7 square seems to be the natural target. 1. Nde6 looks attractive, e.g., 1. ... Bxe6 2. Nxe6 Rd7 3. Rxd7 Nxd7 4. Qg3 g6 5. f5. Let's think for Black: Maybe 2. ... Re8 3. Rxg7+ Kh8 is not so clear. Let's look for an easier White win.

1. Nxh7 Nxh7 (1. ... Qh5 2. Nxf6+ gxf6 3. Qg3+) **2. Qg6 1-0.** (Schlechter - Gavashi, 1918)

95. The Mother of All Sacrifices

1. Bxh7+ Kxh7 (after 1. ... Kh8, Black is down a pawn with a vulnerable King after the simple 2. Bd3) **2. Ng5+ Kg6** (2. ... Kg8 3. Qh3) **3. Qh3!**. The winning threat is 4. Qh7#, and it's okay if you've seen only this far. But did you anticipate 3. ... Nc(or d)xe5 for Black? **3. ... Ndxe5 4. Qh7+ Kf6 5. Nce4+**, and mate next move.

96. Opening the Diagonal for Mate

The White King barely holds his ground. What if Black plays 1. ... Rf3+ 2. gxf3 Bf1+ here? The idea is good, but White still has a defense — 3. Rg2. Is there a better move order?

1. ... Rxd6! (deflection) **2. Rxd6** (otherwise Black is up a piece, with an attack) **2. ... Rf3+** (now!) **3. gxf3 Bf1#**. (Man - Papp, 1962)

97.

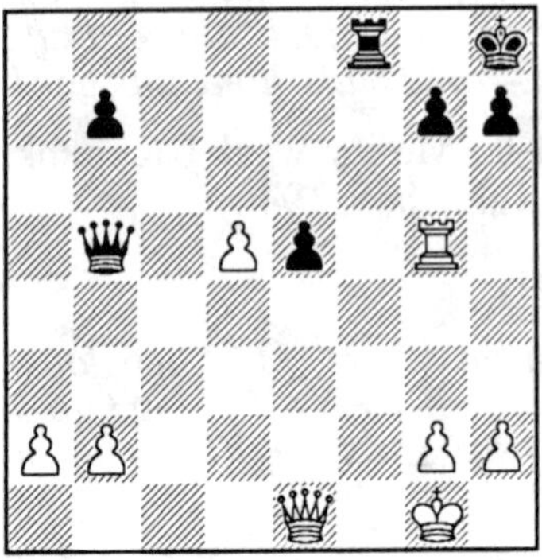

Black to move

98.

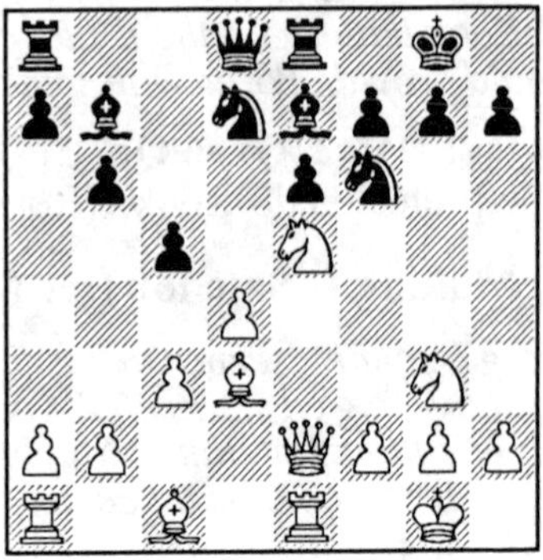

White to move

99.

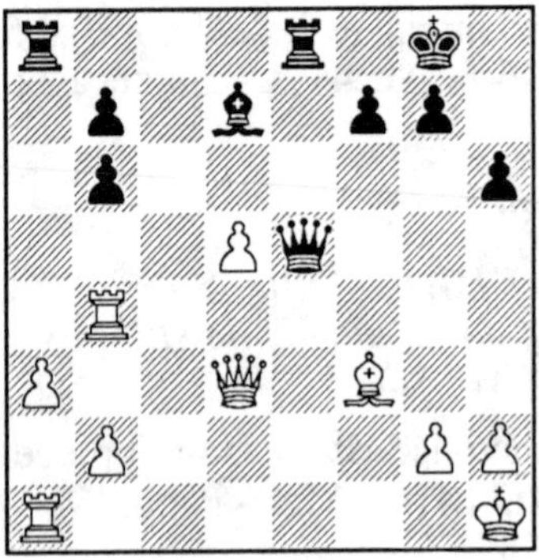

Black to move

100.

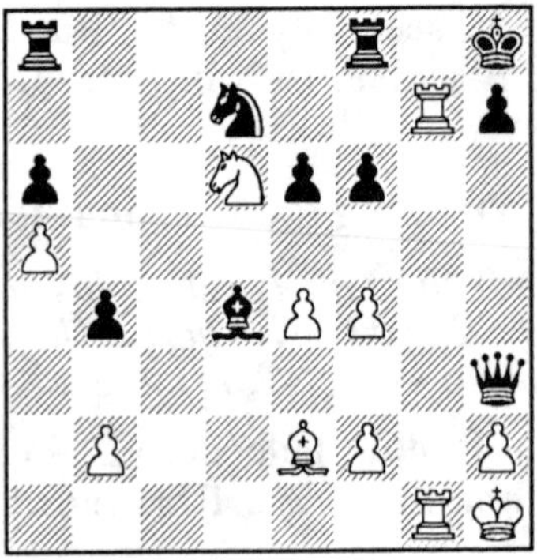

White to move

97. Maneuvering with Checks

1. ... Qc5+! 2. Kh1 Qc4!. The first support position. (Not the double attack 2. ... Qe3? 3. Qxe3 Rf1+ 4. Qg1, winning for White.) **3. Kg1 Qd4+ 4. Kh1**. Use this new support position to assist your calculation. **4. ... Qe4! 5. Qc1** (5. Qg1 Qe2, followed by ... Rf1; 5. Qd1 [or 5. Qa1] 5. ... Qf4) **5. ... Qd3 6. Kg1**. All forced. Note how the Queen improves her position, alternating threats and checks to gain tempi. **6. ... Qd4+ 7. Kh1 Qd2** (this double attack provides a decisive deflection) **0-1**.

This is a difficult one. If you didn't see everything to the end, but still found the first two moves correctly — count it as solved! Now try to do the entire combination in your mind from the starting position. Make sure you see all lines very clearly. Give yourself 20-30 minutes; then check it all by moving the pieces. (Lovitsky - Tartakower, 1935)

98. Vulnerable f7

1. Nxf7! Kxf7 2. Qxe6+ Kf8 3. Bc4, and White will be two pawns up since the only way for Black to avoid mate is to give back a piece. Note that with the d7-Knight still on b8, this combination wouldn't work, because 3. Bc4 is met by 3. ... Bd5 — and now Black is winning! (Rattmann - Haas, corr., 1931-1933)

99. Hit 'em Where They Least Expect It!

Black gains nothing with 1. ... Qe1+ 2. Qf1, so let's look for a typical tool to achieve back-rank mate — deflection.

Black stunned his opponent — and the spectators — with an easy-when-shown but difficult-to-find move: **1. ... Rxa3! 0-1**. This pawn was protected three ways! (Mikenas - Bronstein, 1962)

100. Model Rook & Knight Cut-Off Mate

1. Rg8+ Rxg8 2. Nf7#. (Tolush - Smyslov, 1950)

101.

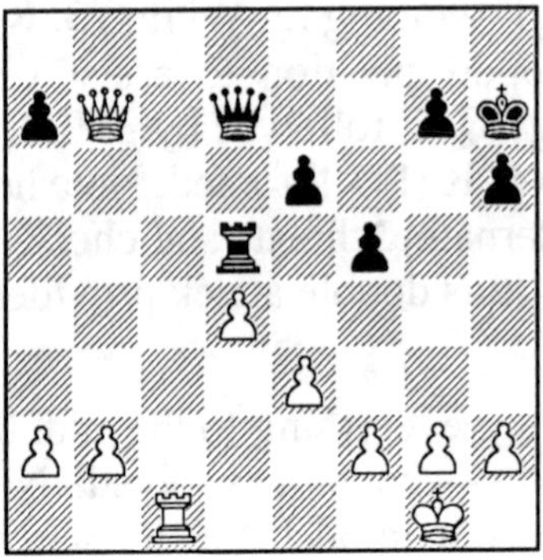

White to move

102.

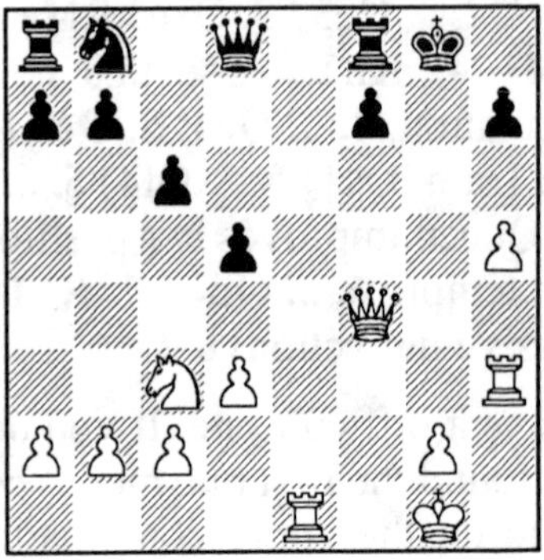

White to move

103.

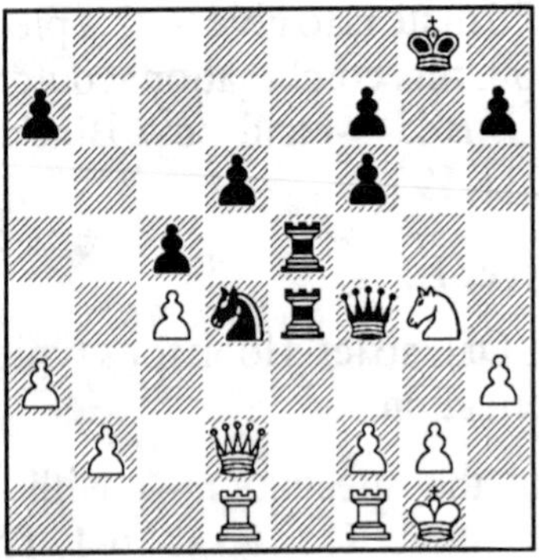

Black to move

104.

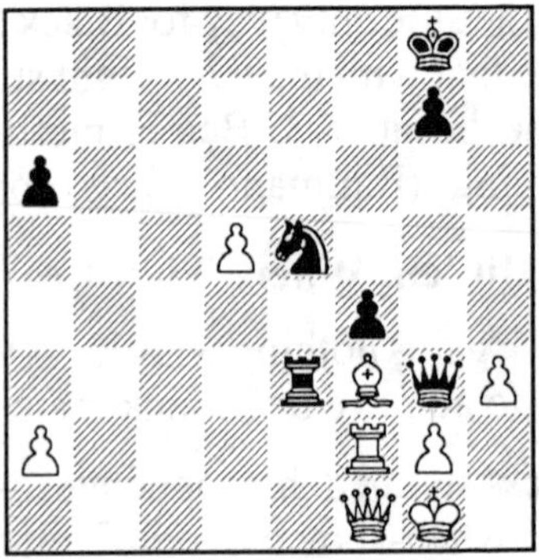

Black to move

101. Scrutinize that "Winning" Move

By exchanging Queens, White of course can get a Rook ending with two extra pawns (and control over the only open file), but shouldn't he look for more?

He should. 1. Rc7 seems to win outright. (If the Queen moves, then White has 2. Rxg7+ etc.). But White then should think hard for his opponent — and, hopefully, find the paradoxical turn-around move 1. ... Rc5! (double pin), winning for Black. White should give thanks and play **1. Qxd7 Rxd7 2. Rc5**, with a decisive (but not instantly winning) endgame edge. The key lesson: Verify your analysis — especially when considering a move that seems to win instantly!

102. Overwhelming Force

1. Rg3+ Kh8 2. Qh6! (2. Qe5+ f6) **2. ... Rg8 3. Re8 1-0**. Either the Black Rook is deflected from protecting g7, or the Black Queen is deflected from protecting f6. Black can't even successfully sacrifice material with 3. ... Nd7, because of 4. Qg7#. (Cardiff - Bristol, correspondence)

103. The Right Road to Rook & Knight Mate

Despite his poor pawn structure, Black's position looks fine because of his dominant pieces. But how should he use them?

1. ... Ne2+!. The right move — and the right idea, with the right move order. (Wrong is 1. ... Qxg4 2. hxg4 Ne2+ 3. Qxe2.) **2. Kh1 Qxg4! 3. hxg4**. (I would try 3. f3, muddying the water a little. Still, with 3. ... Ng3+ 4. Kg1 Nxf1, Black wins a piece and the game.) **3. ... Rh5+ 4. gxh5 Rh4#**. (Guilly - Genneberger, 1941)

104. Sac for a Winning Fork

1. ... Re1! 2. Qxe1 Nxf3+ 0-1. (Perlis - Duz-Khotimirsky, 1911)

105.

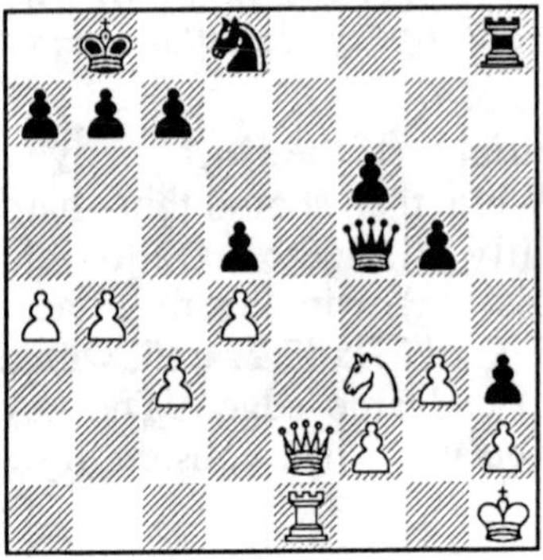

Black to move

106.

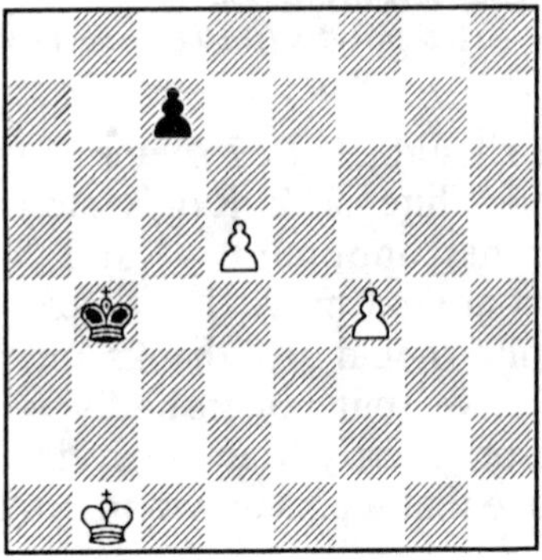

White/Black to move

107.

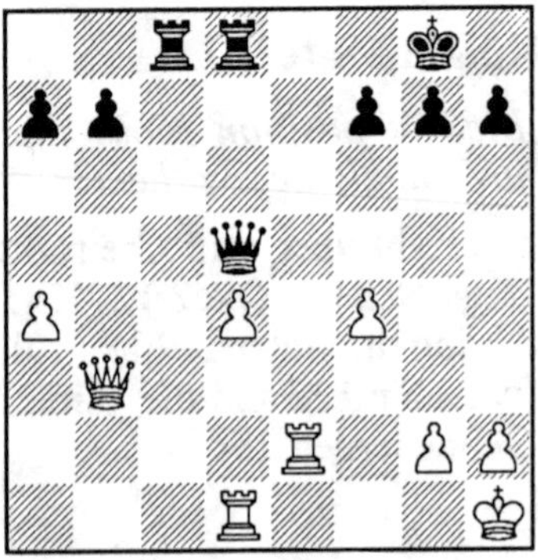

White to move

108.

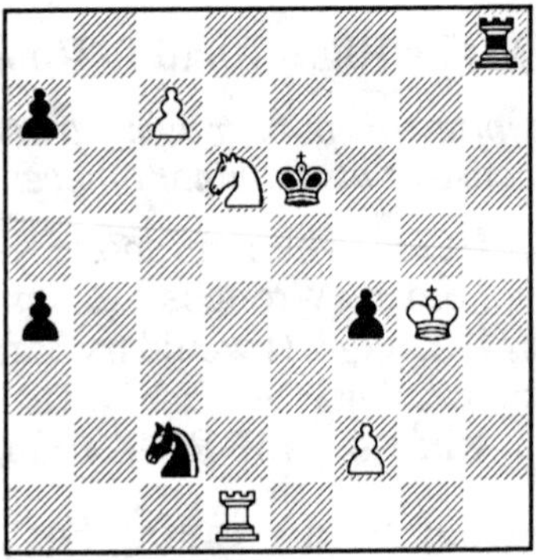

White to move

105. Double Decoy

Black's h3-pawn acts as a wedge in White's pawn cover, sealing up any luft. Bring in more firepower.

If you found **1. ... Re8!**, great! It's even better if you foresaw that after the forced reply **2. Qd1**, you can play the decisive blow **2. ... Qxf3+!**. (Opochensky - Alekhine, 1925)

106. The Rule of the Square

White to move wins by **1. d6!**, and after **1. ... cxd6 2. f5 Kc5 3. f6**, Black's King, hindered by his own pawn, can't remain within the "square" of White's f-pawn. Black to move draws easily with 1. ... Kc5.

107. Model Deflection

1. Re8+ Rxe8 2. Qxd5, winning a Queen for a Rook. Even if Black's h7-pawn were on h6 (providing luft), 1. Re8+ wins after 1. ... Kh7 2. Qxd5 Rxd5 3. Rxc8, snaring a Rook. (Matskevich - Mnatsakanian, 1963)

108. Interfere & Queen Your Pawn!

Winning the Rook for a pawn isn't immediately clear: 1. c8(Q)+?! Rxc8 2. Nxc8 a3. Still, 3. Rd6+ now wins. But simpler is ...

1. Ne8! (clearing the d-file) **1. ... Rxe8 2. Rd8 1-0.** (Salov - Ehlvest, 1989)

109.

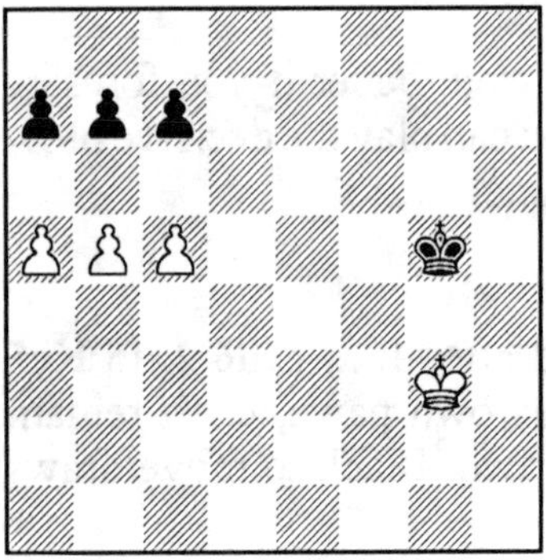

White/Black to move

110.

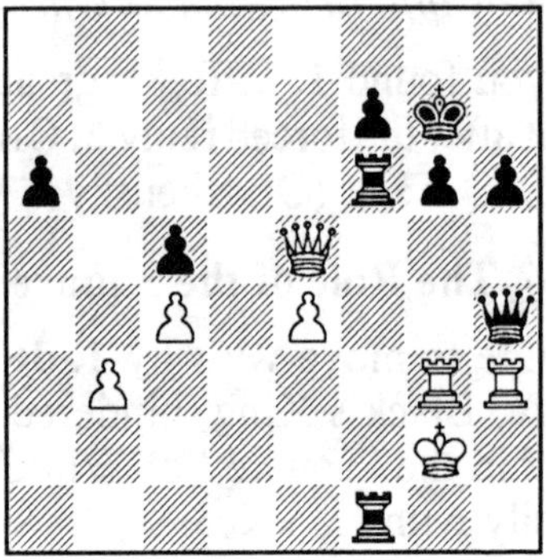

Black to move

111.

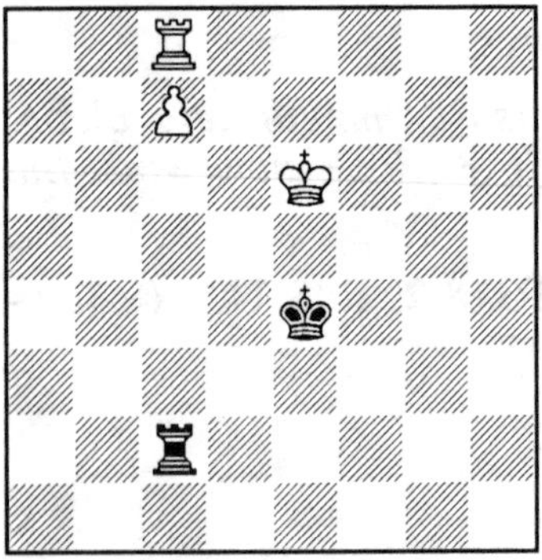

White to move

112.

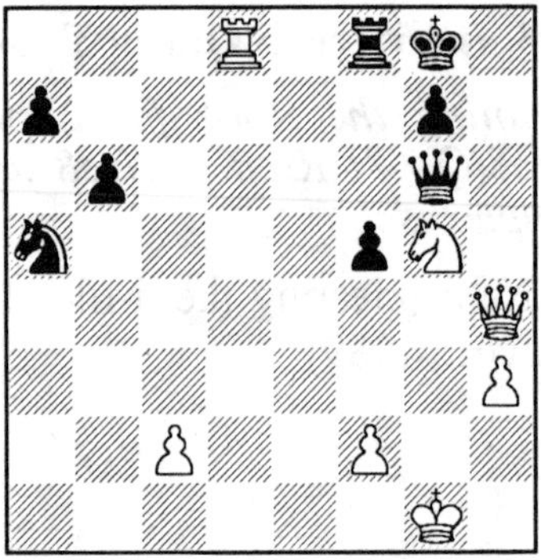

White to move

109. Famous Breakthrough

White to play wins: **1. b6 cxb6 2. a6 bxa6 3. c6**, or **1. ... axb6 2. c6**.

Black to move can stop this breakthrough by **1. ... b6** (not 1. ... a6? 2. c6!, or 1. ... c6 2. a6!) **2. axb6 axb6 3. cxb6**. (This is enough to make a draw, but why not try for more — risk-free — by giving the opponent a chance to go wrong? Here I would play 3. c6, hoping for 3. ... Kf5 4. Kf3 Ke5 5. Kg4! Kd5?. [Greed! Of course Black can draw easily with 5. ... Ke4, taking the opposition and shadowing the White King.] 6. Kf5. Now visualize how White will Queen first, with the Black pawn still on b3, and win.) **3. ... cxb6**. Black will capture the b-pawn, but White will meet **... Kxb6** with **Kb4**, drawing. Wouldn't you prefer my line above, setting up a trap?

Black to play actually wins with **1. ... Kf5**, and now after **2. b6 cxb6!** (2. ... axb6?? 3. c6+-) **3. a6 bxa6 4. c6 Ke6**, he catches the c-pawn. Also losing is 3. cxb6 axb6 4. axb6 Ke5, and when the Black King captures on b6, the White King will be one file too far from the only drawing square (b4).

110. Deflect the Pin

1. ... Qxe4+! 0-1. If 2. Qxe4, then 2. ... R6f2 mate. (Konyagina - Nakhimovskaya, 1963)

111. Setting Up the Discovery

1. Kd6 Rd2+ seems to lead nowhere. Think discovery.

1. Re8! (the setup) **1. ... Rxc7 2. Kd6+** (discovered check) **1-0**.

112. Model Rook & Knight Mate

1. Qh8+ Kxh8 2. Rxf8# yields a back-row checkmate. (Ivanov - Dimitrov, 1957)

113.

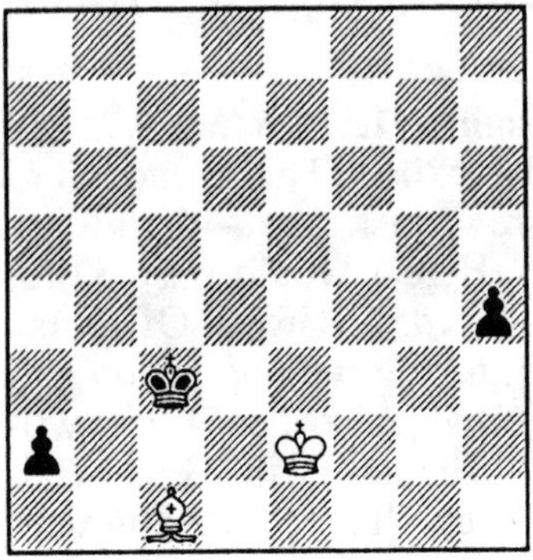

White to move

114.

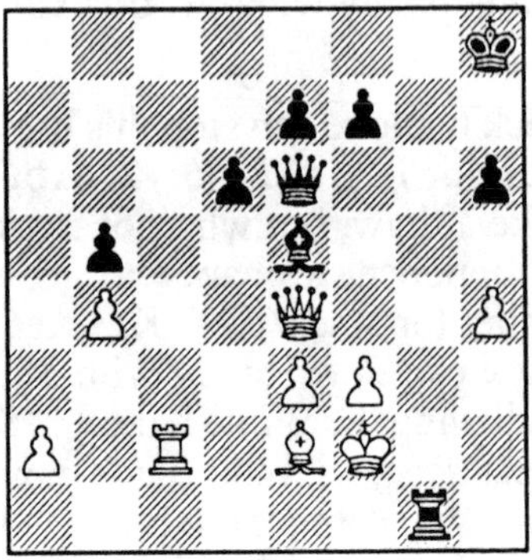

Black to move

115.

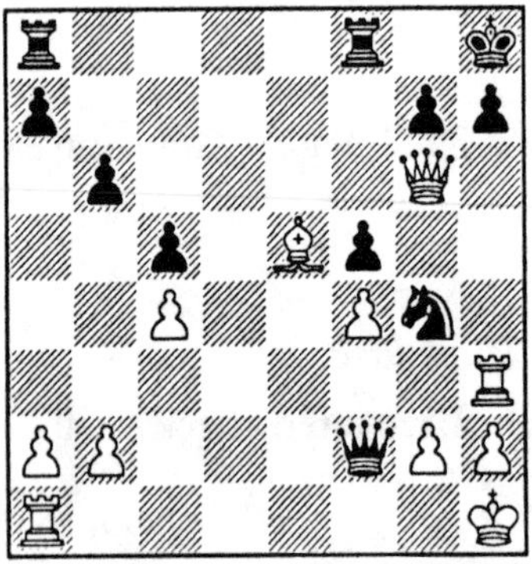

Black to move

116.

White to move

113. Stopping the Pawns

1. Bg5!. (White is ready to meet 1. ... a1(Q) with 2. Bf6+ and 3. Bxa1, using a geometrical motif — Black's King and the new Queen are on the same diagonal, vulnerable to a skewer.) **1. ... h3 2. Bf6+** (followed by **3. Kf2**) draws, since both pawns are stopped. White must be accurate, however. Look at 2. Kf2 h2 3. Kg2??. (It wasn't too late to check on f6 first, taking firm control of the a1-h8 diagonal, and only then stopping the h-pawn.) 3. ... h1(Q)+! —decoy!— 4. Kxh1 a1(Q)+ 0-1.

114. Queen & Bishop Are Enough to Mate!

1. ... Qh3! 2. Kxg1 Bh2+ 3. Kh1 (3. Kf2 Qg3+ 4. Kf1 Qg1#) **3. ... Bg3+ 4. Kg1 Qh2+ 5. Kf1 Qf2#**. These last moves show an important mating mechanism you should memorize. (Larsen - Unzicker, 1966)

115. Active Defense

White's threats (Qxg7# and Qxh7#) are menacing. How can Black defend against both at the same time?

1. ... Qe1+! 2. Rxe1 Nf2+ 3. Kg1 Nxh3+ (all with tempo, all forced) **4. gxh3 hxg6**. Not only has he escaped what seemed overwhelming threats, Black wins the Exchange! (Veijay - Hodza, 1954)

116. Take My Pawn, Please!

Paradoxically, if Black didn't have a pawn, the game would be an immediate draw. Black to move of course draws by 1. ... Kg3 (not 1. ... Kh1?? 2. Ng4 h2 3. Nf2#). But find a win for White if it's his move.

1. Kf2 Kh1 2. Nf1 (*Zugzwang*) **h2 3. Ng3#**.

117.

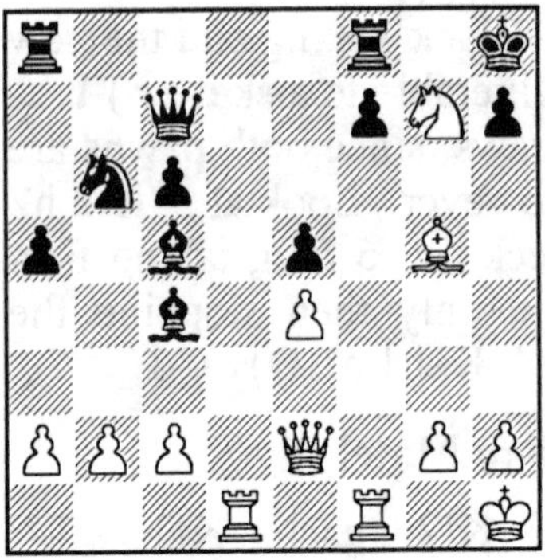

White to move

118.

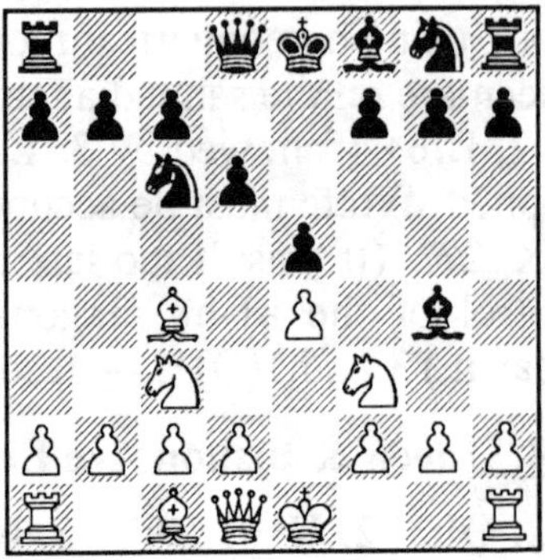

White to move

119.

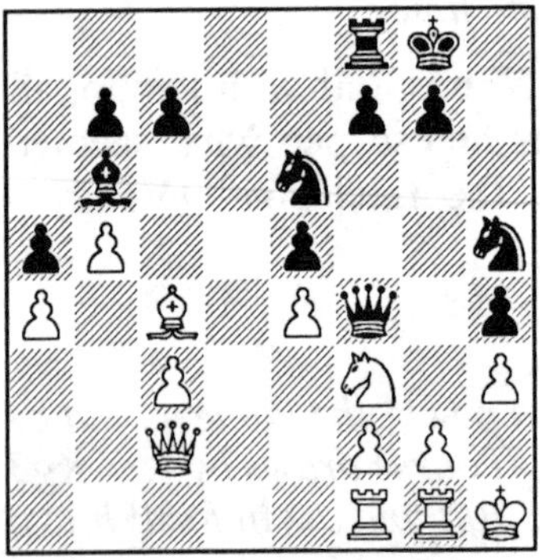

Black to move

120.

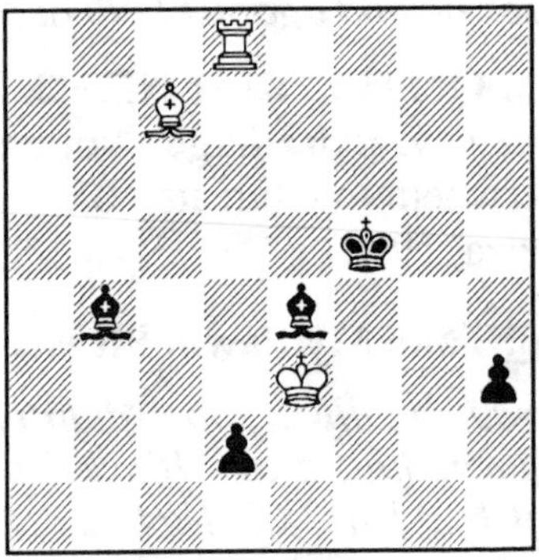

Black to move

117. Variation on the Model Bishop & Knight Mate

Both White's Queen and Knight are en prise. *If the White Queen moves, say to g4, to protect the Knight, Black will get breathing room for his King with ... f6. But Grandmaster Leonid Stein, one of the greatest natural players ever, has another idea in mind.*

1. Bf6! (if 1. ... Bxe2, then 2. Nf5+ and 3. Nh6# — a typical Bishop + Knight mate) **1. ... Be7!**. Lajos Portisch fights back, but White's calm reply renews the mate threat. **2. Qf3**, and White won. (Stein - Portisch, 1962)

118. Ill-Legal's Mate

Don't play the reckless 1. Nxe5?, hoping for 1. ... Bxd1? (or 1. ... dxe5? 2. Qxg4) 2. Bxf7+ Ke7 3. Nd5#, Legal's Mate. Here this try is unsound because of the simple 1. ... Nxe5!, when Black emerges a piece ahead.

A good trap (and a good move) is **1. h3**, and if **1. ... Bh5?**, then **2. Nxe5** wins at least a pawn: **2. ... Nxe5 3. Qxh5 Nxc4 4. Qb5+**. Did you foresee this check?

119. Softening Up the Critical Square

1. ... Bxf2! 2. Qxf2 (2. Rxf2 Ng3+ 3. Kh2 Nf1++ 4. Kh1 Qh2+ 5. Nxh2 Ng3#) **2. ... Ng3+ 3. Kh2 Nxf1++ 4. Kh1 Ng3+ 5. Kh2 Nxe4+ 0-1**. (Bekker - Schneider, 1966)

120. Create Disharmony

Division of duties: The White Rook watches the d2-pawn, and the White Bishop watches the h3-pawn.

1. ... Bd6!!. Double interference. Either the d-file or the h2-b8 diagonal will be blocked, and Black will queen one of his passed pawns and win. (Nenarokov - Grigoriev, 1923)

121.

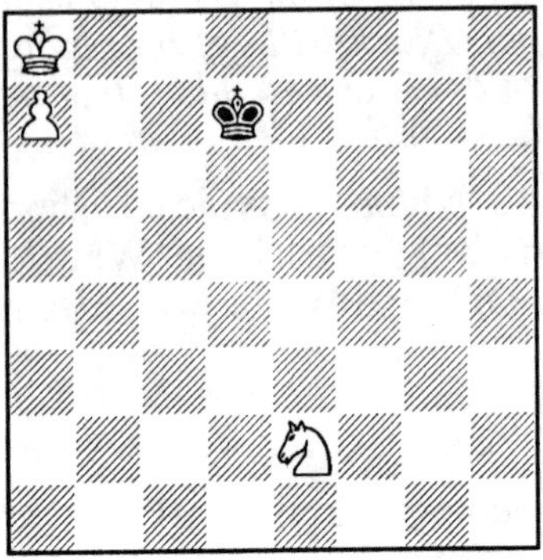

Black to move

122.

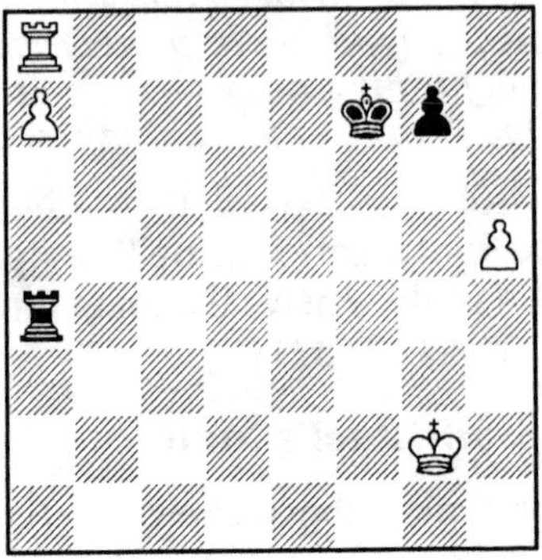

White to move

123.

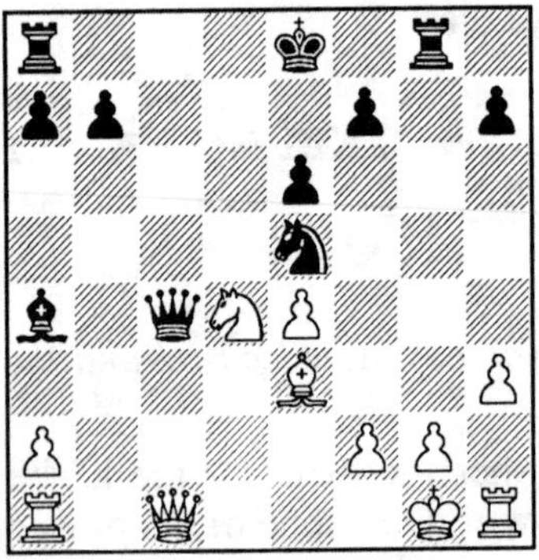

Black to move

124.

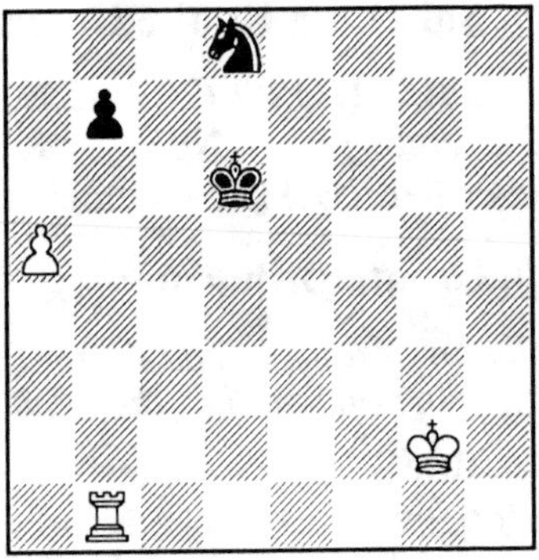

White to move

121. Alternating Colors

To draw, Black must place his King on either c7 or c8, in such a way that it cannot be driven away by the Knight.

1. ... Kc8!. It's important to put the King on the same color square as the Knight, so that when the Knight approaches, it will do so with check, driving Black's King to another safe square. For example, **2. Nd4 Kc7 3. Nb5+ Kc8 4. Nd6+, draw**. It's important to note that in this exercise both the White Knight and the Black King move from light squares to dark, and back again. Losing is 1. ... Kc7?, e.g. — 2. Nd4 Kc8 3. Nb5.

122. Rook-Ending Trap

No matter whose move, White can't win. If his King comes to b6 (or b7) to support the a7-pawn and free up his Rook, Black's Rook will drive away the King with ...Rb1+, then return to the a-file.

White's best chance is to smile broadly and play **1. h6!**, hoping for Black's resignation, or for 1. ... gxh6? 2. Rh8 Rxa7 3. Rh7+. But, of course, the calm 1. ... Kg6 keeps the draw.

123. Queen for a Knight!

Wouldn't it be great to check on f3?

1. ... Qxd4 2. Bxd4 (alas, there is no saving in-between move for White) **2. ... Nf3+ 3. Kf1 Bb5+ 0-1**. (Subaric - Trifunovic)

124. Rook-pawn Beats Knight & King!

If Black succeeds in exchanging pawns, then it's a draw. So White must act quickly!

1. Rxb7! Nxb7 (1. ... Kc6 2. a6) **2. a6**, and the pawn is unstoppable. The Knight blocks his own King's access!

125.

Black to move

126.

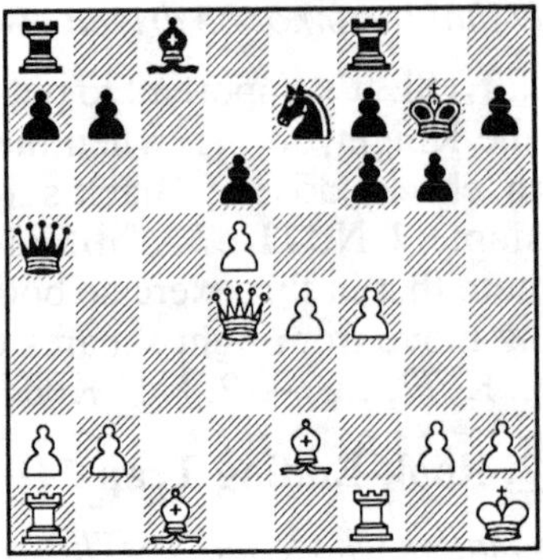

White to move

127.

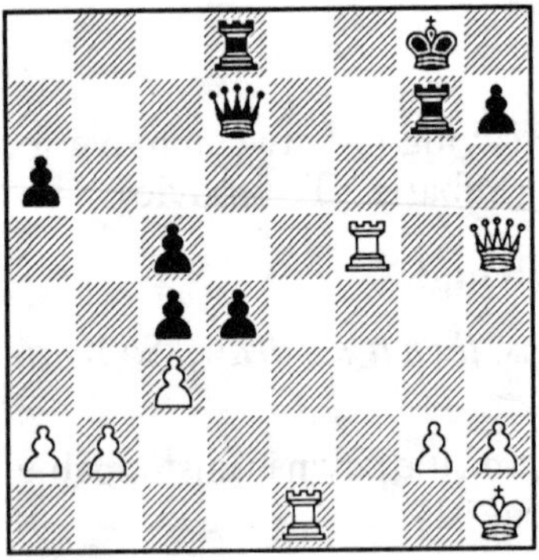

White to move

128.

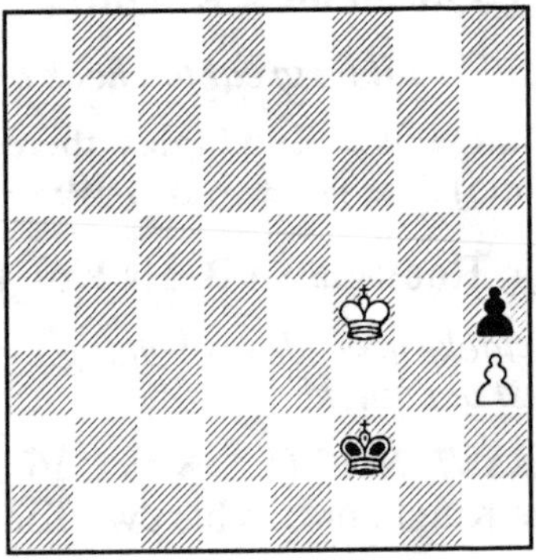

White/Black to move

125. How to Defend Against the Pawn on the 6th

Chess alert! This one's the most basic of all pawn endings. Black has four possible moves, but only one of them draws.

1. ... Kd8!. Yes! Move only on the same file as the pawn. **2. Ke6 Ke8 3. d7+**. (Or 3. Kd5 Kd7! — the safest square. No harm will come when your King is here: 4. Kc5 Kd8!, etc.) **3. ... Kd8**. Remember this position! If the pawn reaches the 7th rank with check, the game is drawn because White must now either give up his only pawn or play **4. Kd6**, giving stalemate. This is why it's always a draw when the weaker side's King blocks the pawn, preventing the opposing King from getting in front of the pawn. With White to move in the original diagram, the position is the same easy draw: 1. Kd5 Kd8!, etc.

126. A Queen's Invitation to the Lion's Den

1. b4! Qd8 (1. ... Qb6 meets the same reply) **2. Qxf6+! Kxf6** (2. ... Kg8 3. Bb2) **3. Bb2#**. (Vanka - Skala, 1960)

127. Mate on e8

1. Rd5 (deflection) **1. ... Qxd5 2. Re8+ Re8 3. Qxe8#** (of course, not the Queen-grabbing 3. Qxd5+??). (Agzamov - Ruderfer, 1974)

128. Throwing the Block on h4

It's a draw no matter who is to move.

White to move: **1. Kg4 Ke3 2. Kxh4 Kf4**. Remember, if Black gets to the queening corner, there's no way to force him out. Thus, blocking White's King on the h-file leads to a draw. Black to move: **1. ... Ke2! 2. Kg4 Ke3**, etc. Wrong is 1. ... Kg2 2. Kg4 Kf2 3. Kxh4 Kf3 4. Kg5! Ke4 5. h4 Ke5 6. h5 Ke6 7. Kg6! (7. h6? Kf7, draw) 7. ... Ke7 8. Kg7!, and by occupying the g7-square, White guarantees the promotion of his h-pawn.

129.

White to move.

Place the Black King on a drawing square. (How many such squares are there?)

130.

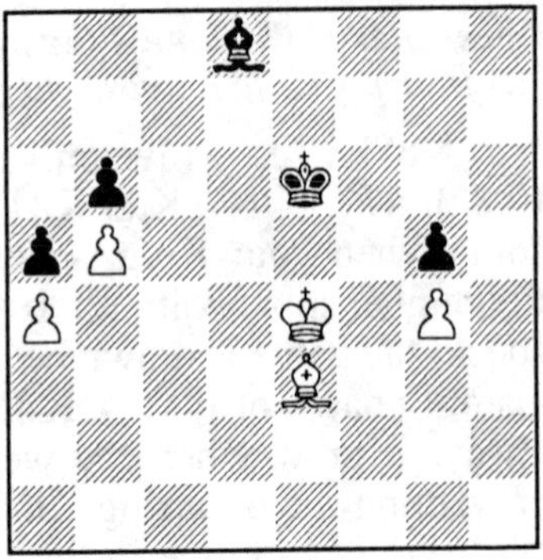

White to move

131.

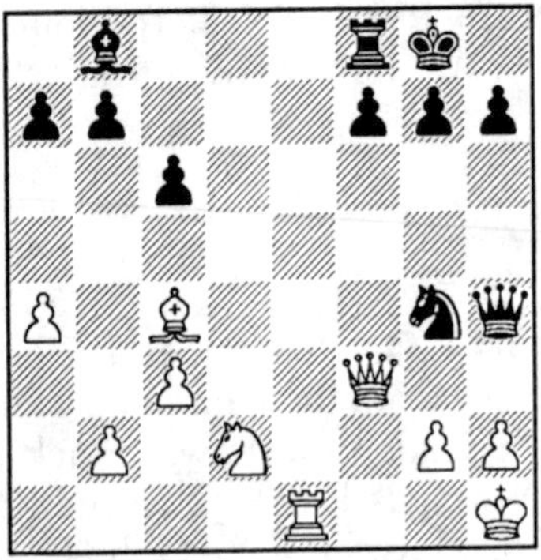

White to move

132.

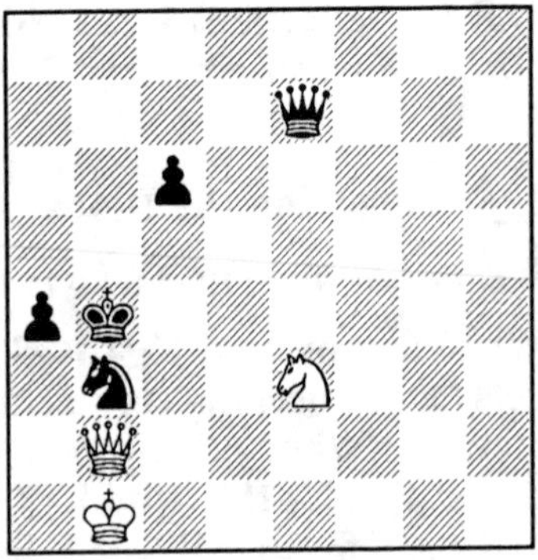

White to move

129. One to Beam Down to Draw, Scotty!

Well, e6 and d6 are pretty obvious. Incidentally, if on e6, the Black King has only one good square to move — d6 — and vice versa. Never move to the side: ... Kc6? and ... Kf6? both lose miserably. And never, ever voluntarily move backward: 1. ... Ke7? loses to 2. Ke5 (grabbing the opposition) 2. ... Kd7 3. Kd5. Taking the opposition when ahead of the pawn diagonally inevitably leads to having the opposition in front of the pawn. With the White King on d5 and Black's King on d7, Black must move over and let White's King gain more space and secure, inevitably, the queening of the pawn. Similarly, 1. ... Kd7 loses to 2. Kd5. So two other safe squares are d8 and e8. Here, Black is never in *Zugzwang*, as he goes back and forth between these two squares. He meets 1. Kd5 with 1. ... Kd7, or 1. Ke5 with 1. ... Ke7, taking the opposition — thus preventing White's King from making any progress.

So Black draws with **1. ... Ke6, 1. ... Kd6, 1. ... Ke8** or **1. ... Kd8.**

130. Lose a Tempo, Win a Game

White needs to reach this same position with Black to move.

1. Bg1 Bc7 2. Bf2 Bd8 3. Be3. White reaches his goal. Black is in *Zugzwang*, and cannot avoid material loss.

131. Counterattack!

White's position looks critical, but ...

1. Qxf7+ Rxf7 2. Re8#. (Harms - Kuppe, 1947)

132. Fantasy is the Key

1. Qa3+!, winning the Queen if the Black King retreats. **1. ... Kxa3 2. Nc2#.** (study by L. Kubbel)

133.

White/Black to move

134.

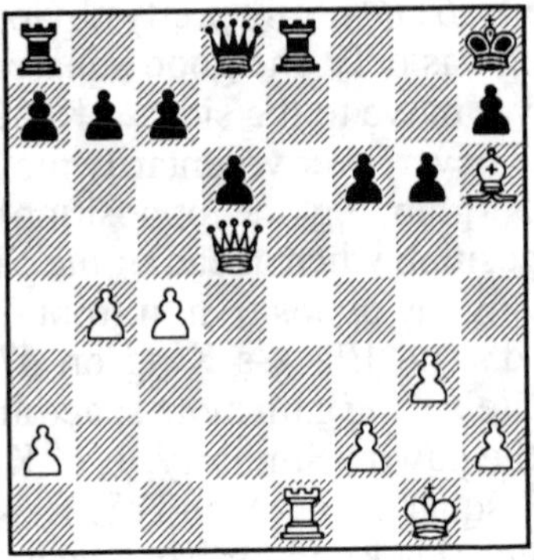

White to move

135.

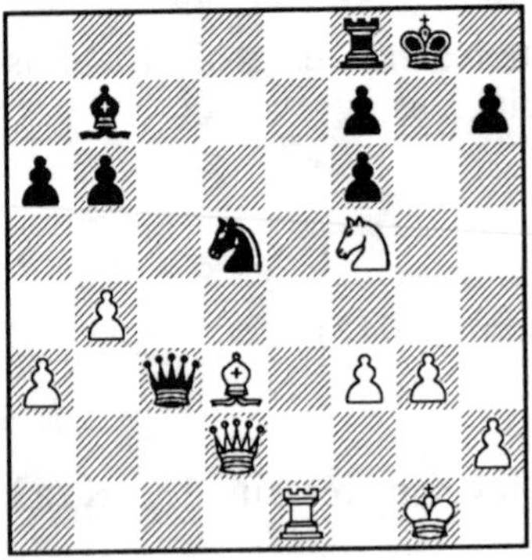

White to move

136.

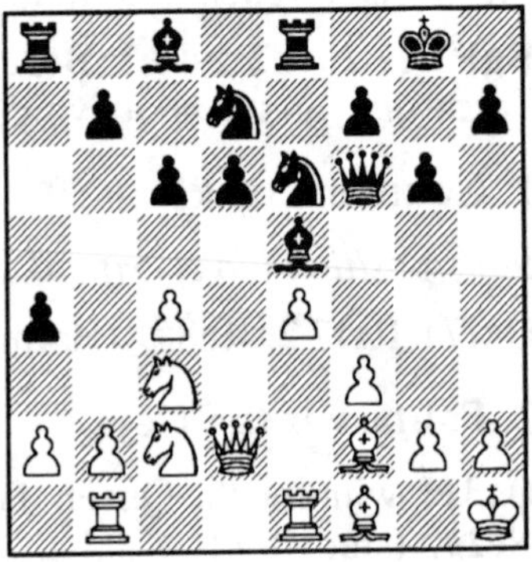

White to move

133. Capturing on the Right Square

It's tempting to attack the pawn with 1. ... Ke3, expecting 2. Kg2, the only way to protect the pawn. And it must be protected (must it not?) as all our chess experiences have "taught" us. Then 2. ... f4 wins the f3-pawn and the game.

The King on the 6th rank in front of a non-Rook pawn always wins*. This is one of those dozen or so maxims every 1600 player must know about pawn endings in order to become an Expert!*

Well, the f3-pawn is doomed. The only question is on which rank it will be taken. Thus, 1. ... Ke3? leads to only a draw after 2. f4 Kxf4 3. Kf2 (Another key position to remember: Here f2 — ***the opposition!*** *— is the only square to which the White King can move to for a draw).*

Black wins with **1. ... f4!** (fixing the pawn on f3) **2. Kf2 Kd3 3. Kf1 Ke3 4. Kg2 Ke2 0-1**. Black won because he always had waiting moves while White didn't. And now we can see that, with White to play, the only move to draw is **1. f4!** (1. ... Ke4 2. Kf1 Kxf4 3. Kf2 =).

134. Rooking Black into a Mating Net

1. Qf7! Rxe1+ (1. ... Rg8 2. Re8, deflecting either the g8-Rook from protecting the g7-square, or the Queen from protecting f6) **2. Kg2 Qe7** (2. ... Qg8 3. Qxf6+) **3. Bg7#**. (Corbett - Taylor, 1963)

135. Forget Material — Go For Mate!

1. Qh6! Qxe1+ 2. Bf1! (2. Kg2? Ne3+), and Black must give away his Queen with **2. ... Qe3+**. (Spielmann - Tartakower, 1925)

136. The Lure of a Pawn

Is 1. Ne2 a blunder?

No, it isn't. The game continued **1. ... Bxb2?** (falling into the trap) **2. Rxb2! Qxb2 3. Nc3 a3 4. Rb1 Ndc5** (the Queen is lost, and so is the game) **5. Rxb2 axb2 6. Nb4 Na4 7. Nb1 Bd7 8. Nd3 1-0**. (Reshevsky - Najdorf, 1952)

137.

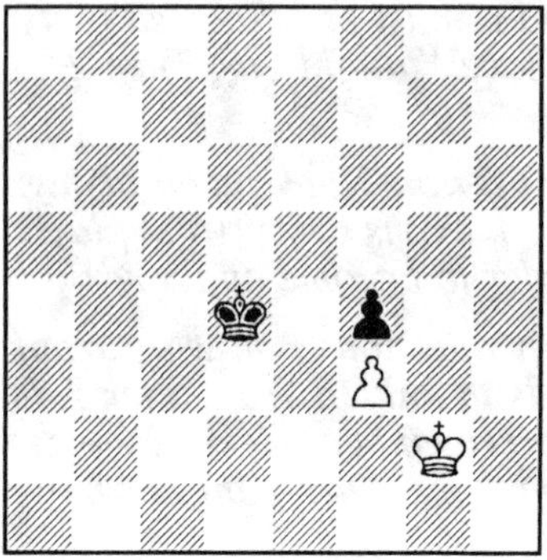

White to move

138.

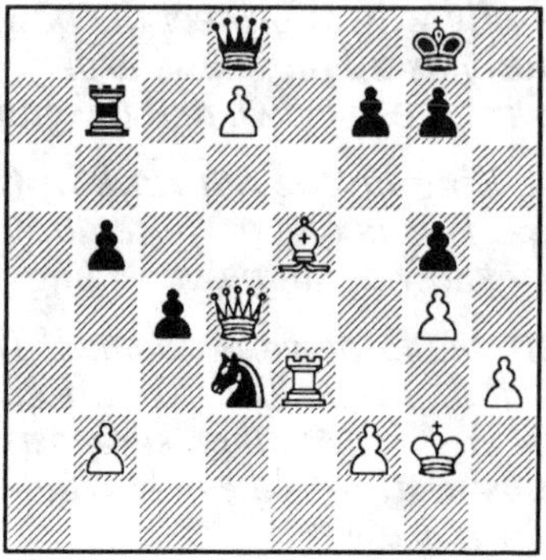

White to move

139.

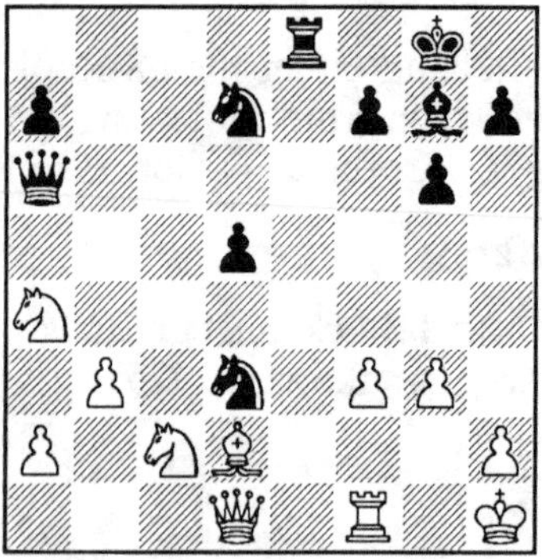

Black to move

140.

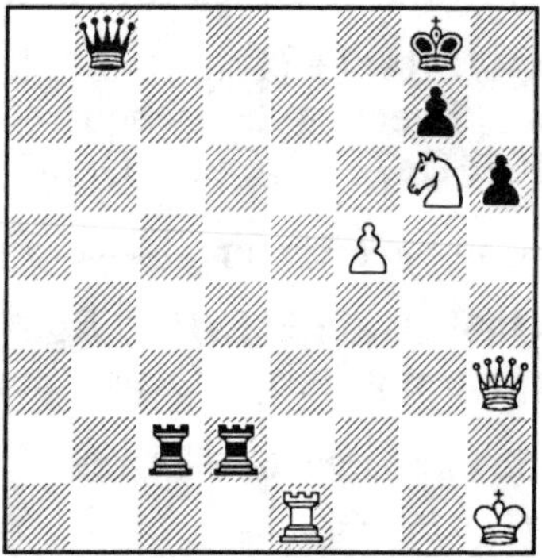

White to move

137. Mutual *Zugzwang*

A very good study tool is to analyze one position in depth and then to expand your knowledge by making small changes to that position. Let's imagine that in diagram #133, White erroneously played 1. Kg2?, and that Black correctly replied 1. ... f4. Can White still save himself? If not, what is his best try?

Sorry, Black is winning. But White can still set a clever trap: **1. Kh3!** (1. Kf2 Kd3 loses without giving White any practical chances) **1. ... Kd3!**. (Avoiding the trap 1. ... Ke3?? 2. Kg4!, and White wins! Remember this important position — whoever moves first, loses.) **2. Kh4**. Still fighting. Here whoever moves first wins because he can enforce the mutual *Zugzwang* position with his opponent to move. Do you see how? **2. ... Ke2!**, forcing **3. Kg4**, and now **3. ... Ke3** wins.

138. To Save & Promote

1. Bc7!. Protects the pawn while clearing the e-file for a decisive check on e8. **1-0**. (Fischer - Di Camillo, 1956)

139. Target f1

1. ... Re1!! interferes with the coordination between White's major pieces. **2. Bxe1** (2. Rxe1 loses to 2. ... Nf2+.) **Nb2! 3. Bc3 Nxd1 4. Rxd1 Qe2, 0-1**. (Jones - Dueball, 1974)

140. A Saving Rook & Knight Mate

Look for a win, even if it's out of desperation.

1. Qb3+! Qxb3 (1. ... Kh7 2. Qxb8, and White's Queen controls the h2-square and prevents checks) **2. Re8+**, and now either 2. ... Kh7 3. Rh8#, or 2. ... Kf7 3. Rf8# — typical Rook + Knight + Pawn mates. (Of course, the Black pawn on g7 is also to be praised — or blamed, if you're playing Black!)

141.

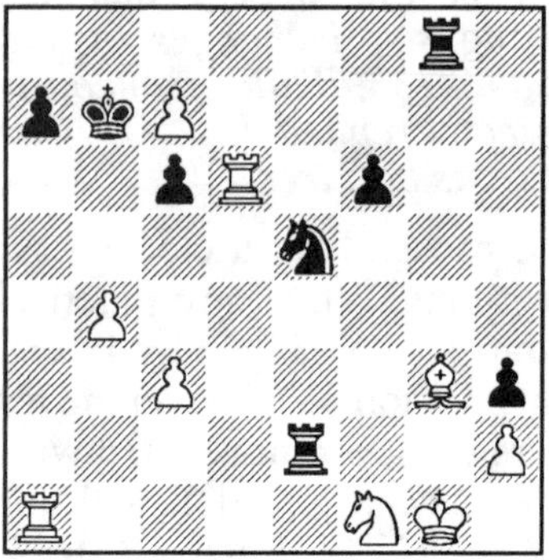

Black to move

142.

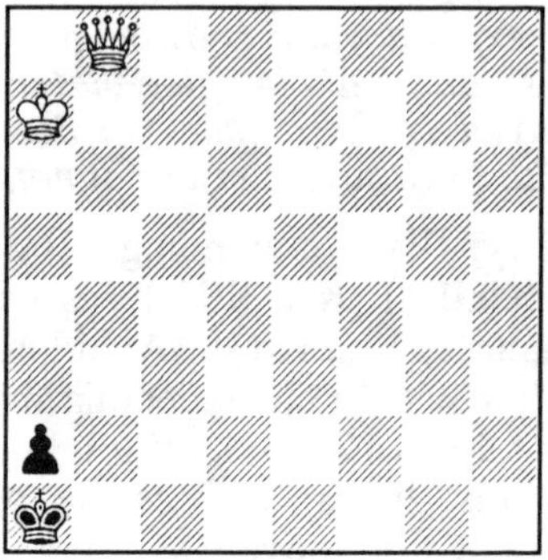

White to move

143.

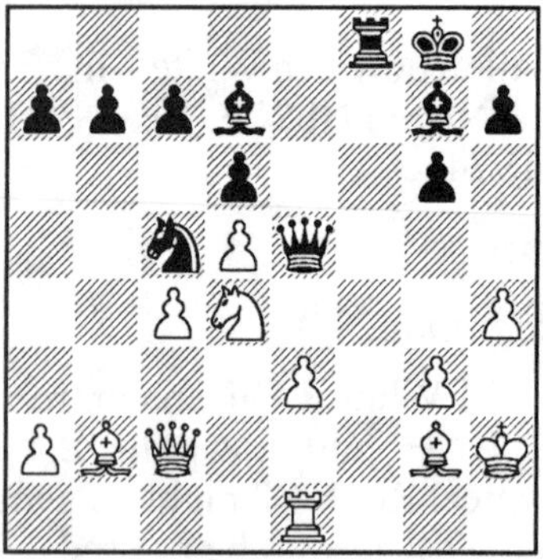

Black to move

144.

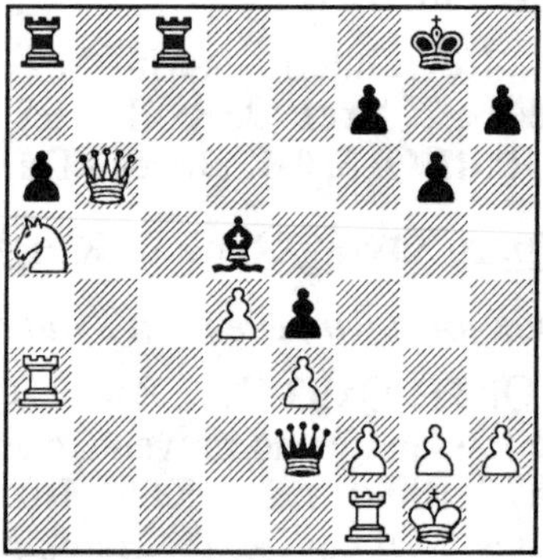

Black to move

141. Arabian Mates

Look for a typical Rook-&-Knight mate in the corner. Verify the move order.

1. ... Nf3+ (not 1. ... Rxg3? 2. Nxg3!, freeing f1 for his King's flight) **2. Kh1 Rxg3 0-1**. The threat is 3. ... Rg1#, and 3. Nxg3 is answered by 3. ... Rxh2#. Queenside diversions such as Rxa7+ or c8(Q)+ just delay the end by a few moves. And after 3. hxg3, Black plays 3. ... Rg2, threatening ... Rg1#. If White moves his Knight to stop this mate, there is another, symmetrical mate on h2. (Orlov - Chistyakov, 1935)

142. The King is Close Enough!

White, to move, wins by quickly bringing his King into the action.

1. Kb6 Kb2 2. Ka5+ Kc2 3. Qh2+ Kb1 4. Kb4 a1Q 5. Kb3, and White wins even with the Black Queen already aboard.

143. Thunder from a Blue Sky

This one is a shock — unless you play the King's Indian Defense or Modern Benoni.

1. ... Qxg3+!. This thunderous move destroys the pawn cover of the White King while decoying him to a dangerous square (2. Kxg3 Be5#) **0-1**. (Novotelnov - Chistyakov, 1949)

144. Botvinnik's Linear Mate

The weakness of White's first and second ranks, exacerbated by Black's pawn-wedge on e4, provides a motif for a successful combination.

1. ... Rab8!. Black brings in his Rook with a tempo. **2. Qd6 Qxf1+ 3. Kxf1 Rb1+ 4. Ke2 Rc2#**. (Goglidze - Botvinnik, 1935)

145.

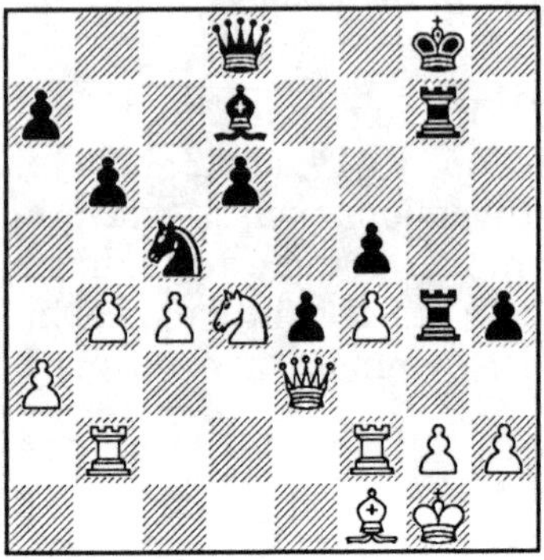

Black to move

146.

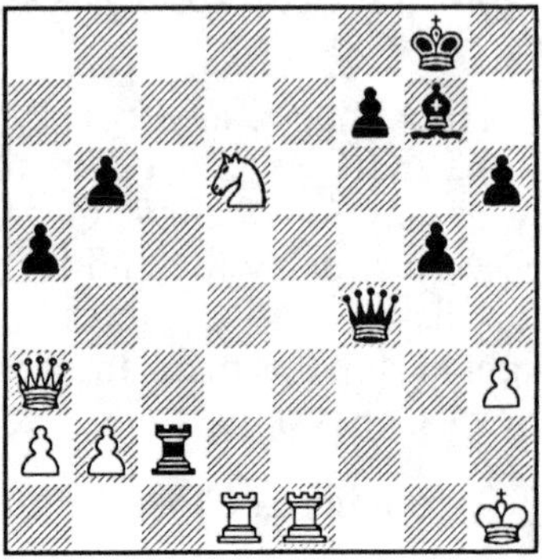

White to move

147.

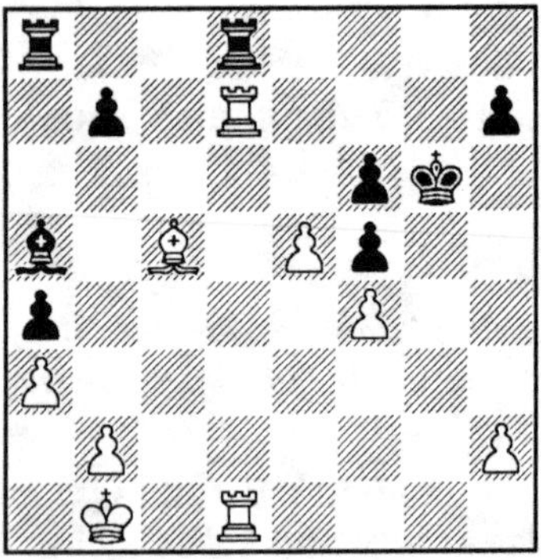

White to move

148.

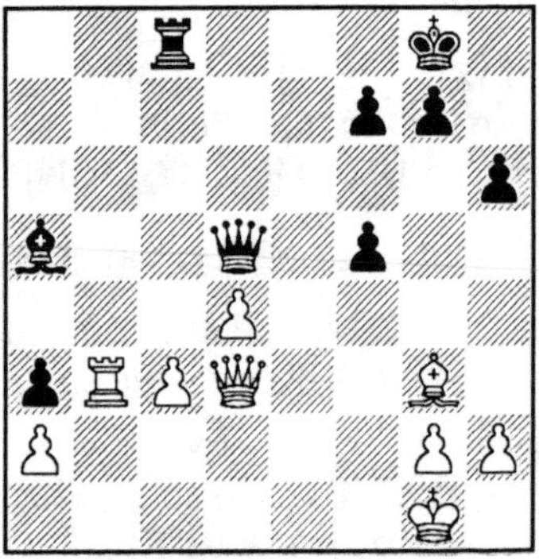

Black to move

145. Tiger's Teeth

Congratulations if you found **1. ... Rg3! 2. hxg3** (perhaps White should not take the Rook, but then he would have the worse position) **2. ... hxg3**, creating a wedge pawn, with the strong threat of ... Qh4 and ... Qh2. If not, look at it now. The further you can calculate this line, the better, up to the definite and successful conclusion. **3. Rfc2 Qh4 4. Be2 Rh7!**. (Bringing up reserves. Not 4. ... Qh2+? 5. Kf1 Qh1+ 6. Qg1.) **5. Kf1**. Former World Champion Tigran Petrosian was known as a very cautious, solid player. But when he had to, he could become Tiger Petrosian! He obviously had this position in mind before sacrificing on g3, and now played **5. ... Qxf4+!** (deflection) **6. Qxf4 Rh1#**. (Keres - Petrosian, T., 1959)

146. Mating Matrix to Memorize

*White is up a Rook, but how can he counter the threat of ... Qh2#? Senseless are 1. Rd2, 1. Re2, and 1. Qg3, so there is only one move to consider, **1. Re8+!**. What's next?*

Black's reply is forced: **1. ... Bf8** (1. ... Kh7 2. Qd3+ and 3. Qxc2) **2. Rxf8+** (decoy) **2. ... Kxf8** (2. ... Kg7 3. Ne8+ and 4. Qd3+) **3. Nf5+** (with a mating position in mind) **3. ... Kg8 4. Qf8+!** (another decoy!), followed by **4. ... Kxf8 5. Rd8#**, or **4. ... Kh7 5. Qg7#**. (Vidmar - Euwe, 1929)

147. Set Up the Linear Mate

1. Rg1+ Kh6 2. Bf8+ (to deflect Black's Rook from the d-file) **2. ... Rxf8 3. Rd3 1-0**. (Polugaevsky - Siladi, 1960)

148. The Hidden Energy of a Far-Advanced Pawn

1. ... Qxb3! 2. axb3 a2 3. Qd1 Bxc3 -+. (Stahlberg - Menchik, 1935, variation)

149.

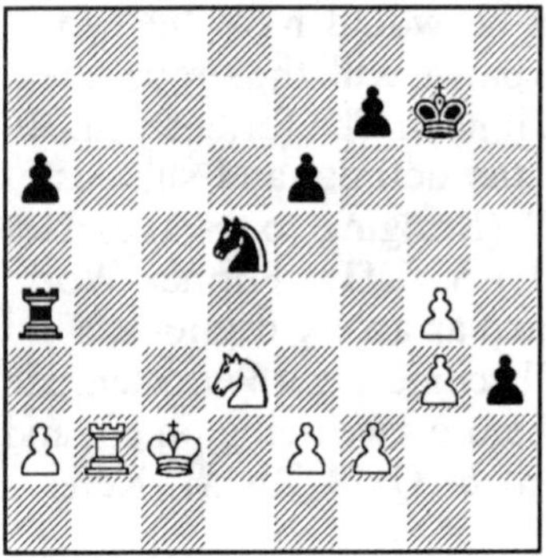

Black to move

150.

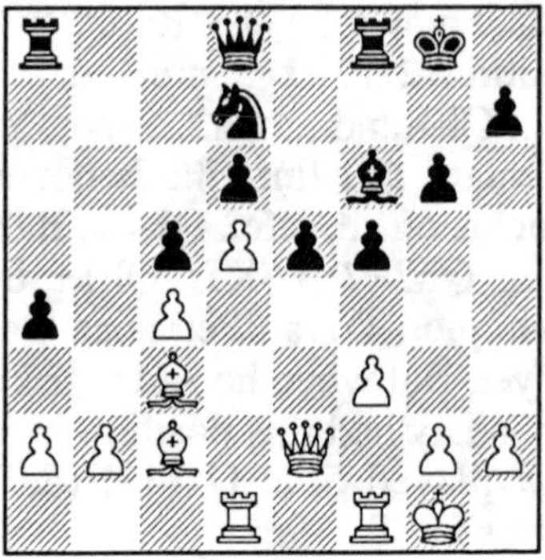

Black to move

151.

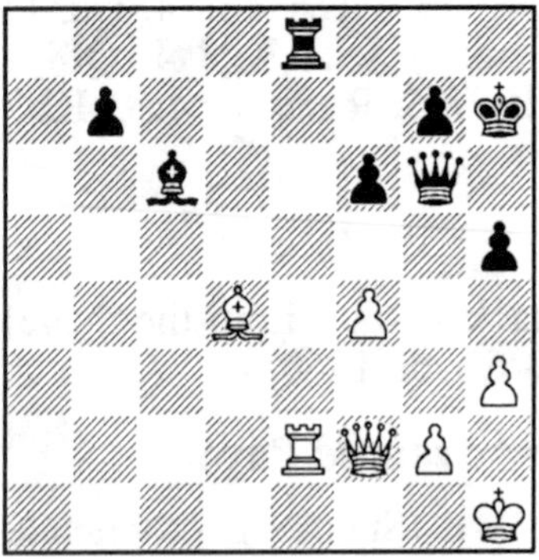

Black to move

152.

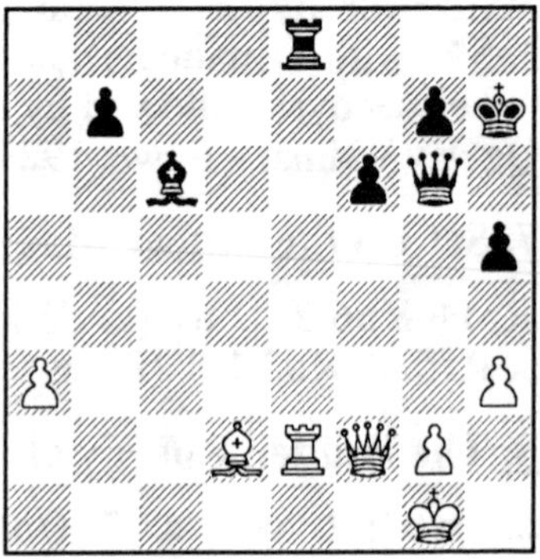

Black to move

149. First-Rank Interference

Black is down a pawn, but his h3-passer is very dangerous. First let's try a natural sample line: 1. ... h2 2. Rb1 Rxa2+ 3. Kb3 Rxe2. This looks promising, so let's look a bit harder for White — yes, 3. Nb2 offers better defense. Let's make a mental note of what we've found so far, then go back to the initial position and search for a more promising candidate move. Wouldn't it be nice to queen our pawn? If only we could eliminate the Rb1 defense ....

1. ... Rc4+! 2. Kd2 Rc1!, blocking the first rank for White's Rook (interference) **0-1**. (Averbakh - Korchnoi, 1965)

150. Get the Dominant Knight with a Pawn Sac

*GM Efim Geller, one of the founding fathers of the modern King's Indian Defense, played **1. ... e4** here. Why?*

This sac changes the dynamics of the position in Black's favor. After **2. Bxf6 Qxf6 3. fxe4 f4!**, followed by **4. ... Ne5**, Black has a powerful Knight vs. bad Bishop, plus excellent attacking chances on the kingside, where he now enjoys a pawn majority. White's extra e-pawn is actually an impediment. Black is clearly better. An important idea to know for any King's Indian player. (Pilnick - Geller, 1955)

151. Absolute Pin Wins Absolutely

Pinning a piece to your opponent's King makes the pin absolute (as opposed to relative). It can't be ignored!

1. ... Qxg2+ 2. Qxg2 Rxe2 0-1. (Kotov - Botvinnik, 1939)

152. Pin Deja Vu

As we'll see, Kotov learned a lesson from his game with Botvinnik (see previous position).

1. ... Bxg2! 2. Rxe8 (2. Qxg2 Rxe2) **2. ... Be4+** and **3. ... Qxe8** with a won position. (Guimar - Kotov, 1946)

153.

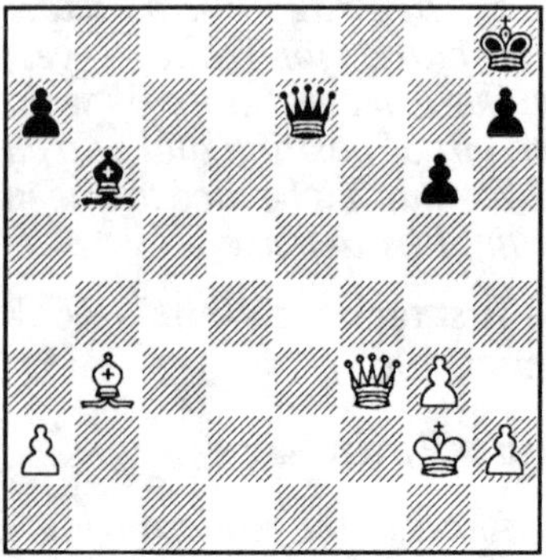

White to move

154.

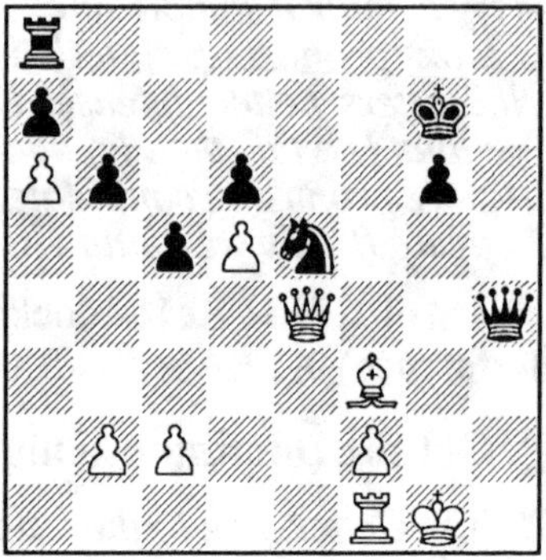

Black to move

155.

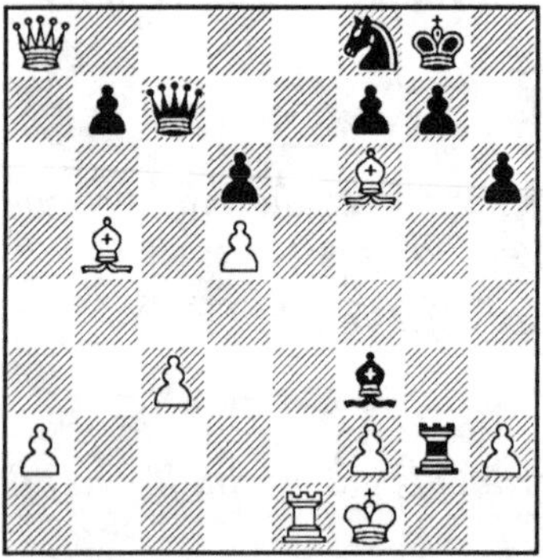

Black to move

156.

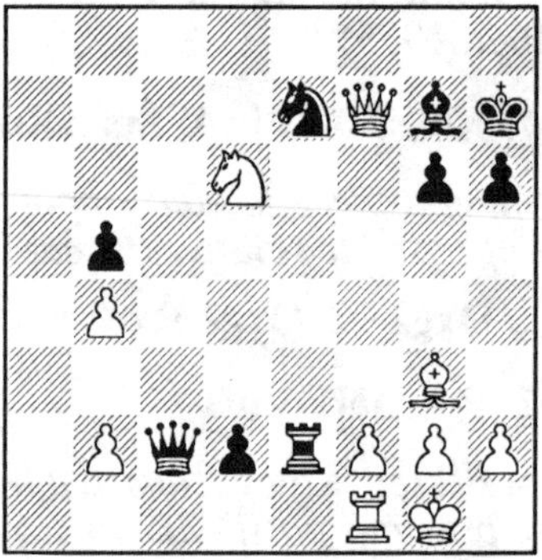

White to move

153. Winning Queen Maneuver

1. Qc3+ Qg7 2. Qc8+, winning.

154. Putting the "Zwang" in *Zugzwang*

1. ... Rf8!, forcing **2. Bh1**, as 2. Qxh4 loses a piece to 2. ... Nf3+. **2. ... Ng4 3. Qg2 Rf3!!** and White is nearly in *Zugzwang*. His only remaining moves are pawn moves, and they will soon run out. After **4. c4 Kh6**, White resigned. (Podgaets - Dvoretsky, 1974)

155. Anything Up Your Rival's Sleeve?

Black has powerful threats: 1. ... Qc5 or 1. ... Rxh2. So it's time to think for your opponent (White).

1. ... Qc4!. (The immediate 1. ... Rxh2 [or 1. ... Qc5] loses to 2. Qxf8+! Kxf8 [2. ... Kh7 3. Bd3+] 3. Re8#.) **2. Bxc4**. And now that the Bishop is decoyed, **2. ... Rxh2** wins. (Bunyan - Crowl, 1933)

156. How Great Ideas Are Born

First look at the natural 1. Ne8, and if 1. ... Nf5 then 2. Nf6+ and 3. Qg8#. But what about 1. ... Qxb2?

1. Be5!! Rxe5 (*1. ... Nf5 2. Nxf5*+-) **2. Ne8!** (now!) and White wins, as the Black Rook on e5 blocks the a1-h8 diagonal. (Keller - Nivergelt, 1960)

157.

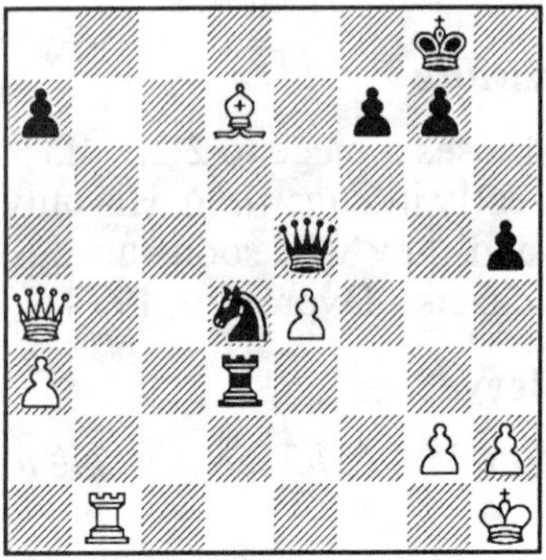

Black to move

158.

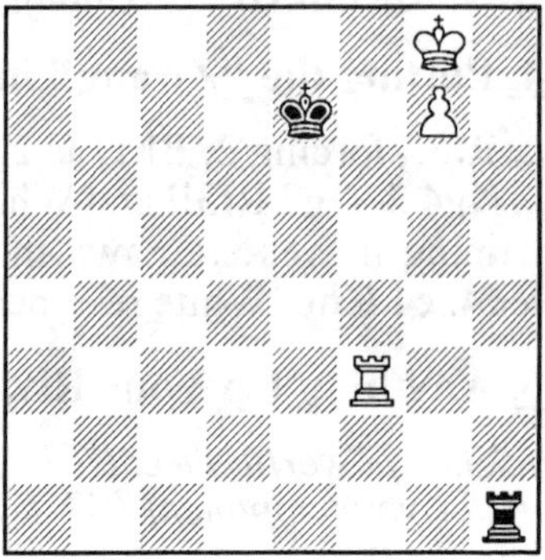

Black to move

159.

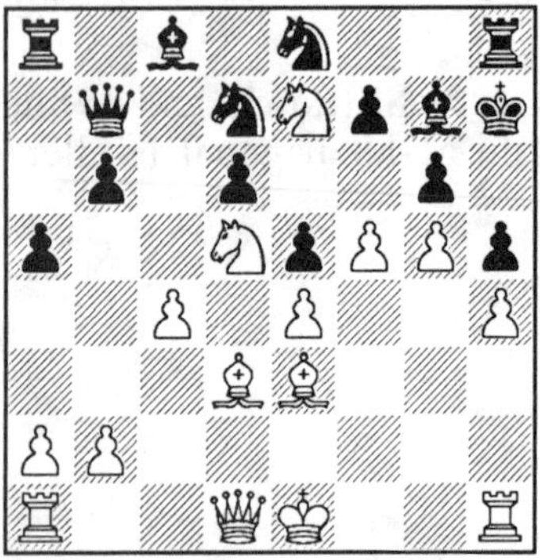

White to move

160.

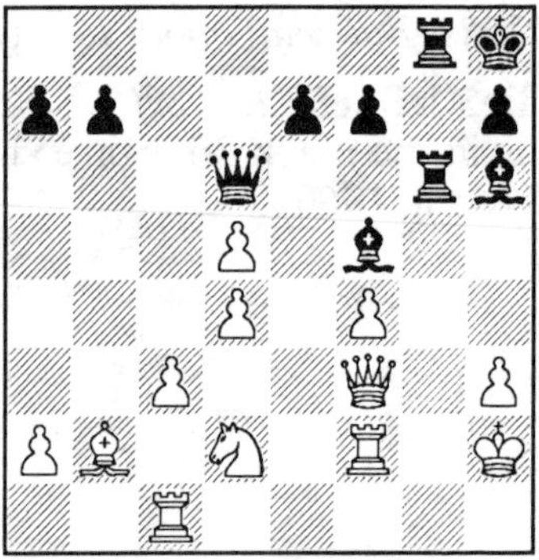

Black to move

157. Pry Open the King

1. ... Nf3! 0-1. On either 2. g3 or 2. gxf3, 2. ... Rd2 leads inevitably to mate. (Stahlberg - Keres, 1936)

158. Lucena's Position: Building a Bridge

This famous and important position is lost for Black no matter who is to move. His best chance is to keep his Rook on the h-file, otherwise White wins more easily, e.g.: 1. ... Re1 2.Rh3, followed by Kh7.

After **1. ... Rh2**, *White wins by building a bridge.*

Here many beginners would try the futile 2. Rf7+? Ke8 3. Rf8+ Ke7 4. Ra8 Rh1 5. Ra7+ Ke8 6. Ra8+, etc.

But the correct way is **2. Re3+ Kd7 3. Re4! Rh1 4. Kf7 Rf1+ 5. Kg6 Rg1+ 6. Kf6 Rf1+** (*6. ... Kd6 7. Re6+ Kd7 [7. ... Kd5 8. Re5+ followed by Rg5] 8. Re5 followed by Rg5*) **7. Kg5 Rg1+ 8. Rg4!**, winning — this is why White puts his Rook on the *4th rank* before bringing out his King.

159. Pawning the Queen

1. Qxh5+ gxh5 2. g6+ fxg6 3. fxg6#. (Kapsenberg - Norman, 1946)

160. The Weakest Point

1. ... Bxf4+ 2. Qxf4 Rg3 0-1. (Relstab - Petrov, 1937)

161.

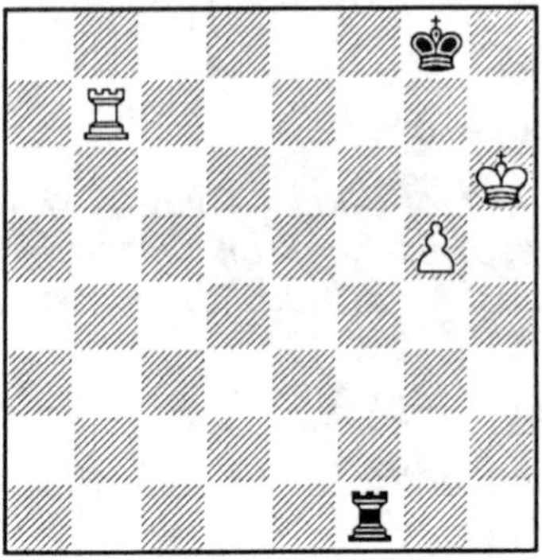

Black to move

162.

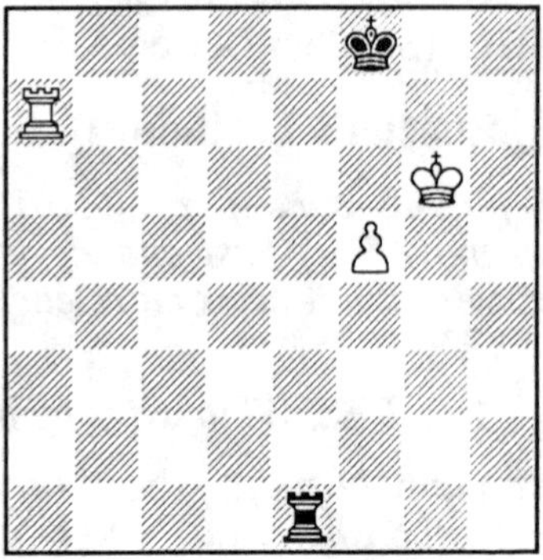

Black to move

163.

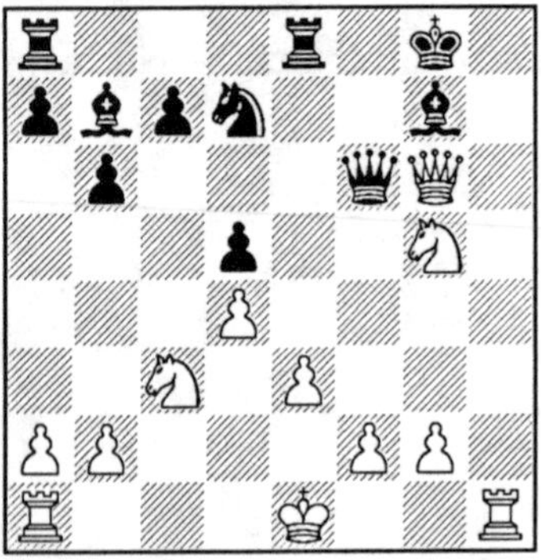

White to move

164.

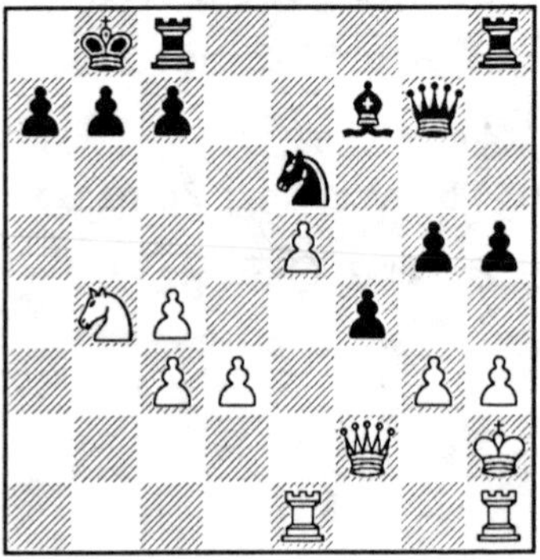

White to move

<u>161.</u> R+NP vs. R: Passive Defense Draws!

White threatens to win by 1. Rb8+. Bad for Black is 1. ... Rh1+ 2. Kg6, or 1. ... Rg1 2. Kg6! Kf8 3. Rb8+ Ke7 4. Rg8! followed by 5. Kh7. White reaches a position with his King on g8 and pawn on g7 and wins by building a bridge. (See position #158.)

But Black can draw by assuming a passive defense: **1. ... Rf8!** and White can't make any progress, e.g.: **2. g6 Ra8 3. Rg7+ Kh8=**. If White tries too hard, he can even lose — *4. Rh7+ Kg8 5. g7?? Ra6+*, winning for Black.

<u>162.</u> When Passive Defense Fails

Here passive defense doesn't work: 1...Re8? 2. f6 Rb8 3. Rh7 Kg8 4. f7+ Kf8 5. Rh8+. Even if Black's King were on g8 initially, passive defense would still fail: 1. ... Re8 2. f6 Rb8 3. Rg7+ (remember this tempo-winning idea) 3. ... Kh8 4. Rh7+ (or 3. ... Kf8 4. Rh7), and White wins.

Passive defense works agains Rook and Knight pawns, but fails against all other pawns.

In the diagram position, Black saved himself with another important technique — *the side attack.* **1. ... Rg1+ 2. Kf6 Kg8!**. (Black puts his King on the *short side*, leaving the *long side* for his Rook to deliver checks.) **3. Ra8+ Kh7 4. Kf7 Rg7+ 5. Ke6 Rb7 6. f6 Rb6+**, when Black's Rook is far enough away from White's King so that this check leads to a draw, e.g.: **7. Ke7 Rb7+ 8. Kd6 Rb6+ 9. Ke7 Rb7+ 10. Kf8 Kg6! draw**.

<u>163.</u> Decoy to Remember

1. Rh8+ Kxh8 2. Qh7#. (Marshall - Burn, 1900)

<u>164.</u> Rip Open the King's Position

1. Nc6+ bxc6 2. Qxa7+ *(2. Rb1+ Ka8 3. Ra1?? c5 -+)* **2. ... Kxa7 3. Ra1+ Kb6 4. Rhb1+ Kc5 5. Ra5#.**

165.

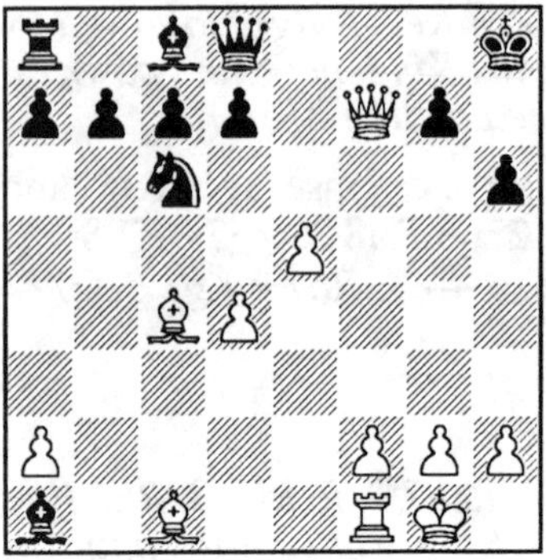

White to move

166.

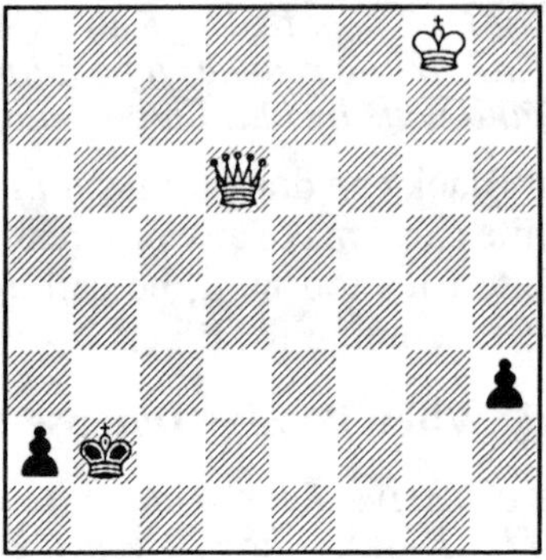

White to move

167.

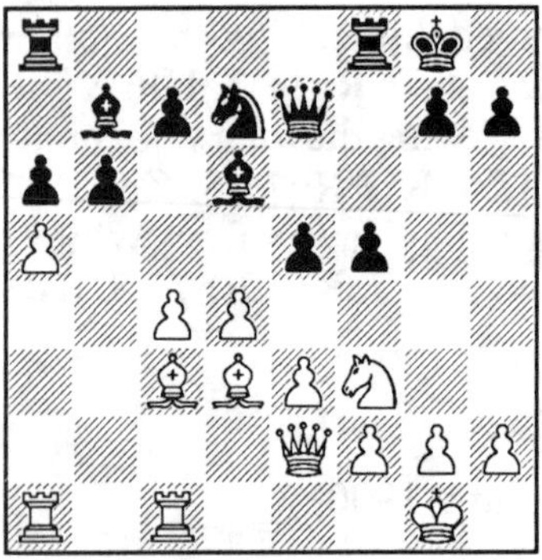

White to move

168.

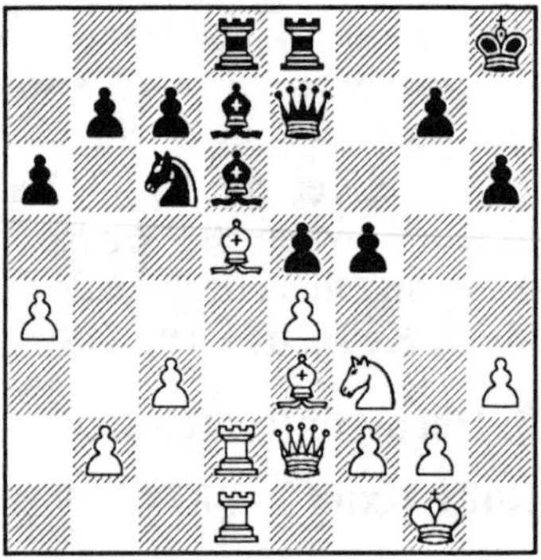

White to move

165. Take Me If You Dare!

1. Bg5!. This taunting move forces resignation. (Felner - Bancroft, 1960)

166. The Rules for Queen vs. Rook Pawns

In Queen-vs-pawn endings, the weaker side can draw only when three conditions exist simultaneously: (1) his pawn has already reached the 7th rank; (2) the opponent's King is far away; and (3) only with a Rook or Bishop pawn, creating a stalemate resource.

Paradoxically, the presence of Black's extra pawn denies him the stalemate possibilities, and he loses: **1. Qb4+ Kc2 2. Qa3 Kb1 3. Qb3+ Ka1 4. Qc2 h2 5. Qc1#.**

167. Forcing Pawn Weaknesses

1. c5! bxc5 (1. ...e4? 2.cxd6 +-) **2. dxe5 Nxe5 3. Nxe5 Bxe5 4. Bxe5 Qxe5 5. Qc2**, and White wins a pawn back, with a better game because of Black's isolated and weak c7-pawn. If 5. ... Rad8, then 6. Rab1. (Pachman - Euwe, 1954)

168. Putting the Queen & Bishop Mate to Use

Here you can use your knowledge of the positions that went before to find the stunner that opens the h-file, and then the hammer-blow that clears the way for the White Queen.

1. Bg5! hxg5 2. Nxe5! (not 2. Nh4? Qf6) **1-0**. (Lukovnikov - Sergeev, 1974)

169.

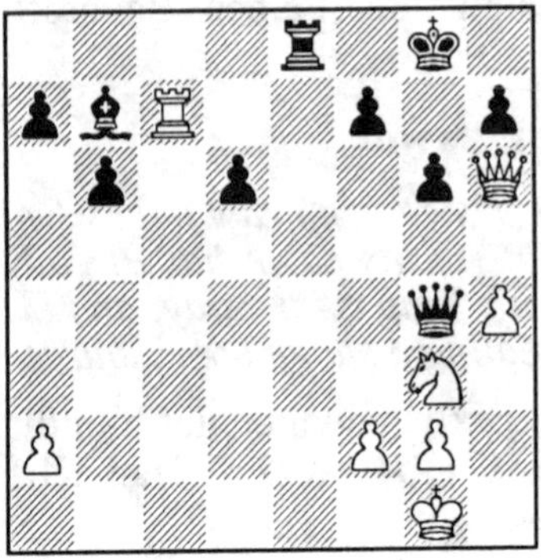

Black to move

170.

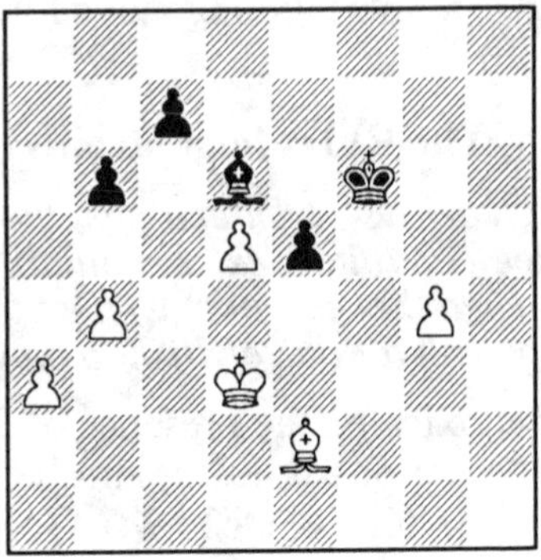

Black to move

Evaluate the position.

171.

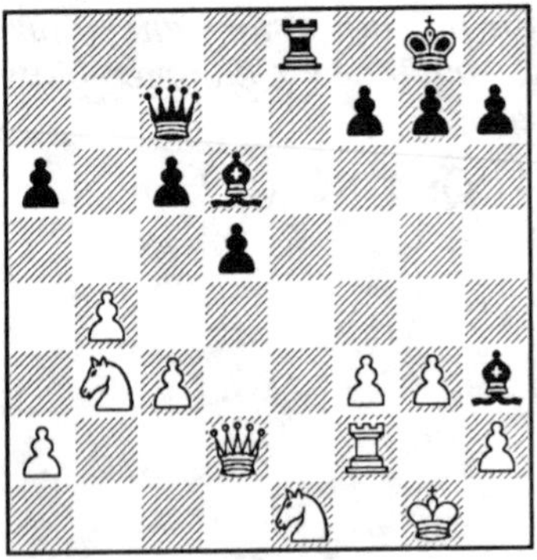

Black to move

172.

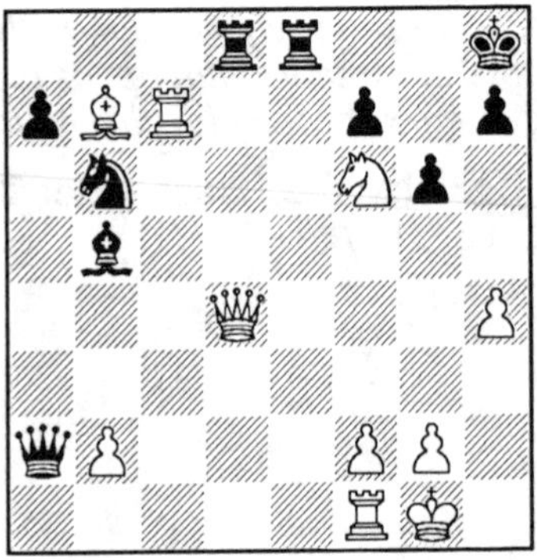

White to move

169. The Suicidal Rook Sets Up a Pin That Mates!

Can't we somehow exploit the weakness of the g2-square?

1. ... Re1+ 2. Kh2 Rh1+! 3. Kxh1. *(A decoy, but if 3. Nxh1 [deflection] then 3. ... Qxg2#.)* Now Black mates using a pin: **3. ... Qh3+ 4. Kg1 Qxg2#**. (Medler - Uhlmann, 1963)

170. Opening a Second Front

White wins by creating a second passed pawn on the a-file. It's important that his Bishop protects the g4-pawn while stopping the advance of Black's only passed pawn, the e-pawn, on the same d1-h5 diagonal.

The game continued **1. ... Kg5 2. Kc4 e4 3. a4 Bg3 4. Kb5 Kf4 5. a5 bxa5 6. bxa5 Bf2 7. Kc6 Ke3 8. Bb5 Kf4**. (Black's counterplay comes too late.) **9. Kxc7 Kxg4 10. d6 Black resigned**. (Chigorin - Vinaver, 1887)

171. Does It Work?

Of course you should look into 1. ... Bxg3 (destroying the White King's pawn cover) 2. hxg3 Qxg3+ (your first support position). Is this a sound sacrifice?

Yes, it is. Black wins after either **3. Ng2 Bxg2 4. Rxg2 Re1+**, or **3. Kh1 Rxe1+!** (elimination of a defender, plus decoy) **4. Qxe1 Bg2+ 5. Kg1 Bxf3+ 6. Kf1 Qh3+ 7. Kg1 Qh1#**. (Lasker, Em - Bogoljubov, 1934)

172. Arabian Mate

1. Bd5! (double interference) **1. ... Rxd5 2. Rxf7! 1-0**. (Urgeanu - Anastasides, 1949)

173.

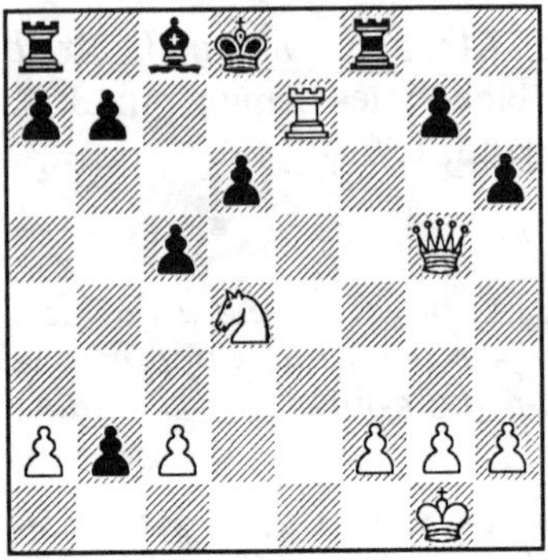

White to move

174.

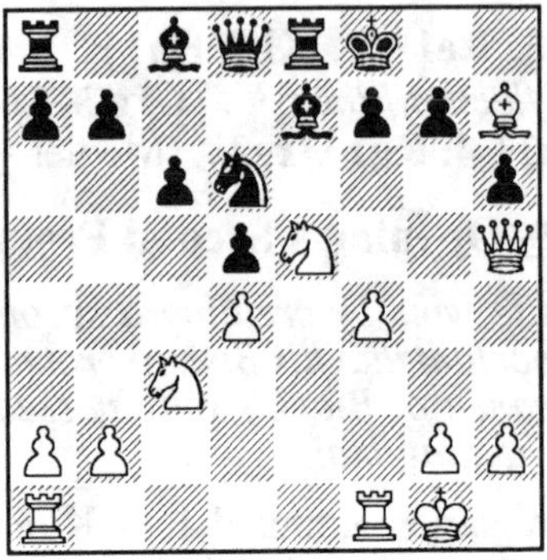

White to move

175.

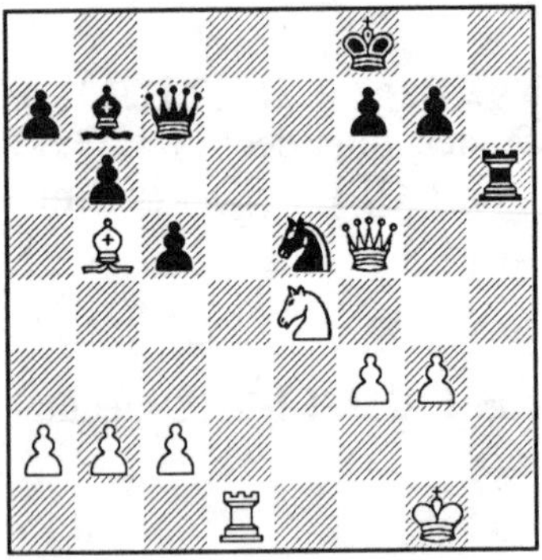

White to move

176.

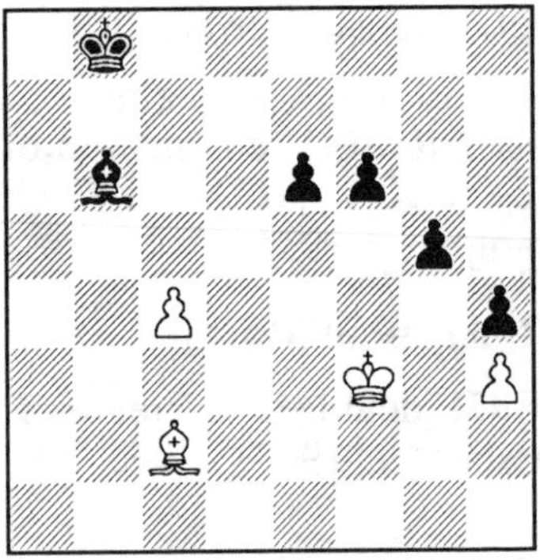

White to move

Evaluate the position.

173. **Discovering a Rook & Knight Mate**

This struggle is over in three moves!

1. Rxb7+! hxg5 2. Nc6+ Ke8 3. Re7#. (Sokolov - Rushnikov, 1967)

174. **No Breathing Room**

1. Qxf7+! Nxf7 2. Ng6#. (Wikstrom - Wood, 1947)

175. **Overloaded Queen**

1. Qxe5! (deflection) **1. ... Qxe5 2. Rd8+ Ke7 3. Re8#**. (King - Bedianian, 1962)

176. **Casting Away a Stone to Build a Fortress**

In endgames with Bishops of opposite colors, the quantity of pawns is much less important than their quality. Here Black wins if he is allowed to bring his King to support his passed e6-pawn. He then will advance his connected passers — the e- and f-pawns — in a way that, at all times, leaves at least one of them on a light square. For example: f6-f5, e6-e5, e5-e4, f5-f4, f4-f3, etc. White would have to give up his Bishop for these two pawns — and lose the game.

Thus, White must force Black to play ... e6-e5, moving his only correctly placed pawn, on e6, to a dark square.

1. c5!. This pawn is of little value anyway, and White needs to clear — now! — the a2-g8 diagonal. **1. ... Bxc5 2. Bb3 e5 3. Be6 Kc7 4. Ke4**. White has *built a fortress* — an impregnable position he can defend effortlessly. Here, for instance, he simply moves his Bishop from f5 to g4 and back.

177.

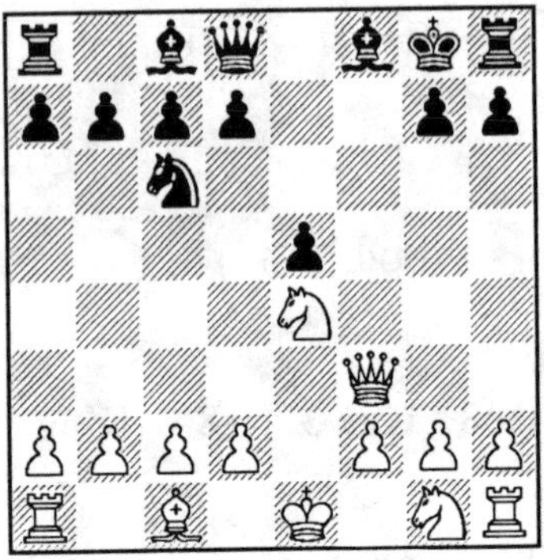

White to move

178.

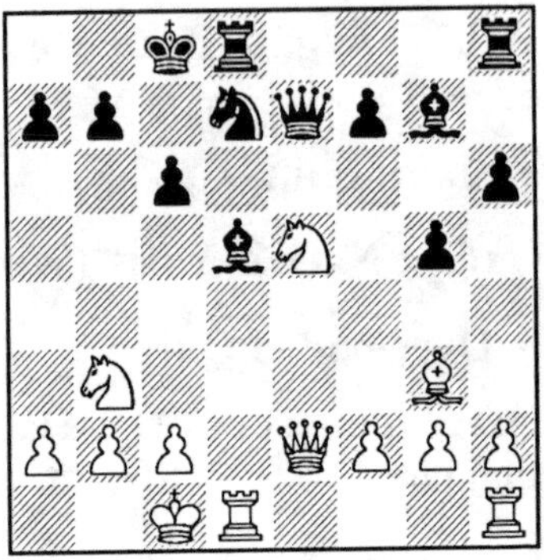

White to move

179.

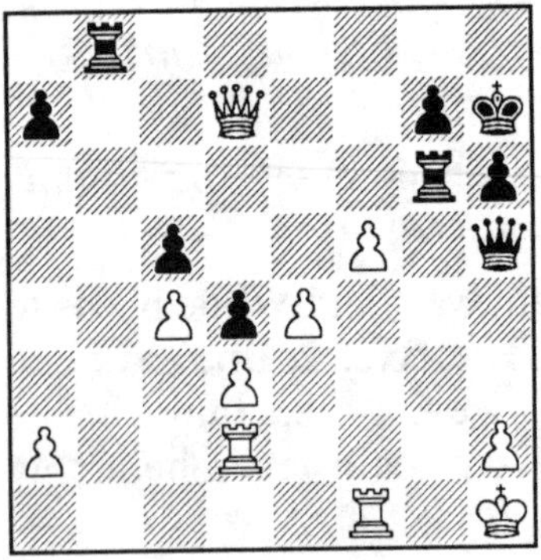

Black to move

180.

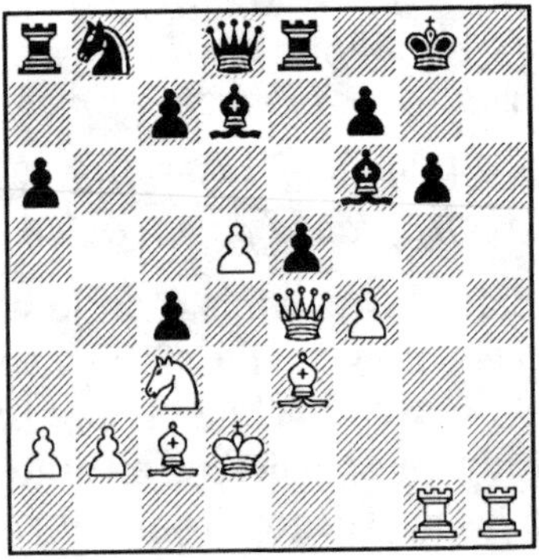

White to move

<u>177.</u> One Knight, Two Mate Threats

1. Ng5! (1. Nd6? Qf6 2. Qd5+ Qe6) **1-0**. (Imbish - Hering, 1899)

<u>178.</u> Uncovering the Truth

1.Nxc6! and Black resigned because 1. ... Qxe2 leads to 2.Nxa7#. (Sharkovsky - Minchev, 1974)

<u>179.</u> Asleep at the Glitch

White's last move (f4-f5) was careless. If he had been wide-awake, Black could have mated brilliantly. Stay alert!

1. ...Qf3+! with a forced mate. In the game, Black played 1. ...Rg3 and eventually *lost!* (Barcza - Tarnovsky, 1950)

<u>180.</u> Decoy Sac to Remember

Try to see clearly in your mind the position after ***1. Rxg6+*** *(destruction of the King's pawn cover)* ***fxg6 2. Qxg6+****. Now consider both of Black's possible replies, and make your judgment — and then your move.*

White won after **2. ... Bg7** *(2. ... Kf8 3. Bc5+)* **3. Rh8+!** (memorize this frequent decoy sacrifice) **3. ... Kxh8 4. Qh7#**. (Pfeifer - Blau, 1952)

181.

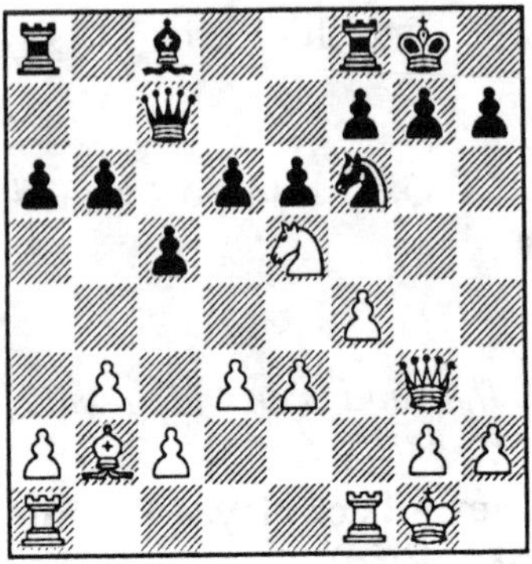

White to move

182.

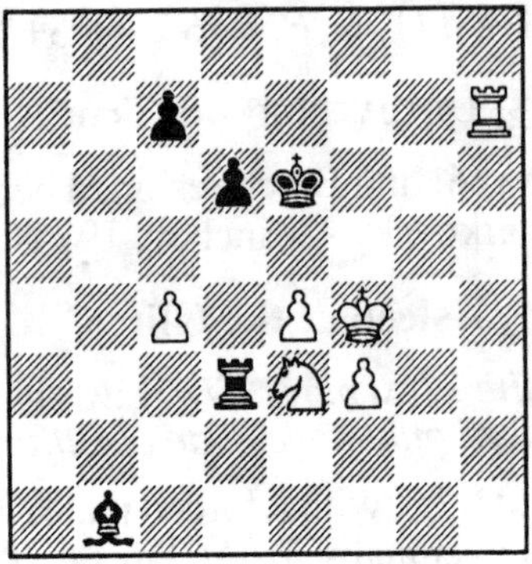

Black to move

183.

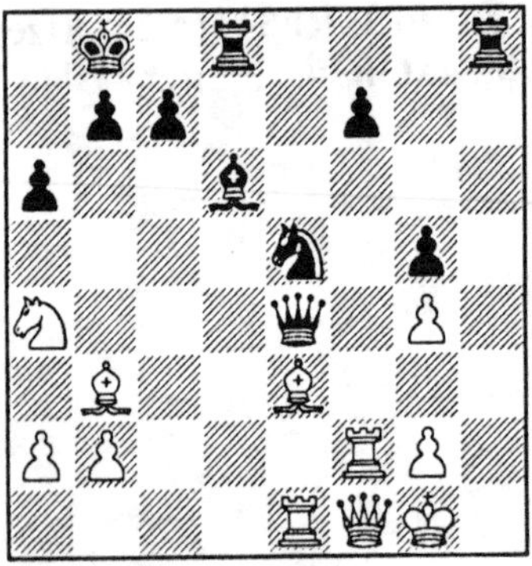

Black to move

184.

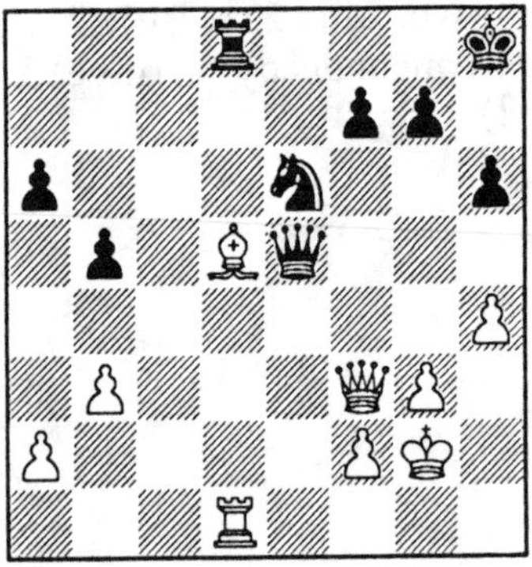

White to move

181. Clearing the Long Diagonal

1. Nd7! Now the Knight can — and can't — be taken by three pieces! **1. ... Qxd7**. If 1. ... Nh5 (or 1. ... Ne8), then 2. Nf6+, with play similar to the game. **2. Bxf6 g6 3. Qg5 1-0**. (Durst - Alster, 1965)

182. Try A Trap

The position is correct — Black is down a pawn and is in deep trouble. Still, what is his best move?

Well, in the actual game Black simply resigned! But unless you are playing against the World Champion, you should try **1. ... c5!?**, hoping for the reckless **2. Nd5??** (now how to stop *3.Re7#* ?) and here comes the fireworks, **2. ... Rxf3+! 3. Kxf3** *(3. Kg5 Rf7)* **3. ... Bxe4+ 4. Kxe4**, stalemate.

Note that the stubborn-looking *1. ... c6* leaves Black few practical chances after *2. Rc7*, winning the second pawn because *2. ... c5 3. Nd5* now leads to a forced mate.

Give your opponent the chance to go wrong, especially when you have little or nothing to lose! (Lasker, Em. - Janowsky, 1909)

183. Double check that mates!

Decoy the King to h2!

1. ... Rh1+! 2. Kxh1 Qh7+! 3. Kg1 Qh2+! 4. Kxh2 Nf3+ 5. Kh1 Rh8#. (Komov - Sydor, 1952)

184. Rejecting the Recapture

1. Bxe6! Rxd1 2. Qa8+!. White aims higher than the normal exchange of heavy artillery. **2. ... Kh7 3. Bxf7 1-0**. (Bilek - Farago, 1973)

185.

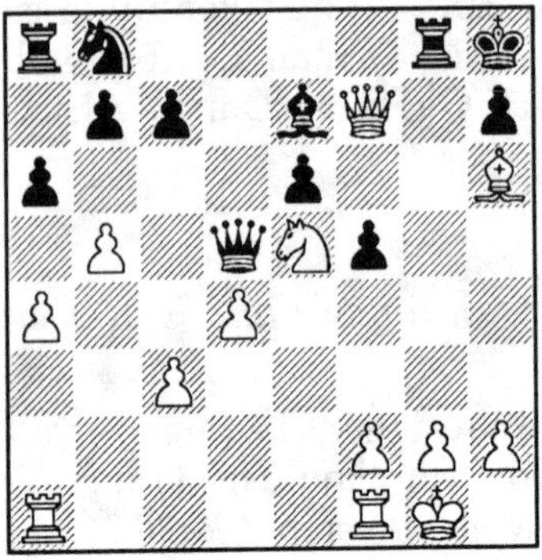

White to move

186.

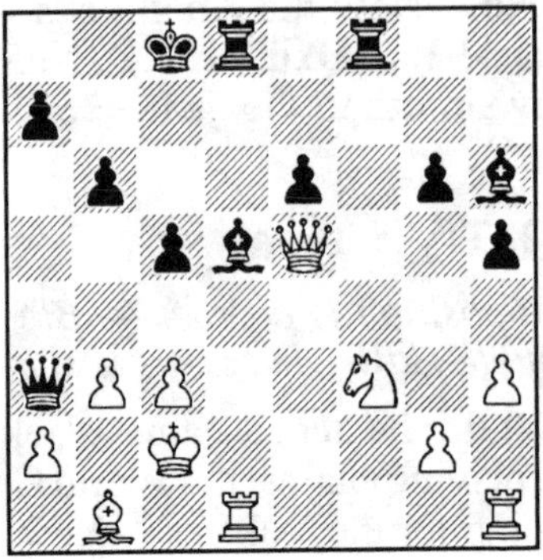

Black to move

187.

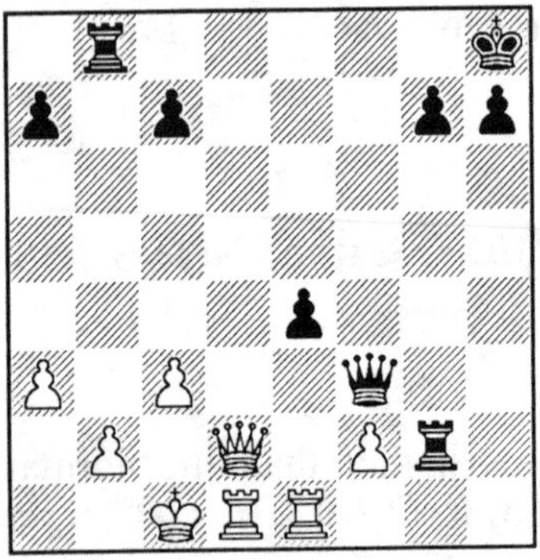

White to move

188.

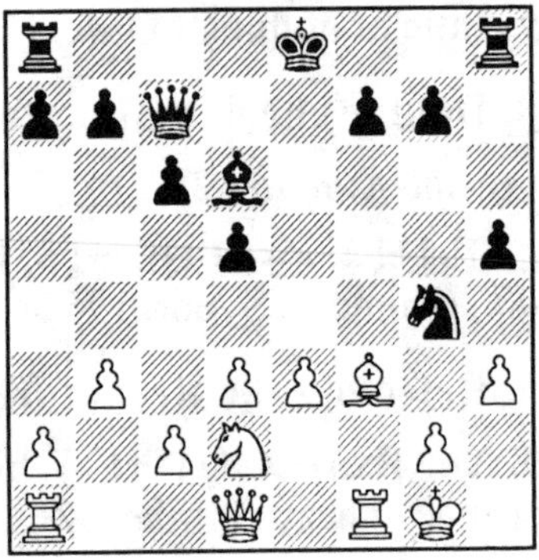

Black to move

185. Clearing the Square

1. Qf6+ Bxf6 2. Nf7#. (Semyonov - Loginov, 1952)

186. Rook and Bishop Smothered Mate

1. ... Rxf3! *(if 1. ... Bxf3 2. Qxe6+)* **2. gxf3**. (Useless is *2. Rxd5* because of *2. ... Rf2+*, but when you're winning, always look out for such "desperados" and in-between moves by your opponent.) **2. ... Bxb3+!** (clearing the d-file) **3. axb3 Qc1+!** (deflection and blocking) **4. Rxc1 Rd2#**. (Bulach - Petrov, 1851)

187. Even Pillsbury Could Fall For A Trap!

After White's 1. Re3, how should Black respond?

Clearly, in the diagram position White is much worse (e.g., *1. Qd8+ Qf8*). So he set a trap with **1. Re3**, which should have failed to 1. ... Rxf2!. Instead, the "natural" **1. ... Qxf2?** followed, only to be met by the crushing **2. Re2!** and White won *(2. ... Qxe2 3. Qd8+ Rxd8 4. Rxd8#)*. (Showalter - Pillsbury, 1904)

188. The Queen's Assistants

1. ... Bh2+! 2. Kh1 Bg1! 0-1. Knowing the model Queen and Knight mate allowed Black to find the two creative tempo-gainers that rolled out the red carpet for the Queen. (Vis - Barcza, 1939)

189.

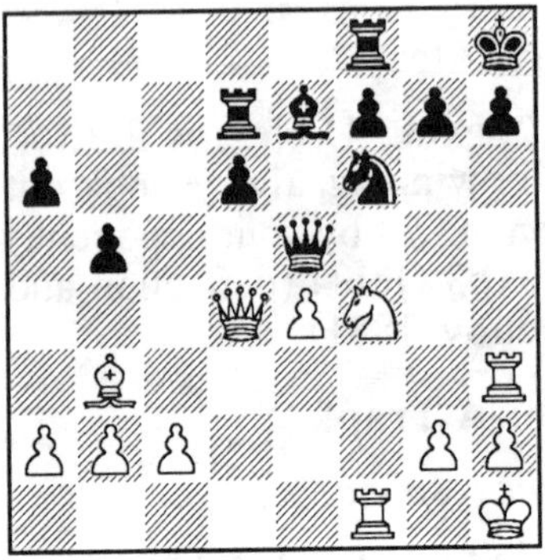

White to move

190.

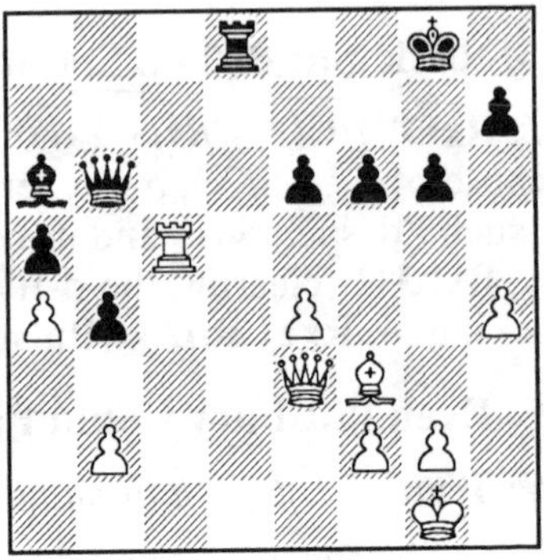

White to move

191.

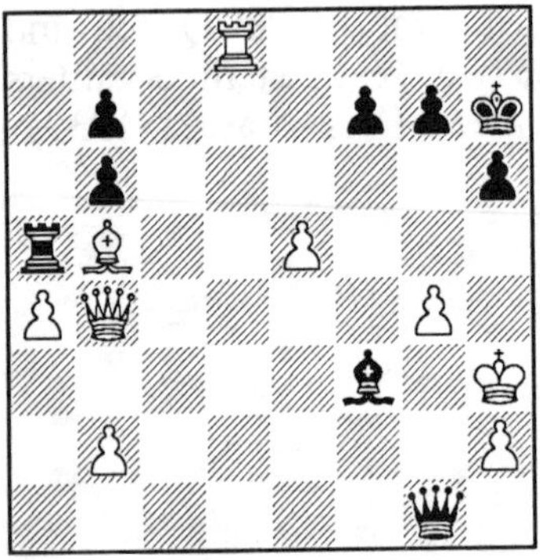

White to move

192.

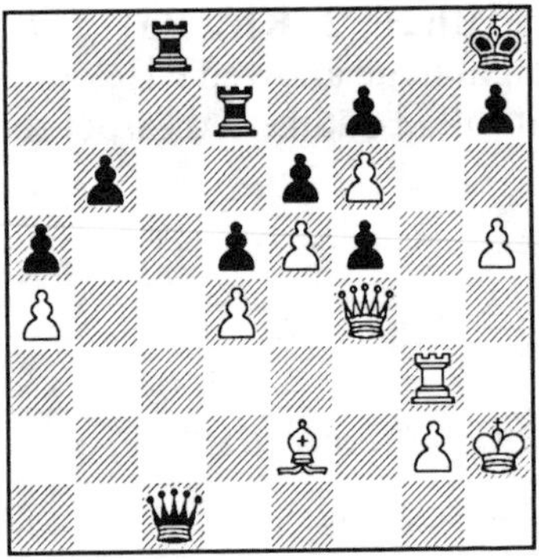

White to move

189. **Making g6 Safe for the Cavalry**

1. Bxf7! and Black resigns, as he will either lose his Queen or be mated. (Wade - Boxal, 1953)

190. **Championship Lesson**

Is 1. e5 a good move?

1. e5! is an excellent *positional* move, which also contains a trap. Notice that instead 1. Rc8?! would be met by 1. ... Qd6.

Black replied **1. ... f5?** in order to keep his pawns intact (1. ... fxe5 æ was a must). The World Champ then delivered a winning blow — **2. Rc8!**. (Alekhine - Flohr, 1931)

191. **Practical Thinking**

Because Black has deadly threats, White must act forcefully — i.e., his moves must give check. Do you see a perpetual for White?

1. Bd3+. (1. Rh8+ leads, after 1. ... Kxh8 2. Qf8+ Kh7 3. Bd3+, to the same position as 1. Bd3+. But it gives Black another option, 1. ... Kg6. For practical purposes, why not limit your opponent's choices?) **1. ... g6 2. Rh8+ Kxh8 3. Qf8+**. When playing 1. Bd3+, you didn't have to see farther than the draw by perpetual check. *Now* — start looking for more! **3. ... Kh7 4. Qxf7+ Kh8 5. Qf8+ Kh7 6. Bxg6+! Kxg6 7. Qg8#**. (Forintosh - Tomovic, 1957)

192. **Free Pass to g7**

1. Rg8+!. This move combines three tactical ideas at once: deflection (1. ... Rxg8 2. Qxc1), decoy, and clearing the square! **1. ... Kxg8 2. Qg3+ 1-0**. (Sturua - Kozlov, 1975)

193.

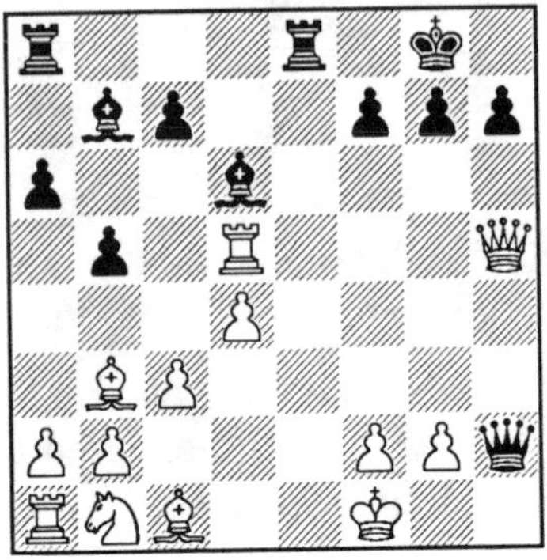

Black to move

194.

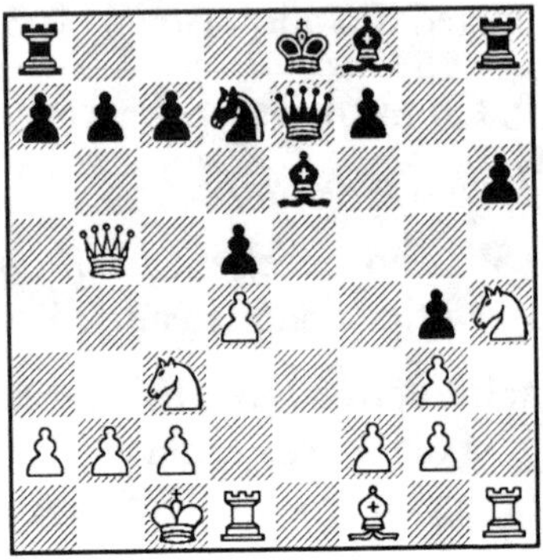

Black to move

195.

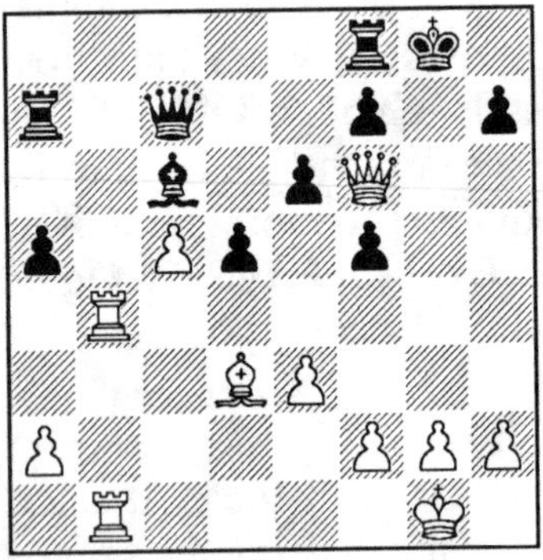

White to move

196.

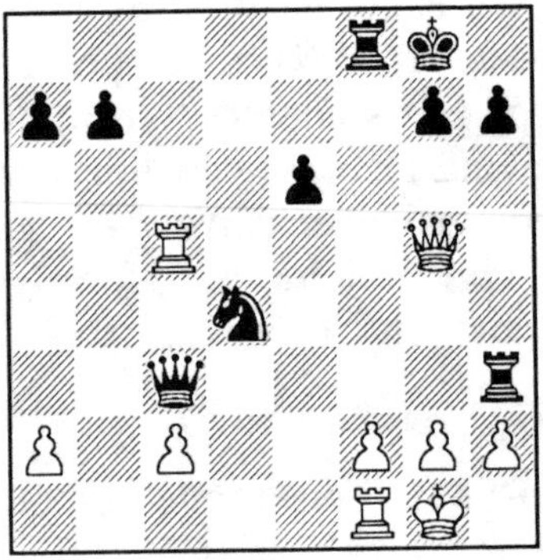

Black to move

193. **Decoy & Mate!**

1. ... Qg1+ 2. Kxg1 Re1#. (Gaiukov - Slucker, 1990)

194. **Surprise Target**

Black has to defend both the b7 and d5 pawns, but how?

Clearly wrong (tactically) is 1. ... Qb4? because of 2. Nxd5 Qxb5 3. Nxc7+.

Black can first defend the d-pawn with a check on g5, and then castle. But he preferred **1. ... 0-0-0**. What's wrong with **2. Nxd5** now?

2. ... Bxd5!! (not *2. ... Qg5+? 3. Nf4*) **3. Qxd5 Qg5+ 4. Qxg5 hxg5**, winning a piece for just two pawns. But Lasker saw through this trap, and didn't take the pawn. (Lasker, Em - Marshall, 1914)

195. **Two Mating Threats**

1. Rg4+! (clearing the diagonal for the Bishop) **1. ... fxg4 2. Qg5+!**. (This important in-between check drives Black's King into the corner, depriving the f8-Rook of its defender.) **2. ... Kh8 3. Qh6** Black resigns. He can't defend against two simultaneous mating threats. (Hort - Portisch, 1973)

196. **This Lady Has Three Suitors**

Black, with both his Queen and Rook en prise, *ended this game with a paradoxical killer move.*

1. ... Qg3! 0-1. 2. Qxg3 Ne2+ 3. Kh1 Nxg3++ 4. Kg1 Nxf1 leaves Black a piece up, while other moves lead to immediate mates. (Levitsky - Marshall, 1912)

197.

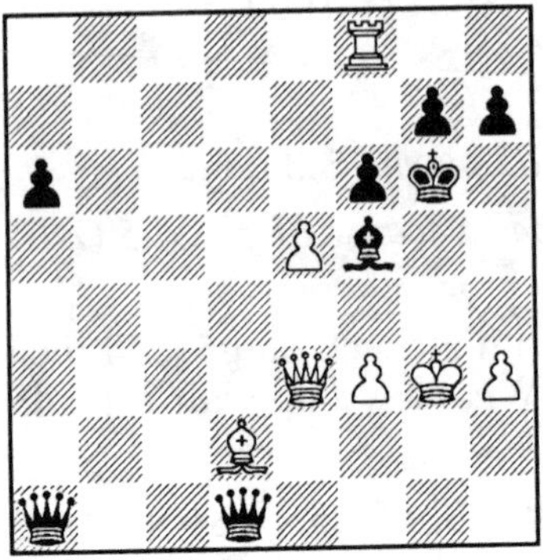

White to move

198.

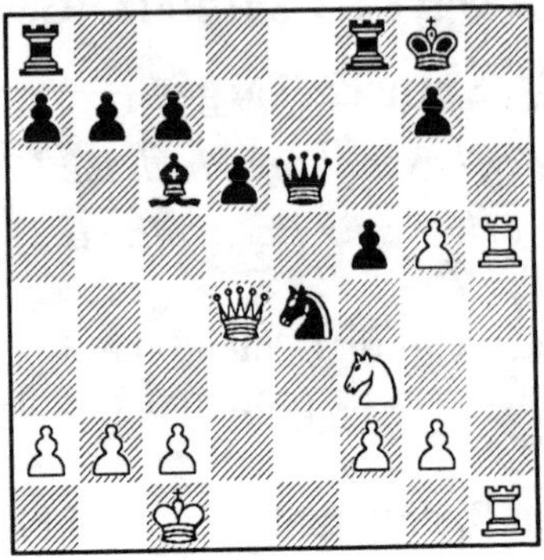

White to move

199.

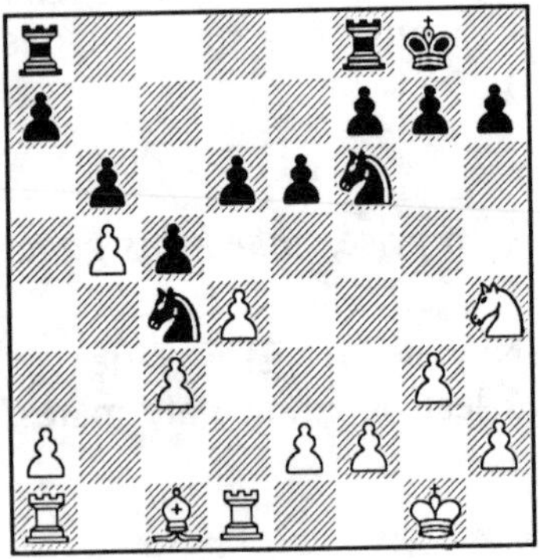

Black to move

200.

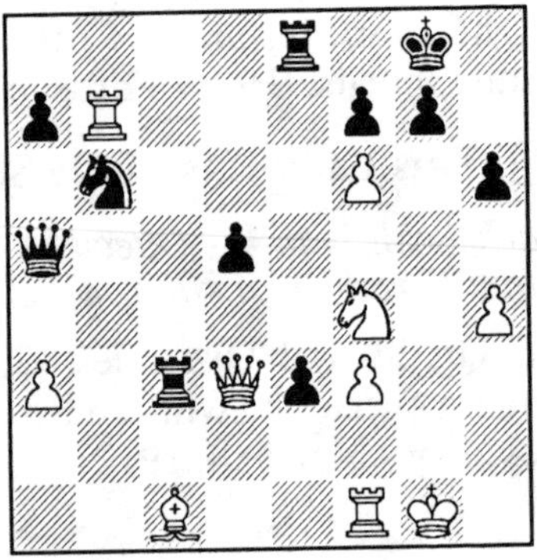

White to move

197. Applying the Rook & Bishop Mate

1. Qh6+ gxh6 2. Rxf6+ and Black resigned, because both retreats lead to mate: 2. ... Kh5 3. Rxh6#, or 2. ... Kg7 3. Bxh6+ and 4. Rf8#. (Novozhenin - Panfilov, 1975)

198. Two-Step Setup

White would love to play 1. g6, creating the unstoppable threat of 2. Rh8 mate, but it would be met by the simple 1. ... Qxg6, and now if 2. Qc4+ (with the idea of forcing Black to block in his own King with 2. ... Rf7 or 2. ... Qf7) then of course 2. ... d5. So the question is, how can he decoy the d6-pawn?

1. Ne5!. (Threatening *2. Rh8#*, as the Knight controls the vital f7-square. Now *1. ... g6 2. Rh8+ Kg7 3. R1h7#*, and *1. ... Qxe5 2. Qxe5 dxe5 3. g6* leads to mate.) **1. ... dxe5 2. g6 Qxg6 3. Qc4+**, followed by mate on h8. (Alekhine - Mindino, 1933)

199. Creating a Second Front

Black is better, and most moves would preserve this advantage, e.g., 1. ... Ne4 or 1. ... Nd5, attacking the c3-pawn. But shouldn't he try to activate his Rooks?

1. ... a6! 2. bxa6 Rxa6 and White won't be able to defend his weak pawns. (Mattison - Nimzovich, 1929)

200. The Queen Clears the 7th

White sets up a Rook & Knight mate, with help from a wedge pawn that supports his Rook.

1. Qg6! 1-0. If 1. ... fxg6 then 2. Rxg7+ and 3. Ng6#. (Bronstein - Geller, 1961)

201.

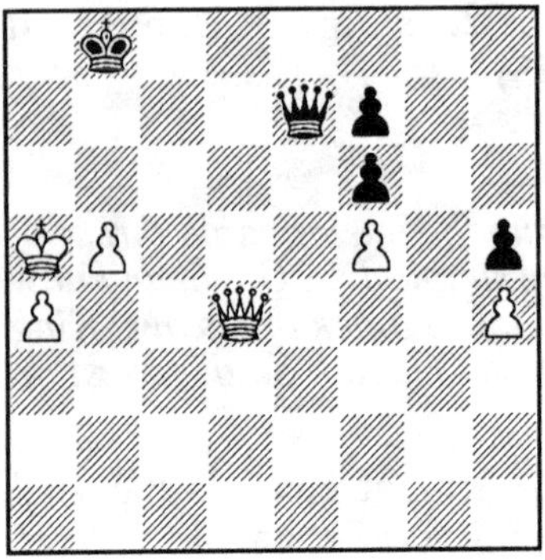

Black to move

202.

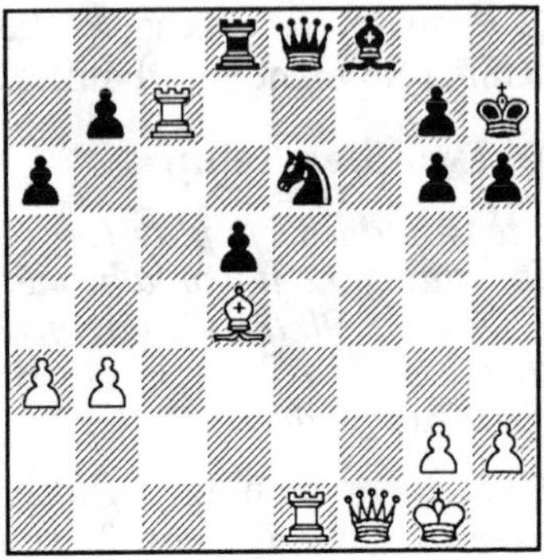

White to move

203.

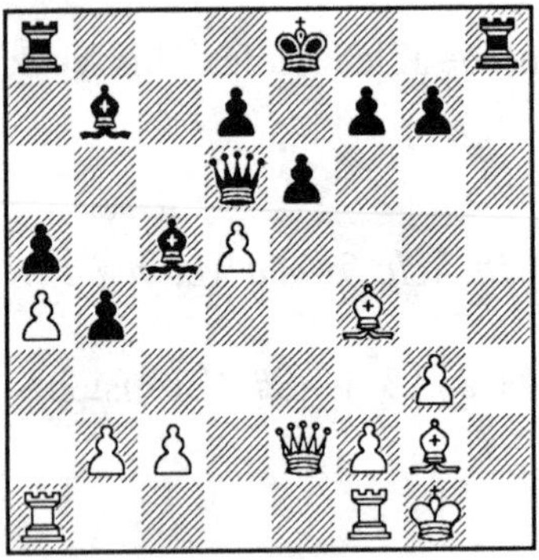

Black to move

204.

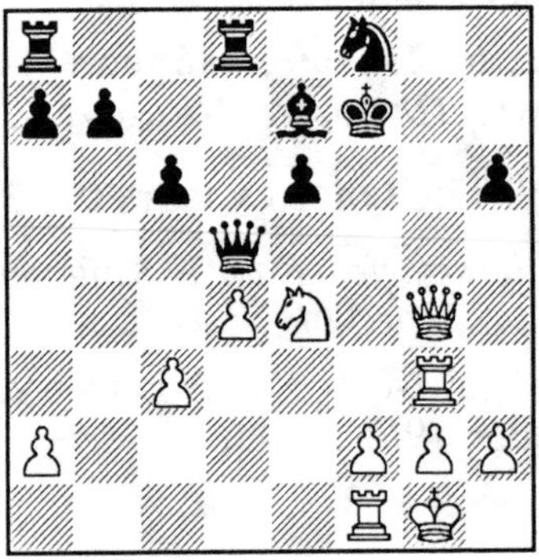

White to move

201. **Stalemate to the Rescue**

White's position should be easily won, as he is effectively two pawns up. Black's only hope is for White to stumble into perpetual check, stalemate, or some other trap. He played 1. ... Qc7+ . What should be White's response?

Certainly not **2. Qb6+??**. White's desire to exchange Queens is understandable, and lures him into a trap. Now **2. ... Ka8!** draws *(3. Ka6 Qc8+ 4. Ka5 Qc7 draw)*

Instead, White would win with **2. b6**, aiming to exchange his Queen and b6-pawn for Black's Queen, with an easily won pawn endgame. (Chigorin - Schlechter, 1905)

202. **Eliminate the Defenders at All Cost!**

1. Rxe6! Qxe6 2. Qxf8 Rxf8 (*If 2. ... Qe1+ then 3. Qf1*) **3. Rxg7+ Kh8 4. Rxg6+!**. (*4. Rxb7+*? fails to *4. ... Rf6*, while *4. Re7+ Qf6!* is better for White but not necessarily winning.) **4. ... Rf6 5. Rxf6**, and no matter where the Black Queen goes, she'll be lost, e.g.: **5. ... Qe1+ 6. Rf1+ 1-0**. (Vasyukov - Dzurashevic, 1961)

203. **Capturing the Diagonal**

Remember the Rook + Bishop mate in the corner? Use brute force if necessary.

1. ... Qxd5! 2. Bxd5 Bxd5 0-1.

Thanks to the c5-Bishop, White's f2-pawn is pinned, making **3. ... Rh1#** unstoppable. (Gutop - Roshal, 1963)

204. **Applying the Epaulet Mate**

1. Qxg7+ Ke8 2. Qxe7+! Kxe7 3. Rg7+ Ke8 4. Nf6#. (Korchnoi - Petrosian, T., 1965)

205.

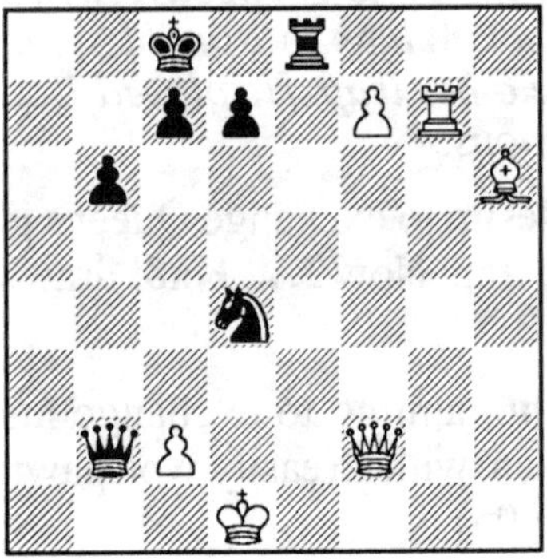

Black to move

206.

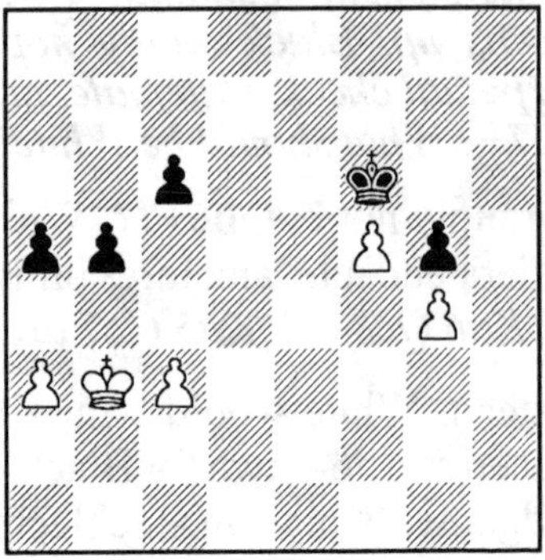

White to move

207.

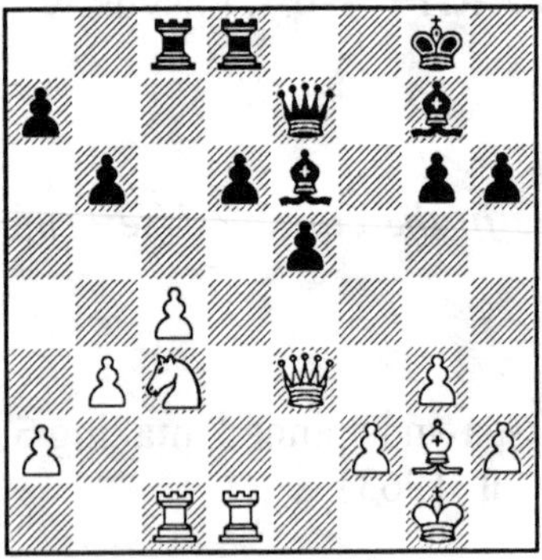

White to move

208.

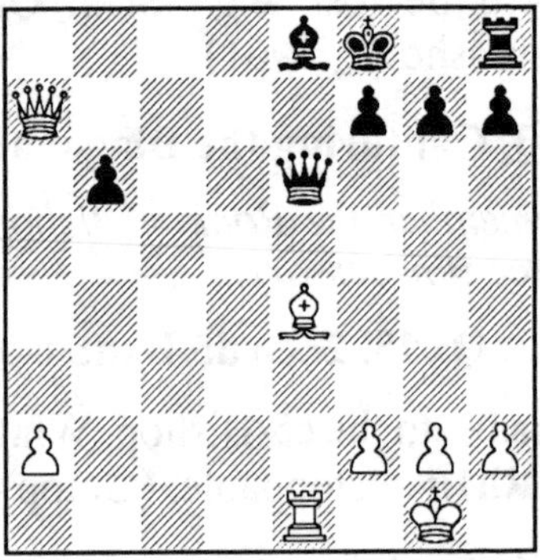

White to move

<u>205.</u> Queen & Knight Duo at Work

1. ... Qb1+ 2. Bc1 Re1+!, and White resigned. (Vatnikov - Borovoy, 1957)

<u>206.</u> Protected Passer

1. a4! Ke5 2. axb5 (*2.c4? b4* is a draw because Black now has his own *protected passed pawn*) **2. ... cxb5 3. c4 a4+** (*3. ... b4 4. c5*, and the Black King can't stop both the c- and f-pawns) **4. Kc3 bxc4 5. Kxc4**. White's King then captures the a-pawn and marches to the kingside to assist the advance of the f-pawn, giving White an easy win.

<u>207.</u> Two Bs or Not Two Bs

White stands better because of Black's backward d6-pawn and "hole" on d5. Additionally, Black's kingside pawns appear vulnerable. How should White proceed?

1. Bd5!. The best. By exchanging light-squared Bishops, White deprives his opponent of his only trump card — the Bishop pair — and leaves himself with a good Knight (to occupy either d5 or e4) vs. bad Bishop. (Smyslov - Denker, 1946)

<u>208.</u> Pinning & Mating!

1. Qa3+! Qe7. (Loses immediately, but 1. ... Kg8 2. Bxh7+ and 3. Rxe6 is also hopeless for Black.) **2. Bc6! 1-0**. A wonderful finale. If 2. ... Qxa3, then 3. Rxe8#. (Evans - Bisguier, 1958)

209.

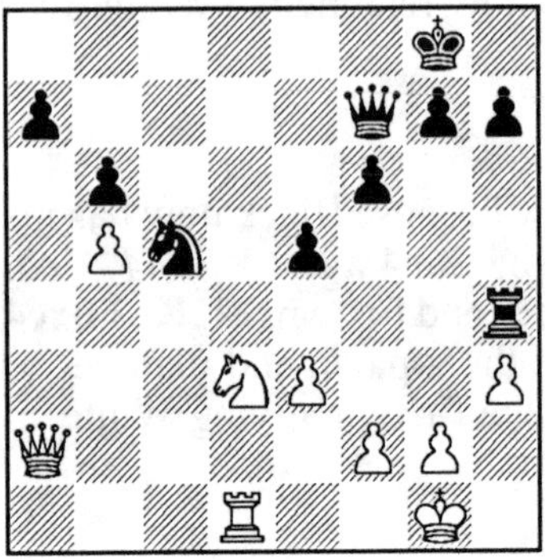

White to move

210.

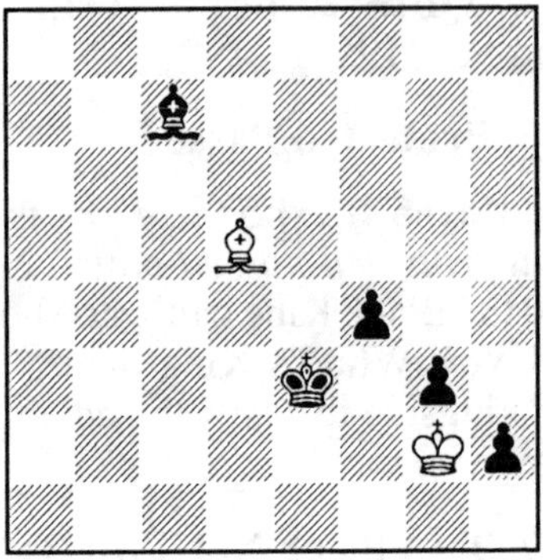

White to move

211.

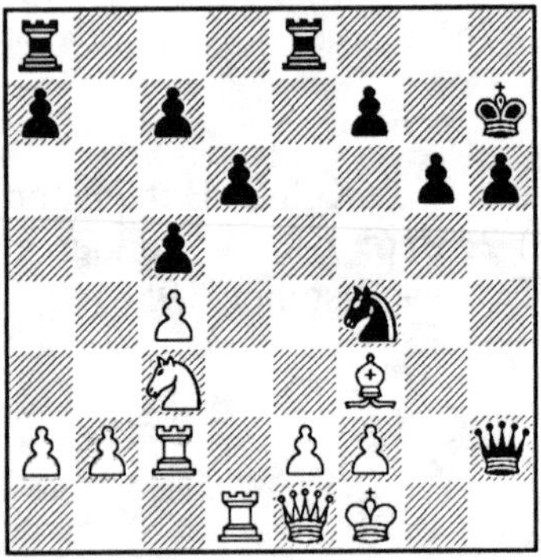

Black to move

212.

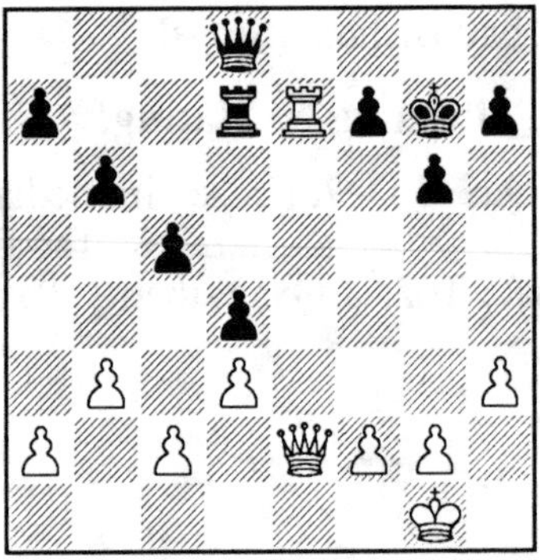

White to move

209. Queen Be Damned!

Set up the back-rank mate!

1. Nxe5! 1-0. (Bronstein - Vasyukov, speed game 1973)

210. Fighting Stalemate

"The qualities required to find stalemate opportunities are a fighting attitude, creativity, and a knowledge of thematic stalemate positions."

— *GM Edmar Mednis*

Black's threat is to play 1. ... f3+ 2. Bxf3 (2. Kh1 g2#) 2. ... h1(Q)+, winning. Even so, White — although three pawns down — can hold a draw!

1. Kh1! to meet **1. ... f3** with **2. Bxf3**, leading to a stalemate.

211. Jamming Up the Escape Route

1. ... Nh3 seems to be the right idea, but after some thought you'll find a defense for White, 2. e3, that lets the White King slip away.

1. ... Re3! and now **2. ... Nh3** leads to immediate mate. (Friedman - Tornblom, 1974)

212. Natural Moves Are Often Best

1. Qe5+! 1-0. It's enough when playing 1. Qe5+! to see that after 1. ... Kf8 (1. ... Kh6 2. Qf4+) 2. Rxd7 Qxd7 3. Qh8+, White wins a pawn. Of course, if your opponent plays 1. ... Kf8, you should search to see if there's something better — and find 2. Qf6, winning immediately. (Kviletski - Roslinski, 1954)

213.

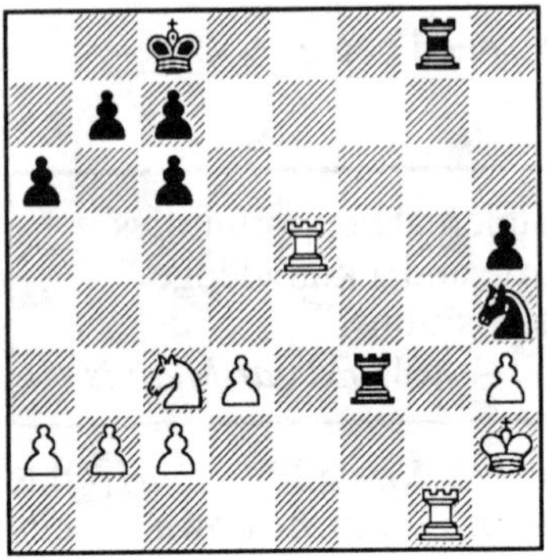

Black to move

214.

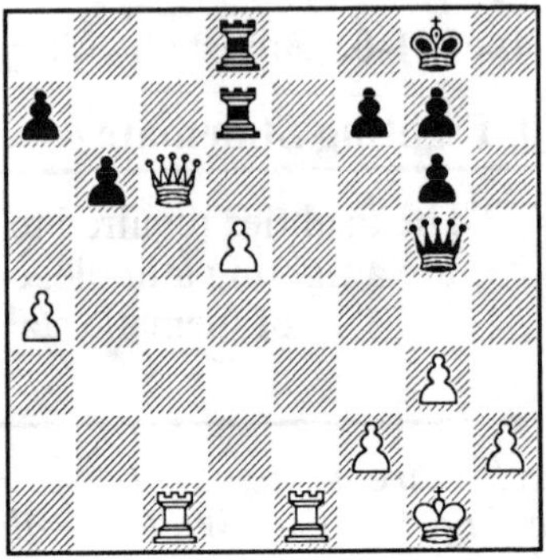

White to move

215.

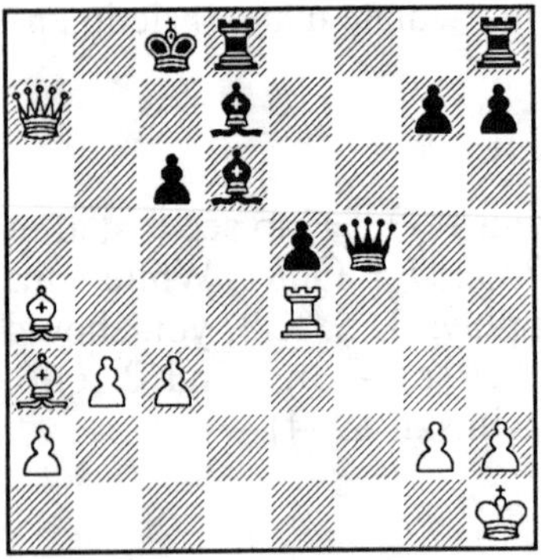

White to move

216.

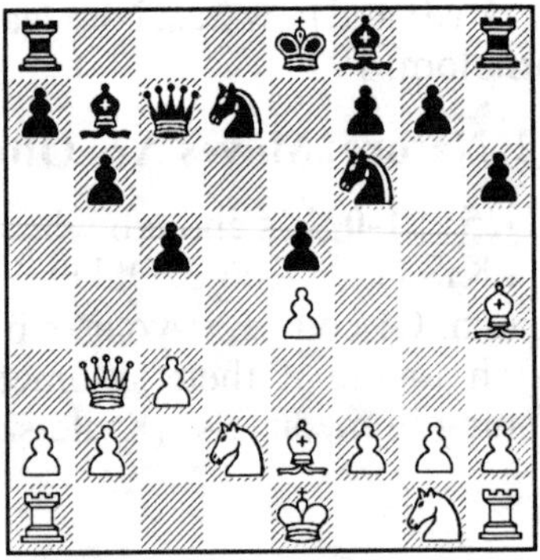

Black to move

213. **Check, Check, Check, Mate!**

1. ... Rf2+ 2. Kh1 Rh2+! 3. Kxh2 Nf3+ 4. Kh1 Rxg1#. (Tartakover - Schlechter, 1908)

214. **With Friends Like These ...**

Look how the Black King's colleagues stand around in his way! A classic example of the havoc two Rooks can wreak on the back rank.

1. Qxd7 Rxd7 2. Re8+ Kh7 3. R1c8 and wins. The g6-pawn blocks the King's escape, and the Black Queen blocks the pawn! (Alekhine - Colle, 1925)

215. **Guard a Mate, Threaten a Mate!**

1. Bb5!. Defends against 1. ... Qf1 mate, while threatening checkmate with 2. Ba6. Black resigned here since 1. ... cxb5 loses to 2. Qa6+ and 3. Bxd6#. The strongest Black defense, **1. ... Rdf8 2. Bxd6 Qf1+ 3. Bxf1 Rxf1+ 4. Qg1 Rxg1+ 5. Kxg1**, leaves Black, after the inevitable loss of the e5-pawn, two pawns down. (Ljubojevic - Durao, 1974)

216. **Win a Pawn, if You Can**

Yes, Black can, and perhaps should, win the e4-pawn by first playing 1. ... g5.

Instead, he hurried with **1. ... Nxe4?**, only to be mated after **2. Qe6+! fxe6 3. Bh5+**. (Mueller - Wolz, 1940)

Winter - Capablanca, 1919:
A Classic Battle in Four Snapshots

1. e4 e5 2. Nf3 Nc6 3. Nc3 Nf6 4. Bb5 Bb4 5. 0-0 0-0
6. Bxc6 dxc6 7. d3 Bd6 8. Bg5 h6 9. Bh4

217.

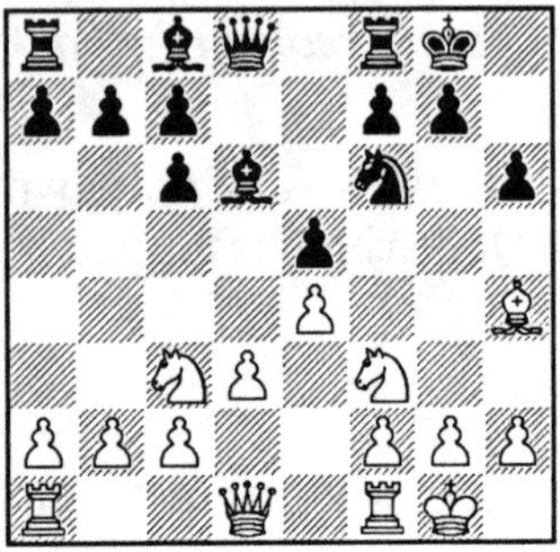

Black to move

218.

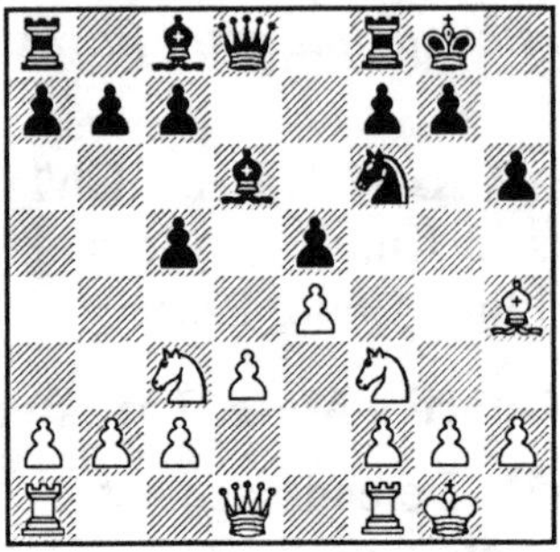

White to move
Should White play 10. Nd5 here?

219.

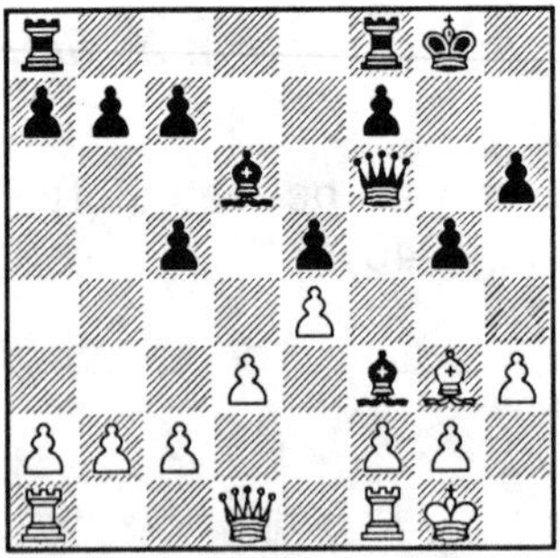

White to move

220.

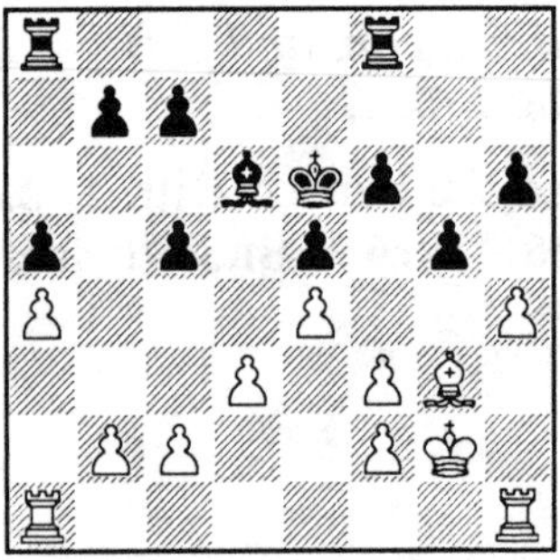

Black to move
Formulate a plan.

217. A Classic Battle Begins

Should Black play 9. ...c5 here?

The answer is yes! True, the pawn makes the Bishop on d6 technically "bad" for a while, but more importantly, it stops White from playing 10. d4, achieving a better pawn structure. (If 9. ... Bg4, also aimed at stopping 10. d4, then 10. h3 and White is better after either 10. ... Bxf3 11. Qxf3; or 10. ... Bh5 11. g4 Bg6 12. Bg3, followed by 13. Nh4 and 14. Nf5.)

So, **9. ... c5** is justified positionally, but what about tactically?

218. How Strong is This Pin?

10. Nd5 g5! (breaks the pin and locks the kingside pawn structure in Black's favor) **11. Nxf6** (after 11. Nxg5 Nxd5!, White has no compensation for his sacrificed material) **11. ... Qxf6 12. Bg3 Bg4 13. h3 Bxf3** and White is faced with a Hobson's Choice. (See diagram #219.)

219. Hobson's Choice

14. gxf3!, keeping more forces on the board, was White's best try. But Winter played **14. Qxf3?** and after **14. ... Qxf3 15. gxf3 f6**, White's once good Bishop is completely cut off from the action. White's chances of survival are slim.

The game continued **16. Kg2 a5 17. a4 Kf7 18. Rh1 Ke6 19. h4**.

220. Playing Where the Bishop Isn't!

Black wins by opening up the game on the queenside, where he is in effect a piece ahead, a great contribution to general chess theory.

19. ... Rfb8 20. hxg5 hxg5 21. b3 c6 22. Ra2 b5 23. Rha1 c4! 24. axb5 cxb3 25. cxb3 Rxb5 26. Ra4 Rxb3 27. d4 Rb5 28. Rc4 Rb4! 29. Rxc6 Rxd4 0-1. In addition to his *de facto* extra piece, Black has a very real, *de jure* extra pawn. He will play his pawn to a3, exchange one pair of Rooks, and win.

221.

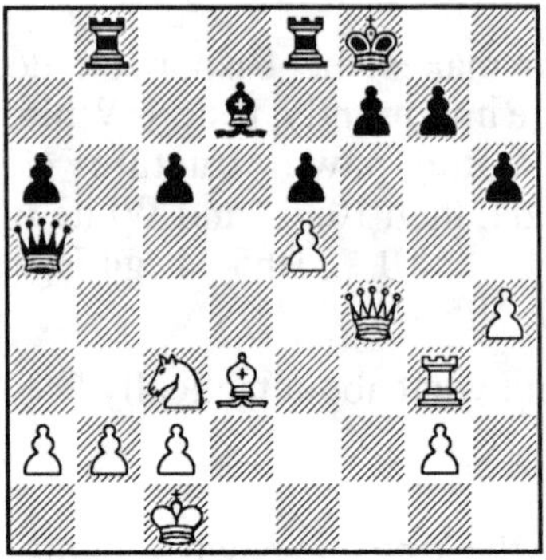

White to move

222.

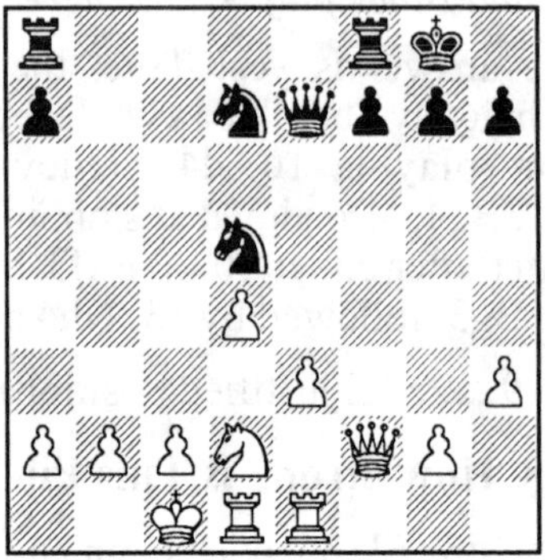

Black to move

223.

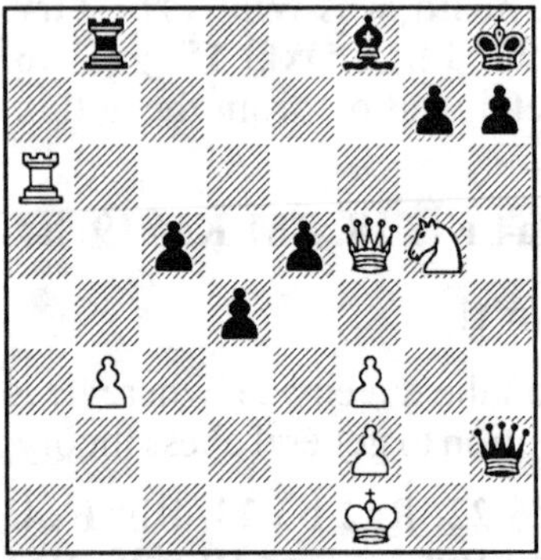

White to move

224.

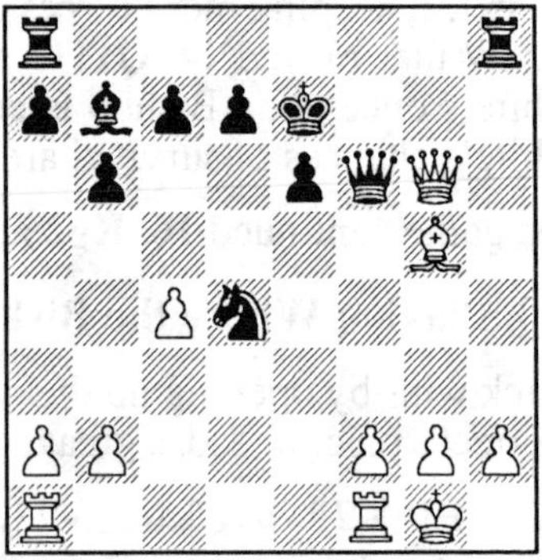

Black to move

221. Thematic Queen & Bishop Mates

Here a Rook sacrifice leads to forced mate.

1. Rxg7 Kxg7 2. Qf6+ Kf8 (2 ... Kg8 3. Qxh6, and there is no defense against the thematic 4. Bh7+ Kh8 5. Bg6+ Kg8 6. Qh7+ and 7. Qxf7#. Neither 3. ... Re7 nor 3. ... f6 helps, because of 4. Qh7+ Kf8 5. Qh8#, or 4. Bh7+ Kf7 5. Qxf6#, respectively.) **3. Bg6**, and Black resigned here. The only defense against 4. Qxf7# is 3. ... Re7, blocking the e7-square and allowing 4. Qh8#. An important example of various typical, and frequently occurring, Queen and Bishop mates. (Keres - Szabo, 1955)

222. "Time Cannot Wither ..."

1. ... Nc3! 2. bxc3 Qa3+ 3. Kb1 Nb6!, and White resigned. There is no adequate defense against 4. ... Na4 (if 4. Ka1, then 4. ... Qxc3+ 5. Kb1 Na4). Note that the immediate 3. ... Rab8+ is inaccurate, because of 4. Nb3 Nb6 5. Ka1, and White holds. Good moves are still good moves, even after more than a century and a half! (Bilguer - Angerstein, 1835)

223. Breaking the Connection on the h-file

1. Rh6! 1-0. (Kireev - Mironov, 1963)

224. Using the Rook & Knight h-file mate

White hoped to win Black's Queen. However, it was Tarrasch, one of the 10 best chess players of all time, and perhaps the best chess writer ever, who wins by a tactical maneuver that is well known — today!

1. ... Ne2+ 2. Kh1 Rxh2+ 3. Kxh2 Rh8+ 4. Bh6 Qh4#. (Richter - Tarrasch, 1892)

225.

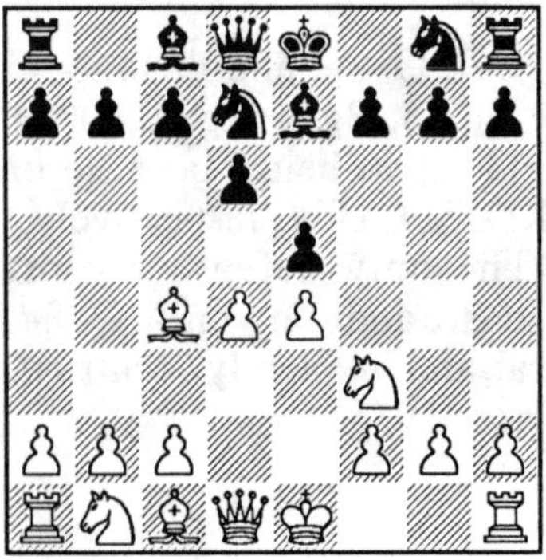

White to move

226.

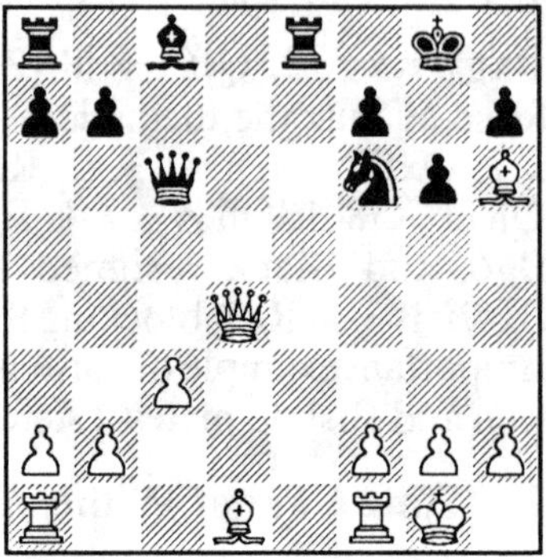

White to move

227.

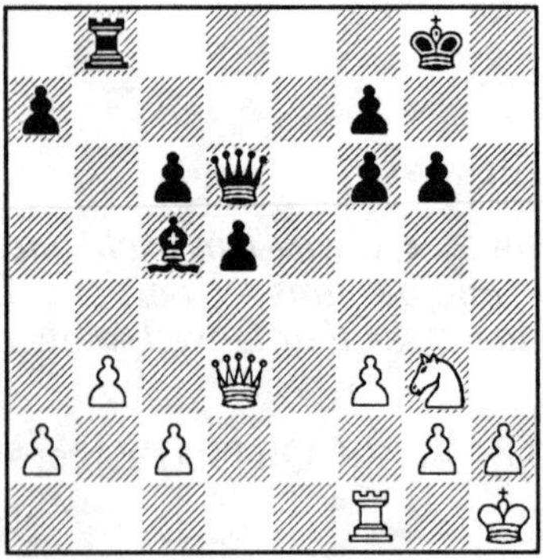

Black to move

228.

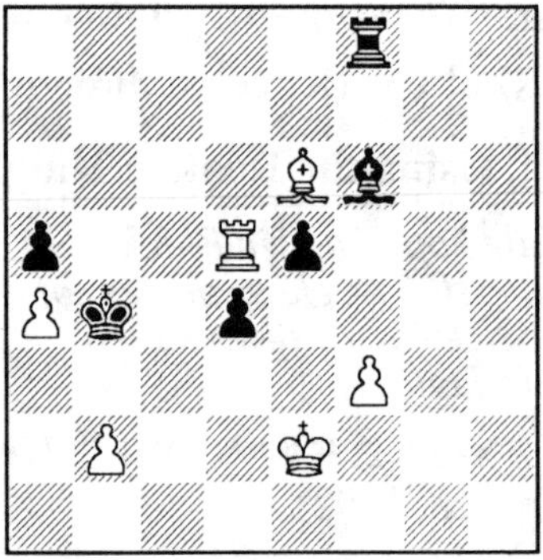

White to move

<u>225.</u> Failed Philidor

After **1. e4 e5 2. Nf3 d6 3. d4 Nd7 4. Bc4 Be7?**, White wins a pawn with **5. dxe5 Nxe5** (even worse is 5. ... dxe5 6. Qd5, winning a piece after 6. ... Nh6 7. Bxh6) **6. Nxe5 dxe5 7. Qh5**, a typical double attack by a Queen.

Black's fourth move was a grave error. The correct line in the Philidor's Defense is 4. ... c6. Black is then ready to meet 5. Ng5 with 5. ... Nh6. If 5. 0-0, only now 5. ... Be7, because the d5-square is protected from the intrusions of White's Queen by the c6-pawn.

<u>226.</u> Beleaguered Queen

The Black Queen tries desperately to protect her Knight, which in turn shelters the Black King. But the future Dean of American Chess wins by multiple deflection.

1. Ba4! b5 2. Bxb5 Qxb5 3. Qxf6 Qe5. White won a pawn, and in a real game — and you should treat these exercises as you would real games — you shouldn't look any further than that. Now with this position on the board, it is easier to find the final winning deflection, **4. Rae1**, and Black resigned. (Koltanowski - Garcia, 1959)

<u>227.</u> The King Stands Aside

1. ... Qxg3! 2. hxg3 Kg7!. An elegant touch! The Black King takes time to step out of the way of his heavy guns. His counterpart is so hemmed in by his own pawns, and out of touch with the rest of his troops, that mate on the h-file can't be stopped. Perfect cooperation between Black's Rook and Bishop! (Alapin - Schiffers, 1902)

<u>228.</u> Pushed to the Edge

1. Rb5!+ Kxa4 2. Rb7, and there is no defense against Bb3#. (Selivanovsky - Yaroshevsky, 1958)

229.

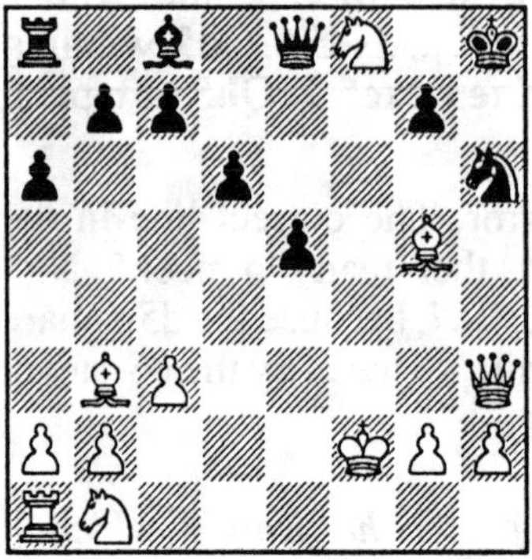

White to move

230.

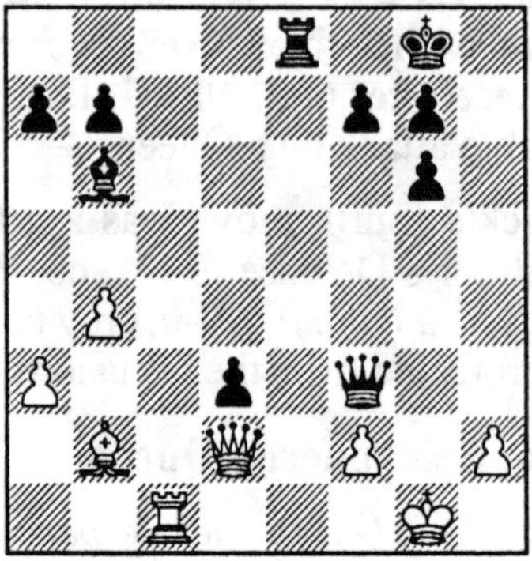

Black to move

231.

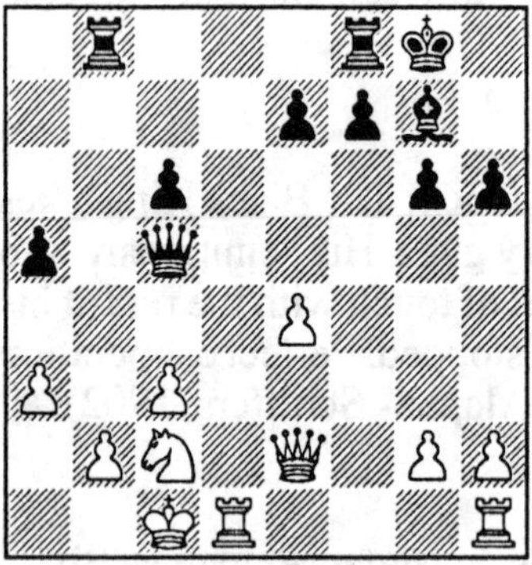

Black to move

232.

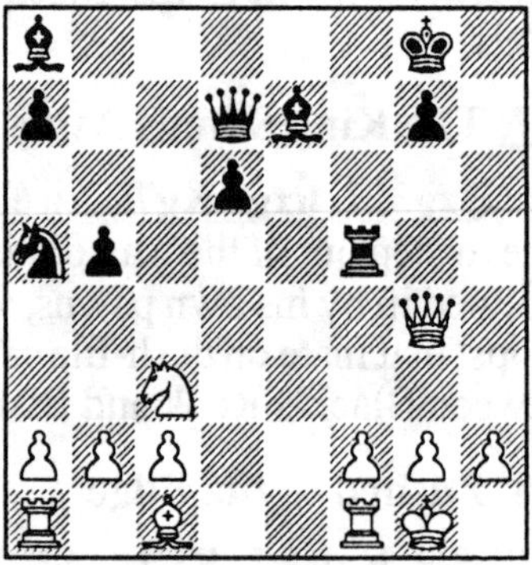

Black to move

229. On Her Own Terms

White's Queen is attacked by a Bishop. So she forces a lowly pawn to capture her, leaving a mate for minor pieces.

1. Qxh6+! gxh6 2. Bf6#. (Exner - Englund, 1902)

230. The Art of Not Losing a Won Position

Black is two pawns up and has an overwhelming positional advantage. He should win easily, unless he falls into a trap. The trick here is to know when to pass up temptingly aggressive candidate moves to take a moment to consolidate.

1. ... f6! followed by 2. ... Re2 is the easiest, but certainly not the only way to win. For instance, also good is the more forceful 1. ...Qxf2 2. Qxf2 d2. But in the actual game, Black, himself a famous tactician, played **1. ... Re2??**, missing **2. Rc8+ Kh8 3. Rh8+!!** (overlooked by Spielmann) **1-0**, because **3. ... Kxh8** loses to **4. Qh6+** and **5. Qxg7#**. (Fazekash - Spielmann, 1938)

231. What's the Follow-Up?

*Of course you'll be considering **1. ... Rxb2 2. Kxb2 Qxc3+ 3. Kc1**. Try to visualize this new position (your support position) very clearly. What — if anything — can Black do now?*

3. ... Rb8!, and there is no effective defense against **4. ... Rb1+** (the archetypal decoy) and **5. ... Qb2#**. (Kapengut - Vaganian, 1970)

232. Target g2

1. ... Rg5! 2. Qxd7 Rxg2+ 3. Kh1 Rxf2+! 4. Kg1 Rg2+ 5. Kh1 Rg3+ 0-1. (Moura - Roha, 1955)

233.

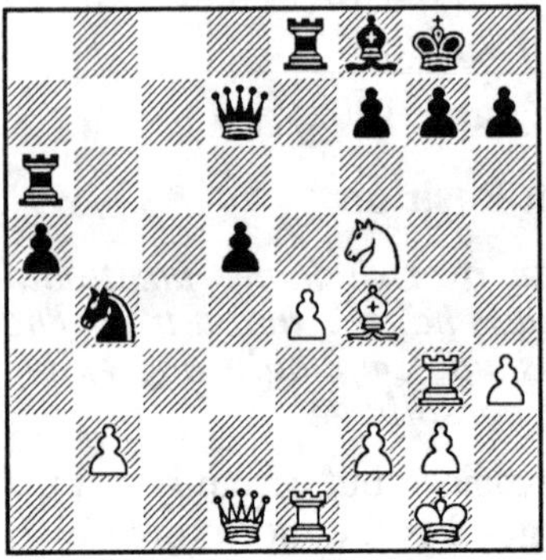

White to move

234.

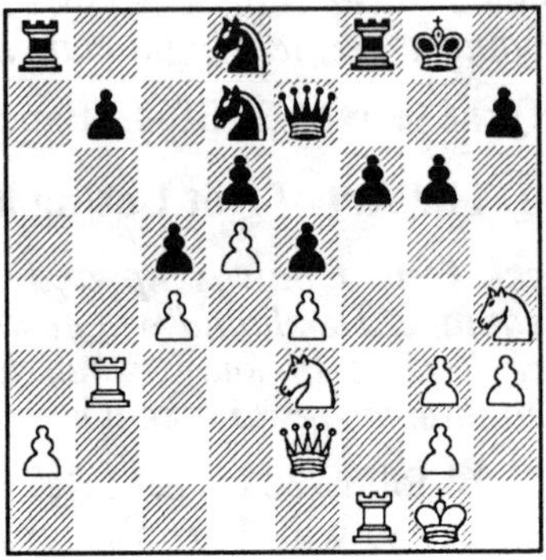

White to move

235.

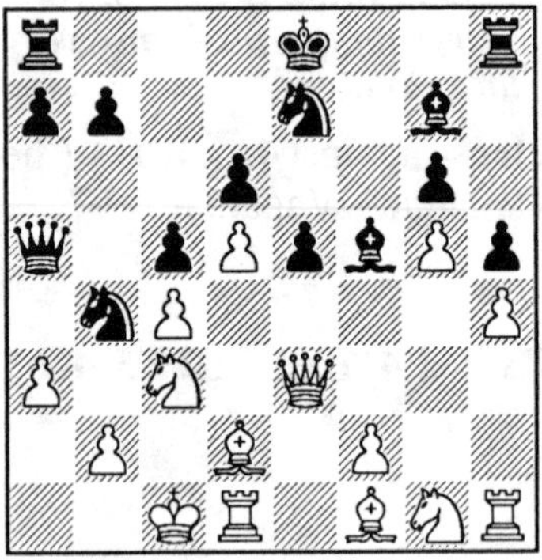

Black to move

236.

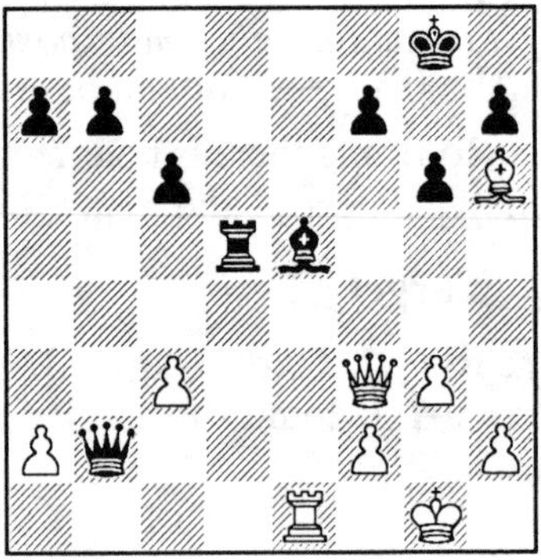

White to move

233. Dangerous Square

The square g7 is under attack, and in addition, the Black Queen is unprotected. Look for a double attack.

1. Rxg7+. (Not the straightforward 1. Qg4 Qe6, and Black holds.) **1. ... Bxg7 2. Qg4**. (Now! If Black defends against 2. Qxg7#, he'll lose his Queen after 3. Nh6+.) **1-0**. (Keres - Gligoric, 1959)

234. Dangerous Square, Part II

In this game, Black loses his Queen in a way reminiscent of his rout by Keres (see position #233).

1. Nhf5 gxf5 2. Nxf5, and the Queen is lost, e.g.: 2. ... Qf7 3. Nh6+, or 2. ... Qe8 3. Qg4+ Qg6 (otherwise Qxg7#) 4. Ne7+. Queen-snatching forks are everywhere, so Black resigned. (Bilek - Gligoric, 1957)

235. Applying the Knight & Bishop Mate

With Black's Bishop on f5 cutting off White's King from b1 and c2, mating threats are likely. Indeed, if it weren't for White's c3-Knight, Black could deliver mate on a2.

1. ... Qa4! 2. Bd3 (2. Nxa4 Na2#) **2. ... Bxd3 0-1**. (Minsheev - Motylev, 1971)

236. Surprise Defense

*White played **1. Qf6!?** (1. Rxe5 Rxe5 2. Qf6 Qb1+, leads to a draw by perpetual check). He won nicely after 1. ...Qxc3? with 2. Qg7+ Bxg7 3. Re8+ Bf8 4. Rxf8#. Could Black play better?*

Yes, **1. ... Qc1!** would save Black. The position after **2. Qxe5** (best) **Qxh6 3. Qb8+ Kg7 4. Qxb7 Qd2** is razor sharp — and unclear. (Kunnerman - NN, 1934)

237.

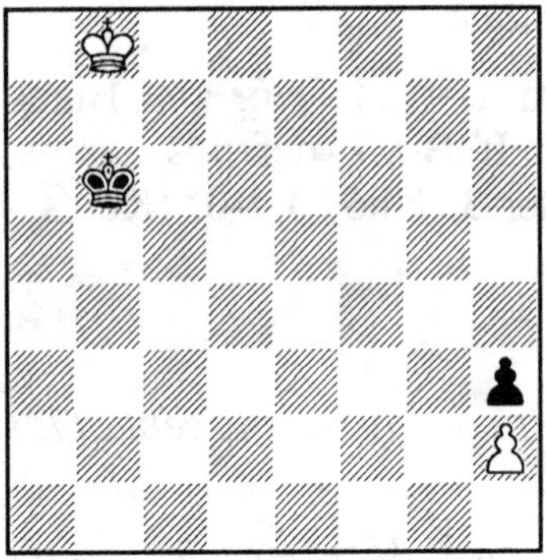

White to move

238.

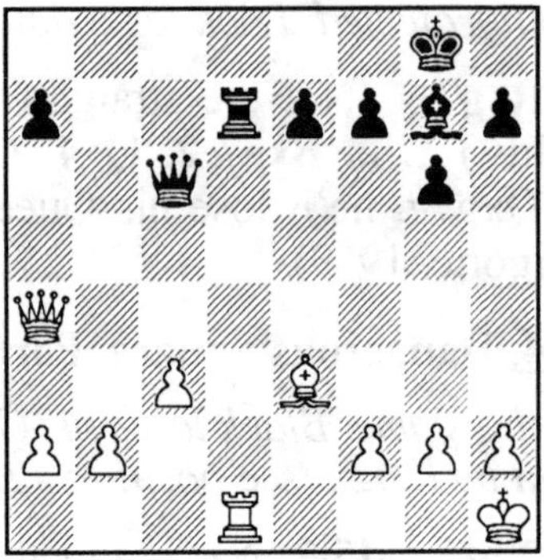

White to move

239.

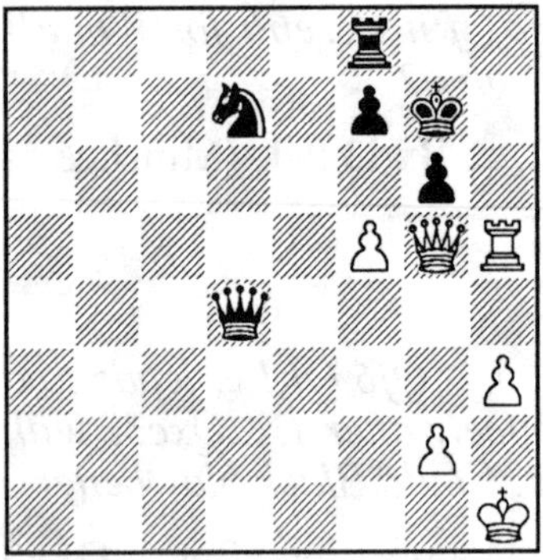

White to move

240.

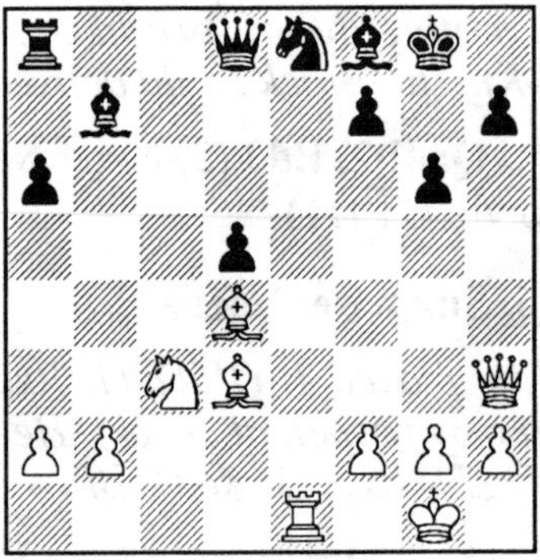

White to move

237. Race to the Key Square

When Black's King comes to g2, White's King needs to be on e3 to lock him in the corner. **1. Ka8!** Paradoxical but logical, considering the hint above. After 1.Kc8? Kc6 the Black King is on the straight road (diagonal) to g2, and en route he will advance one rank per move. White's King will meanwhile be somewhere on the 4th rank, and to draw he must be on the 3rd (e3). **1. ... Kc6 2. Ka7! Kd5 3. Kb6 Ke4 4. Kc5 Kf3 5. Kd4 Kg2 6. Ke3 Kxh2 7. Kf2 draw**. And with Black to move, it should be easy: **1. ... Kc6 2. Ka7**, or **1. ... Kc5 2. Kb7 Kd4 3. Kc6 Ke3 4. Kd5 Kf2 5. Ke4 Kg2 6. Ke3 draw**.

238. Healthy Skepticism

Black's last move (... Qc7-c6) is "pretty" (1. Qxc6? Rxd1#). Of course, White can play 1. Qc2, holding a solid extra pawn. But here he correctly decides to examine the validity of Black's combination. **1. Rxd7! Qxa4 2. Rd8+ Bf8 3. Bh6**. To avoid the archetypal R & B mate, Black will have to play 3. ... Qd1+, with a lost position. (Koltanowski - Krause, 1957)

239. Create a Wedge Pawn

White is down a piece, so he must attack. **1. f6+!** (not *1. Qh6+ Kf6* and the Black King has escaped) **1. ... Qxf6** (*1. ... Nxf6 2. Qh6+* and *3. Qh8#*; *1. ... Kg8 2. Rh8+ Kxh8 3. Qh6+*, etc.) **2. Qh6+ Kg8 3. Qh7#**. Note that if the Black Rook were not on f8, but instead, say, on e8, there is no mate in the last line, and Black wins.

240. An Easy Move is Hard to Find!

All White's pieces are aimed at the Black King, whose position is slightly weakened. To find a decisive blow — a quick, forced win — you should overcome a natural prejudice. We rarely consider sacrificing material when the opponent has two or more ways to capture it, assuming subconsciously that at least one of the captures must be good for him.

1. Bxg6!! 1-0. (Malesic - Masic, 1965)

241.

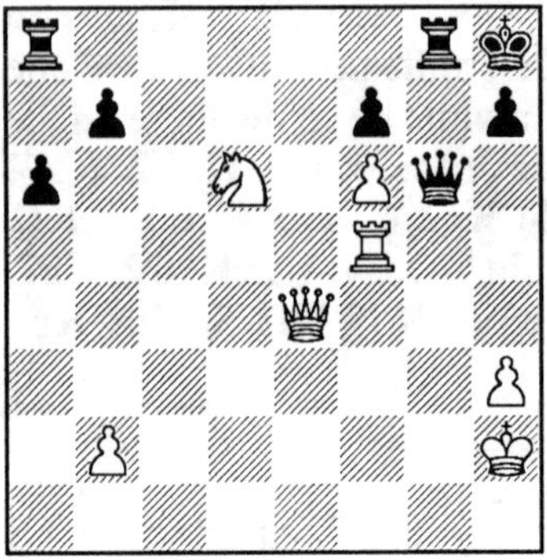

White to move

242.

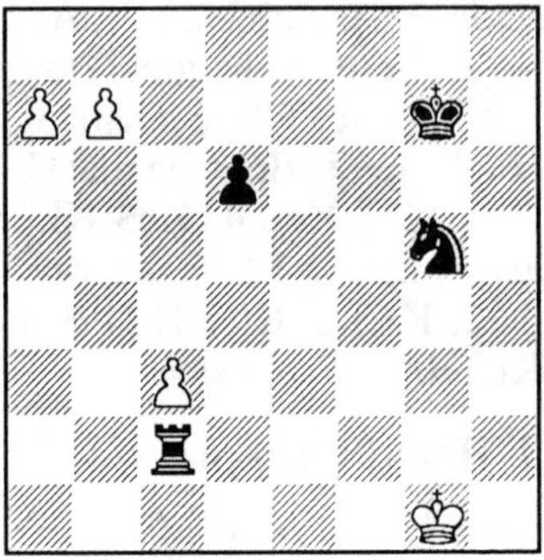

Black to move

243.

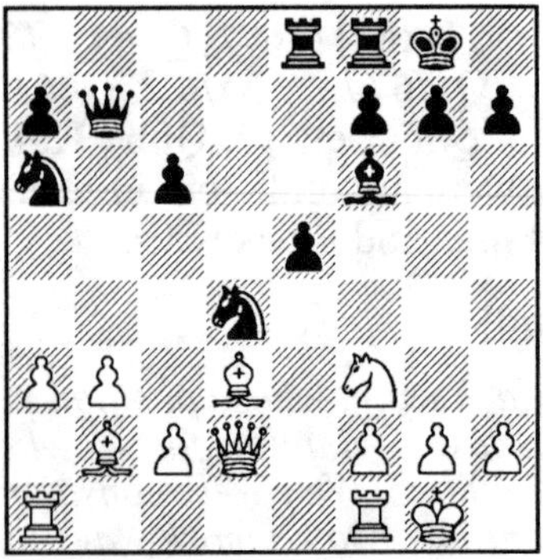

White to move

244.

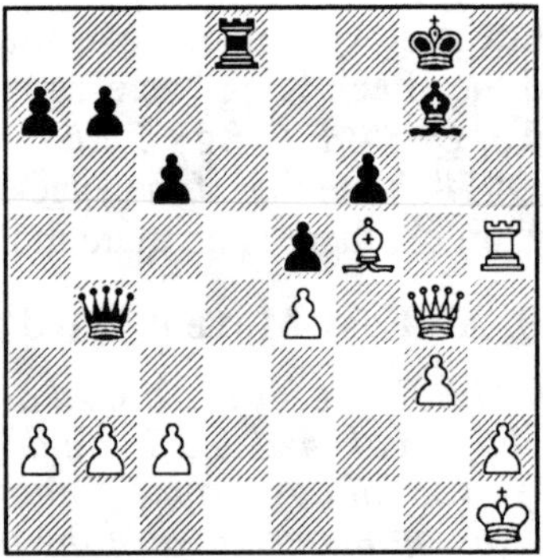

White to move

241. Applying the Rook & Knight Cutoff Mate

Black is up an Exchange and a pawn, but his King is cramped. If not for the Queen on g6, White would mate with Nxf7.

1. Rg5!. An easy-to-find move. White tries to deflect the Black Queen from defending the f7-square. If you saw Black's only defense and White's final blow, great! **1. ... Qxf6 2. Qd4!**. The rest is easy. **2. ... Rg6 3. Rxg6**, and Black resigns. (Zuta - Sutey, 1953)

242. Like a Check Machine

Try to win. If you can't, look for a draw. (Isn't that what you should do, even without a hint?)

1. ... Nf3+ 2. Kf1 (2. Kh1? Rh2#) **2. ... Rd2** (Black's moves could also be reversed — 1. ... Rd2 followed by 2. ... Nf3+) **3. b8(Q) Nh2+ 4. Ke1 Nf3+**.

The perpetual check mechanism set up by Black's last two moves works perfectly. See how the Knight on f3 protects the d2-Rook. The Rook, in turn, cuts off the White King's escape to the queenside, where he would be out of the Knight's reach. Draw!

Notice, however, that without the Black pawn on d6, White will control the h2-square and win by 4. Qxh2. For this drawing method to work, it is crucial that your opponent lacks control of the Knight's checking squares, h2 and f3.

243. Tempo-Gaining Double Attacks

Bring the Lady to f5!

1. Bxd4 exd4 2. Qa5, winning a tempo to relocate forcefully to f5. Queens are very good at such tricks! **2. ... Nc7 3. Qf5**. An important position. Black loses because the only defense against mate, 3. ... g6, surrenders the Bishop on f6. (Henkin - Lebedev, 1961)

244. Bishop of Opposite Color On the Attack!

1. Rh8+ Kxh8 (1. ... Kf7 2. Qg6+) **2. Qh5+**, with a mate in two. (Petrosian, A. - Moldagaliev, 1969)

245.

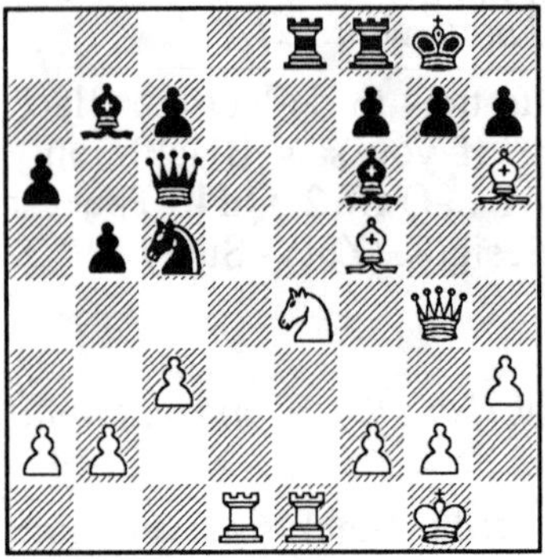

White to move

246.

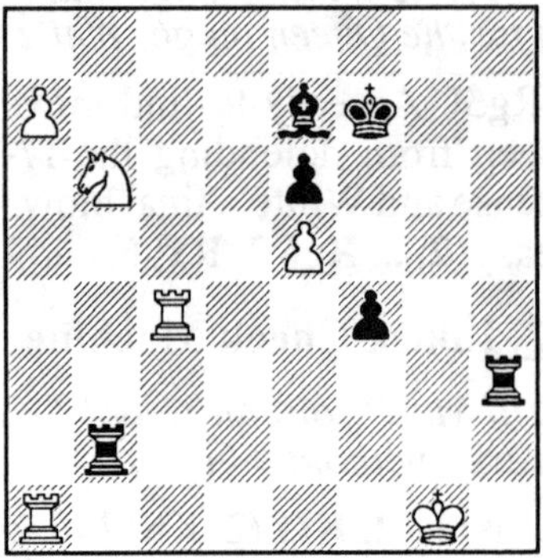

Black to move

247.

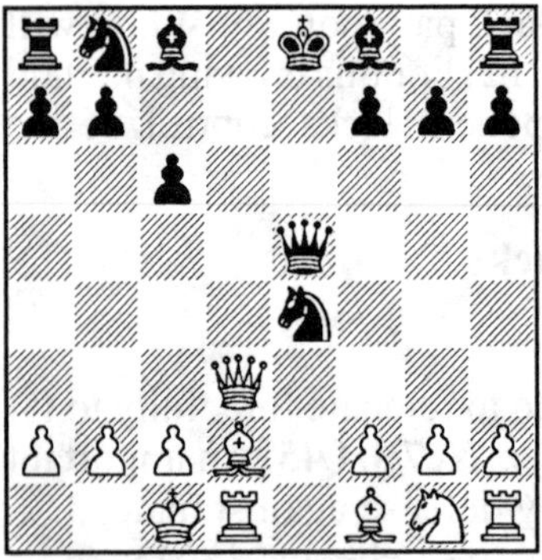

White to move

248.

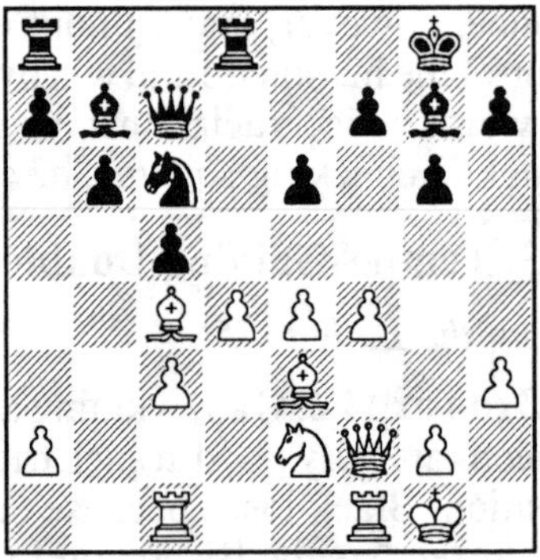

Black to move

245. Decoy & Double Attack

1. Nxc5! Qxc5 2. Bxg7! Bxg7 3. Qh5. White's main threat is 4. Qxh7#, which forces **3. ... h6**. But then he unveils a second threat, a discovered attack — **4. Bh7+!** — winning the Queen. (Vasyukov - Kholmov, 1964)

246. Give Me A Place to Stand and I'll Move the Earth

1. ... f3 creates a threat of 2. ... Rg2+ and 3. ... Rh1#. But there is a defense — and what a defense! — 2. Rf4+!. Grateful that we didn't play a hasty 1. ... f3, we then find ...

1. ... Bc5+!!. Deflecting the Rook. **2. Rxc5 f3**, and now the mate is unavoidable. (Grigorian, K. - Seredenko, 1972)

247. A Shocking Blow

When capturing on e4, Grandmaster Tartakower expected his opponent to continue with 1. Re1, winning a Knight back. Instead a mate in three followed.

1. Qd8+!! (decoy) **Kxd8 2. Bg5++**. (Not all double checks are created equal; 2. Ba5++ doesn't lead to mate and thus loses.) Now there follows a typical Rook + Bishop mate with **2. ... Ke8 3. Rd8#**, or the less common Bishop mate after **2. ... Kc7 3. Bd8#**. (Reti - Tartakower, 1910)

Be alert and double check (don't just announce double-check), especially when planning to sacrifice your Queen!

248. Fighting the Pawn Center

Although it doesn't mate or win material immediately, this series of forced moves gives Black a dominating game.

1. ... Na5 2. Bd3 f5! 3. e5 c4! 4. Bc2 Nc6. Now the center is fixed. The Knight goes to e7 and then to d5, supporting Black's advances on the queenside. Black is clearly better. (Gligoric - Smyslov, 1959)

249.

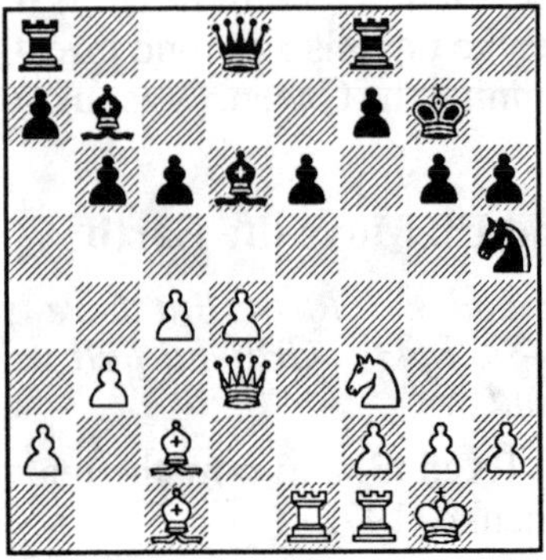

White to move

250.

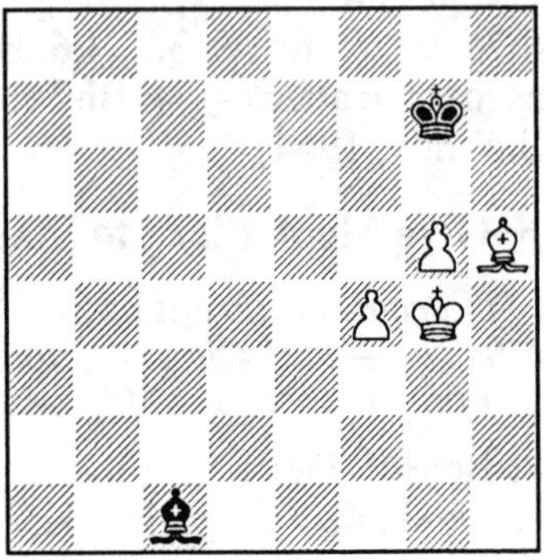

Black to move

251.

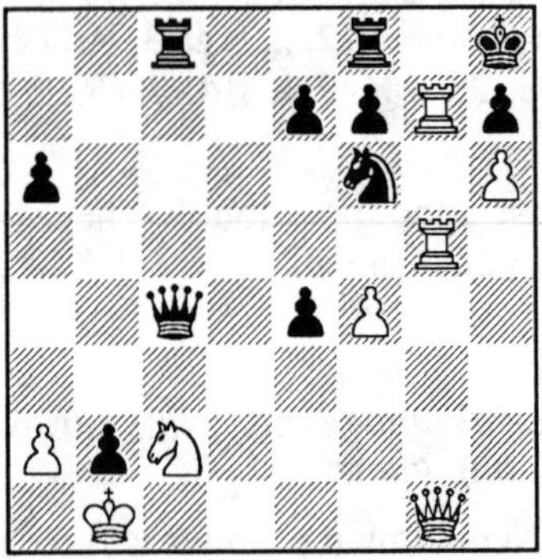

White to move

252.

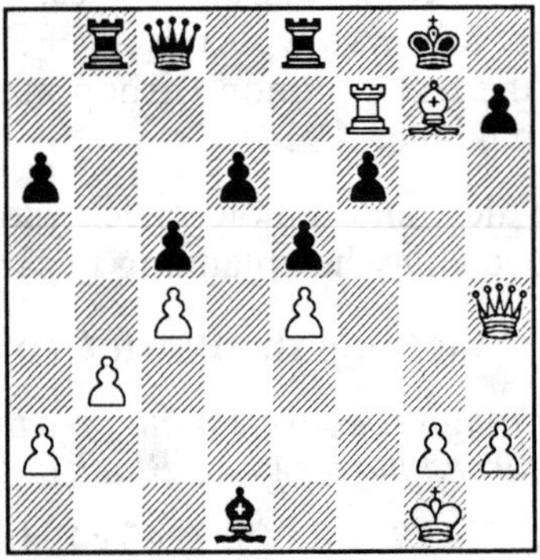

White to move

249. High Voltage Battery

1. Rxe6!. This wins a pawn, because 1. ... fxe6 loses to 2. Qxg6+ and 3. Qh7#. In a real game, you shouldn't look any further! Now watch how White went on to win, using the same powerful Queen and Bishop battery.

1. ... Nf6 2. Ne5! c5? loses immediately. Relatively better was 2. ... Bxe5 3. Rxe5, although White would be a pawn up and have a much better position as well. Not good was 2. ... fxe6 3. Qxg6+ Kh8 4. Qxh6+ Kg8 5. Qg6+ Kh8 6. Bg5 Qe7 7. Ng4. **3. Bxh6+ Kxh6 4. Nxf7+!**, and Black resigns. Capa's sacrifices of Bishop and Knight completely destroyed the Black King's cover, making way for the battery of Queen and Bishop to deliver mate. (Capablanca - Joffe, 1910)

250. Bishop of Opposite Color Endings: Three Rules

White to move plays 1. f5 Bb2 (to meet 2. f6+ with 2. ... Bxf6, draw) 2. Kf3, and White's King marches to e6 to support f5-f6, winning. If Black moves first, can he draw?

Yes, by **1. ... Ba3!**, meeting 2. f5 with 2. ... Be7. Now not only does Black's Bishop (1) control the f6-square, and (2) have reserve moves to d8 and back, but also, by attacking the g-pawn, (3) prevents the White King from coming to e6. (This last requirement explains why 1. ... Bb2 wouldn't draw.) These three criteria are, together, *always* enough to secure a draw in similar situations.

251. Clear the Queen's Path

1. Rc5!. A clearance sacrifice, freeing the g-file by getting rid of the Rook that stands in the Queen's path to g7. Importantly, this is a tempo-gaining move, attacking the Black Queen while also defending against ... Qxc2+. **1. ... Qxc5 2. Rxh7+ 1-0**. (Heemsot - Haisenbuttel, 1958)

252. Ready to Mate

1. Bh8! 1-0. (Tal - Rantanen, 1979)

253.

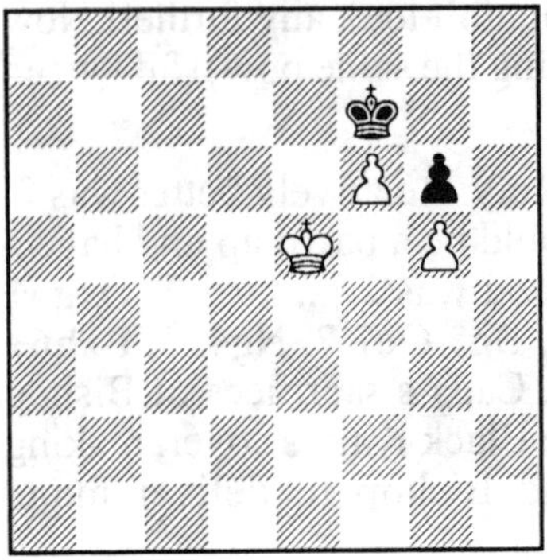

White to move

254.

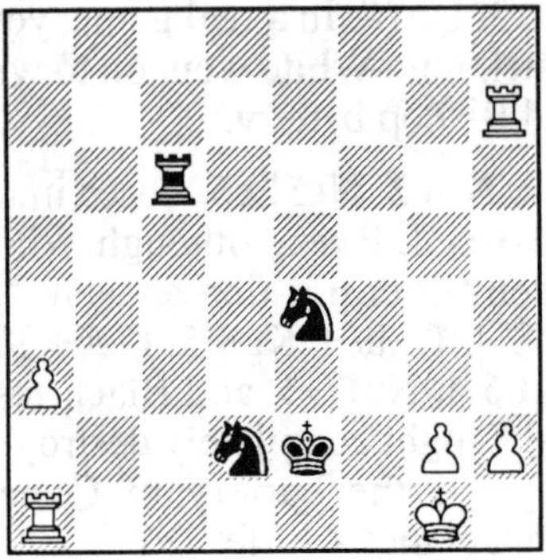

Black to move

255.

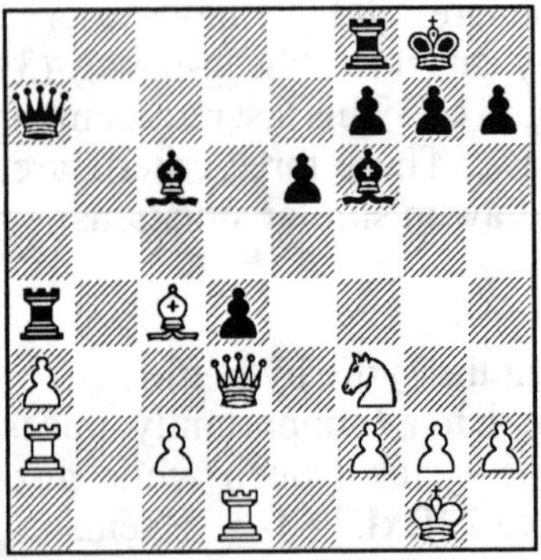

Black to move

256.

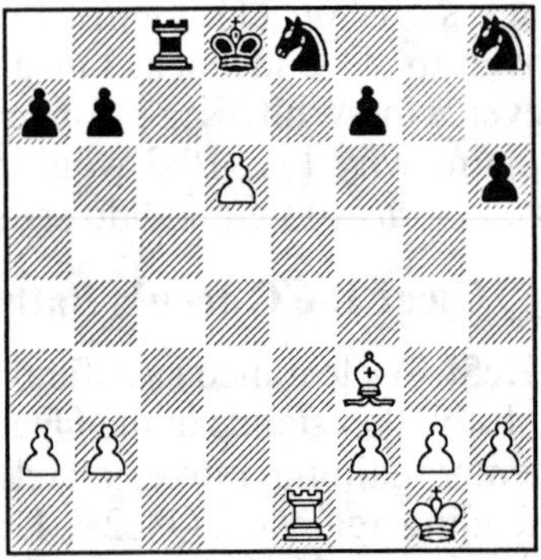

White to play

253. Go for the Known Win

It seems likely (and indeed it is correct) that here it doesn't matter which side is on move, since White can always win/lose a tempo by moving his King to d5 or d6, while the Black King doesn't have this luxury. But can White win? Let's try a sample line: **1. Kd5 Kf8!** *The only move, as usual, is to go along the line of the opponent's passed pawn.* **2. Ke6 Ke8**. *Now if it weren't for the g-pawns, the position would be an easy, theoretical draw.*

Many players under 1800 (and even some Experts) will try in vain here to outmaneuver Black to achieve this position with Black to move. They will usually spend nearly all their time on futile tries, then give up. Look for a better, more creative idea.

Yes! The g-pawn alone can win the game! (Remember that the King on the 6th in front of the pawn ...) So **3. f7+ Kf8 4. Kd6! Kxf7 5. Kd7 Kg7 6. Ke7**. The g6-pawn is doomed — White has waiting moves; Black doesn't. **6. ... Kg8 7. Kf6 Kh7 8. Kf7 Kh8 9. Kxg6 Kg8**. Now — be careful! Most players will automatically play **10. Kf6** (toward the center) **10. ... Kh7!**. (Hoping for 11. g6+? Kh8, draw). Here White must recognize his error and calmly repeat the position: **11. Kf7 Kh8 12. Kg6 Kg8 13. Kh6! Kh8 14. g6 Kg8 15. g7** (without check) **1-0**.

254. Karpov's Surprise Mate

1. ... Nf3+ 2. gxf3 (2. Kh1 Nf2#) **Rg6+ 3. Kh1 Nf2#**. (Korchnoi - Karpov, 1978)

255. Diagonal Robbery

1. ... Rxc4 0-1. If 2. Qxc4, then 2. ... Bd5. (Tal - Petrosian, T., 1962)

256. The Light-Squared Debacle

1. d7! wins a Rook for a pawn. **1-0**. (Kikovic - Fortinosh, 1957)

257.

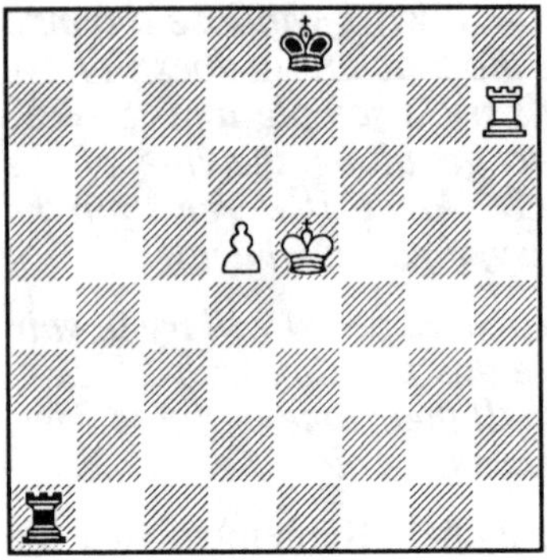

Black to move

258.

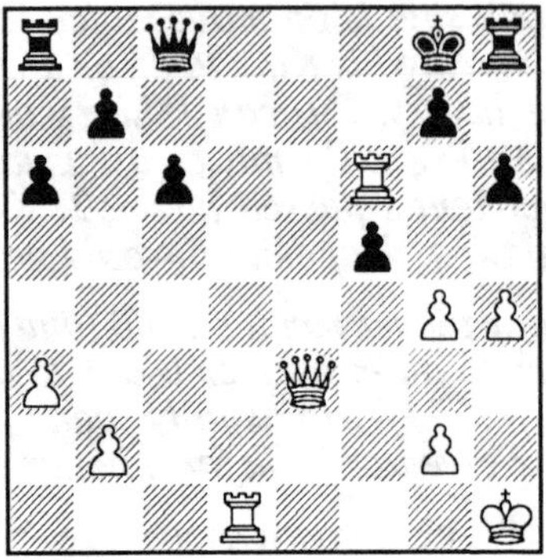

White to move

259.

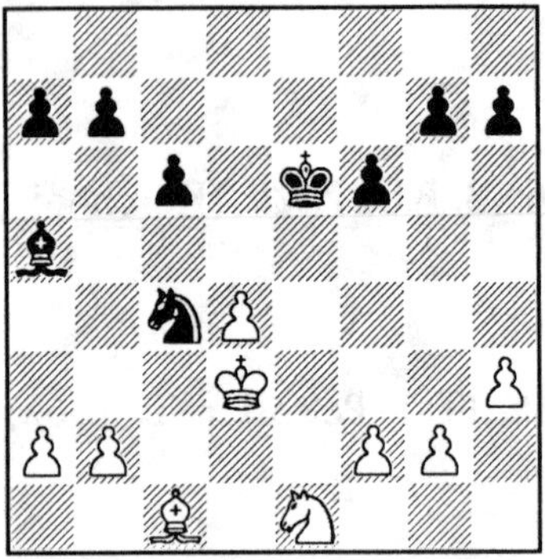

White to move

260.

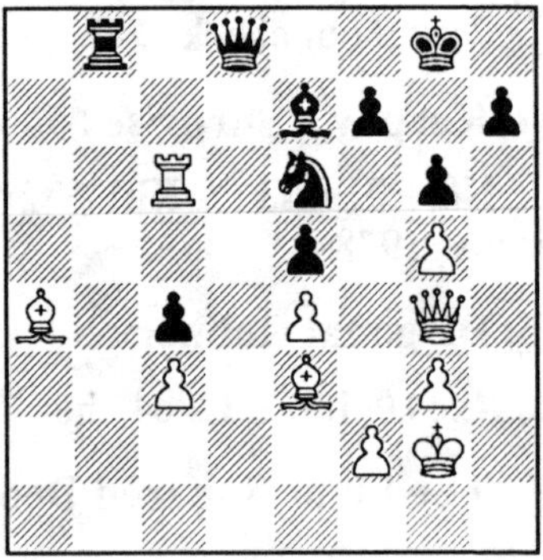

White to move

257. Philidor's Position: An Easy Draw

White's threat is 1. Ke6, in order to answer 1. ... Re1+ with 2. Kd6, hiding his King ahead of his pawn. While Black can still hold, it isn't easy: 2. ... Rd1! 3. Rh8+ Kf7 4. Rd8 (4. Kc6 Ke7!) Ra1! (the side attack) 5. Kc7 Ra7+ 6. Kb6 Ke7!, draw — but was it ever hard to find!

With the move, however, Black can draw easily with **1. ... Ra6**, barring the White King from the 6th rank and achieving to so-called Philidor's Position. Black waits until White advances his pawn to the 6th rank. (There is no other promising idea for White — for example, 2. Rc7 Kd8! 3. Rc6 Rxc6, draw.) Then after **2. d6, Ra1** draws because the White King has nowhere to hide from vertical checks by the Rook.

258. Setting Up the Epaulet Mate

1. Rd8+ (deflection) **Qxd8 2. Qe6+ Kh7 3. Rxh6+** (destroying the King's pawn cover) **gxh6 4. Qf7#**. (Steinitz - NN, 1861)

259. In-between Move That Wins a Piece

1. b4! Bxb4 2. Nc2 1-0. White's Knight is no longer under attack, while both Black's pieces are hanging. (Lasker, Em. - Euwe, 1936)

260. How Far Should One See?

1. Rxe6 fxe6 2. Qxe6+ Kf8 3. Qxe5 gives White a decisive attack for free (material is even), so let's think harder for Black.

1. Rxe6! Qc8! 2. Bd7! 1-0. Eighteen-year-old Fischer foresaw Black's reply and prepared the decisive counter-blow. If 2. ... Qxd7, then 3. Rxg6+ and 4. Qxd7. (Fischer - Shocron, 1959)

261.

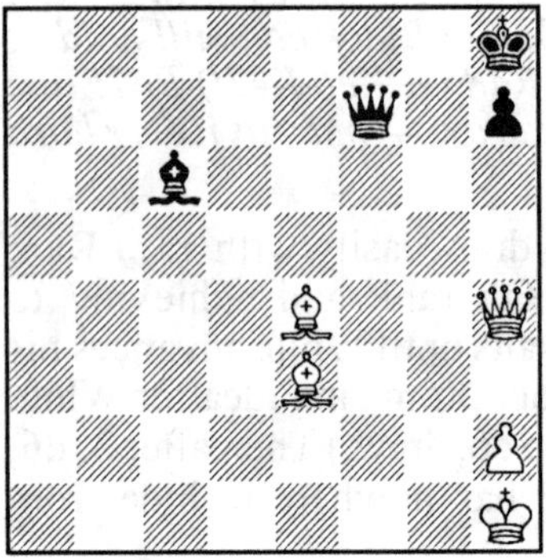

Black to move

262.

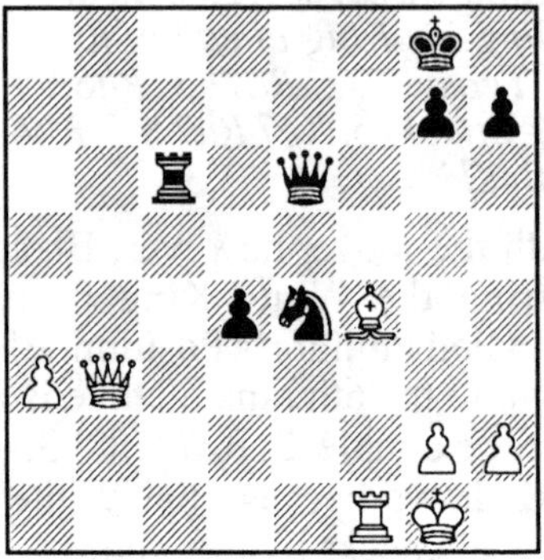

White to move

263.

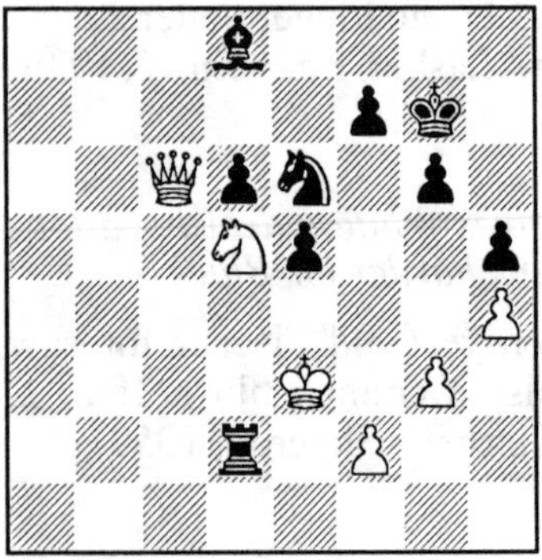

Black to move

264.

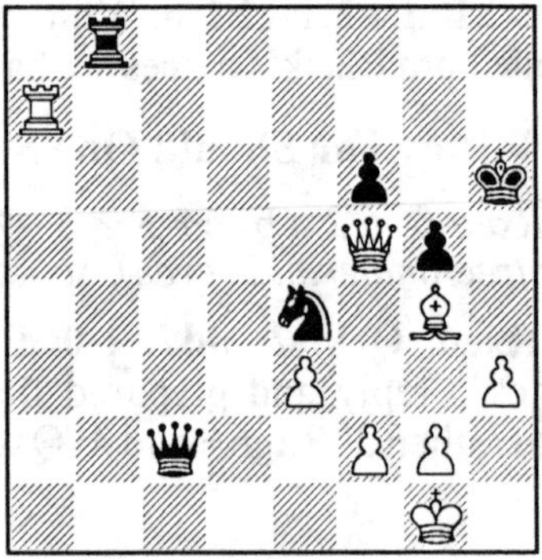

Black to move

<u>261.</u> Bishop's Smothered Mate

1. ... Qf1+ 2. Bg1. Now the White King is smothered. **2. ... Qf3+ 3. Bxf3 Bxf3#**. (NN - Pillsbury, 1899)

<u>262.</u> Highly Disruptive

1. Bd6! is a highly unusual specie of double attack. The threats are 2. Qxe6+ or 2. Rf8#. On **1. ... Rxd6**, White mates with **2. Qb8+**, and on **1. ... Nxd6**, the Queen is lost after **2. Qxe6+**.

<u>263.</u> Deadly Forks

1. ... Re2+! 2. Kd3. Of course the Rook can't be taken because of the Knight fork on d4, and 2. Kf3 fails for the same reason. **2. ... e4+ 3. Kc4** (3. Kc3 Rc2+ 4.Kxc2 Nd4+) **3. ... Rc2+ 4.Nc3 Bf6** (the game is over) **5. Qxe4 Rxc3+ 6. Kd5 Rc5+ 7. Kxd6 Bxe5+**, and White resigned, as after 8. Kd7 Rc7+ 9. Ke8 Bf6, the threat of mate on e7 is decisive. (Alburt - Kasparov, 1982)

<u>264.</u> Win or Escape?

Escape! **1. ... Rb1+ 2. Kh2 Rh1+! 3. Kxh1 Ng3+ 4. fxg3 Qxg2+ 5. Kxg2, stalemate**. (Osnos - Batoczky, 1951)

265.

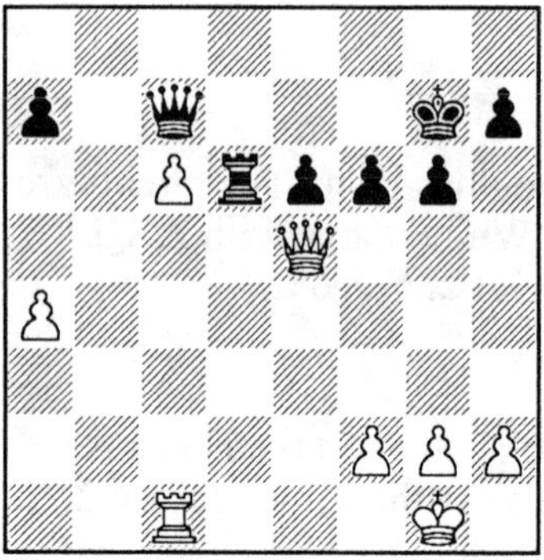

White to move

266.

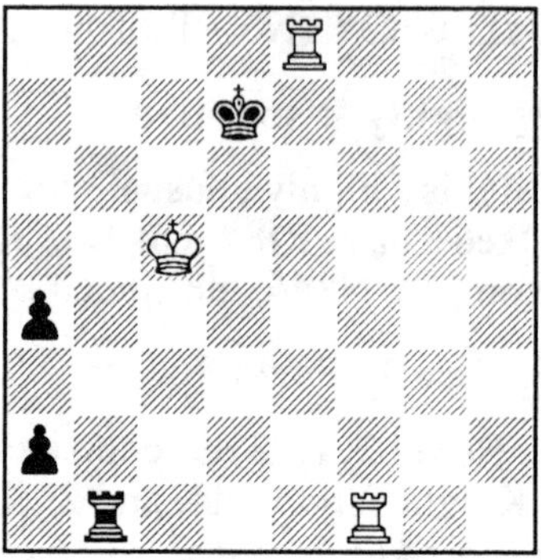

White to move

267.

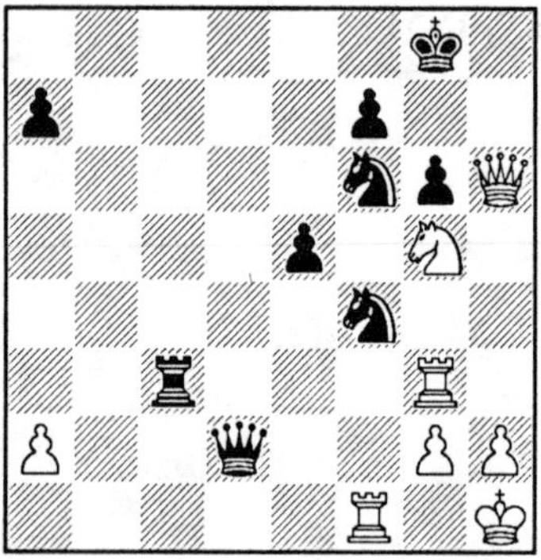

White to move

268.

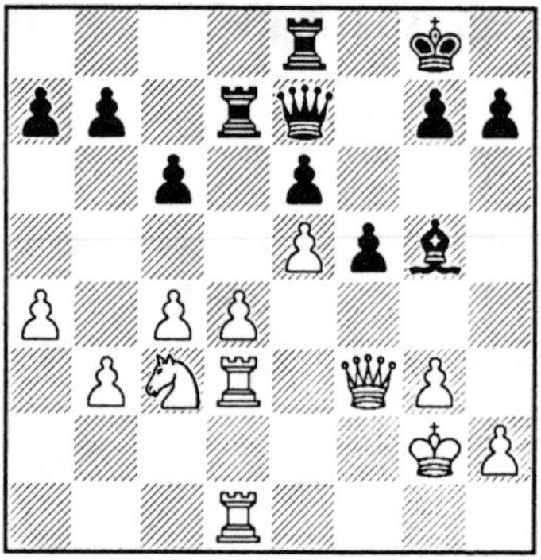

White to move

What plan would you choose?

265. Lust to Expand

1. Qxd6 Qxd6 2. c7, and White wins.

266. The Threat

1. Rfe1, and White wins (1. ... Rxe1 2. Rxe1; 1. ... a1(Q) 2. R1e7#). (study by Wotava, 1948)

267. Alternative Target

A direct winning assault on the h-file remains outside White's reach, so he switches the target. **1. Ne6!**, and Black's position collapses.

268. Iron Grip on d6

1. c5!. White now has two promising ideas: (1) the advance of the b-pawn, and (2) transferring his Knight to d6. **1. ... a5** (preventing 2. b4) **2. Nb1 Qf8 3. Na3 Bd8 4. Nc4 Bc7**. Black has no active plan of his own and can't stop White's **5. Nd6**. White has a big advantage. If Black ever captures on d6, White gets a very strong protected passed pawn. (Botvinnik - Flohr, 1936)

269.

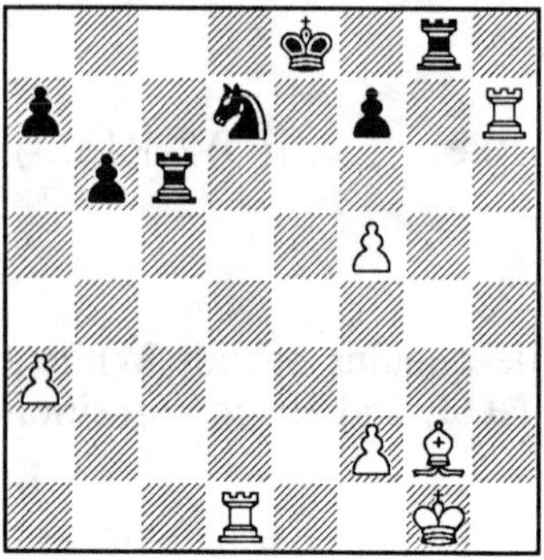

White to move

270.

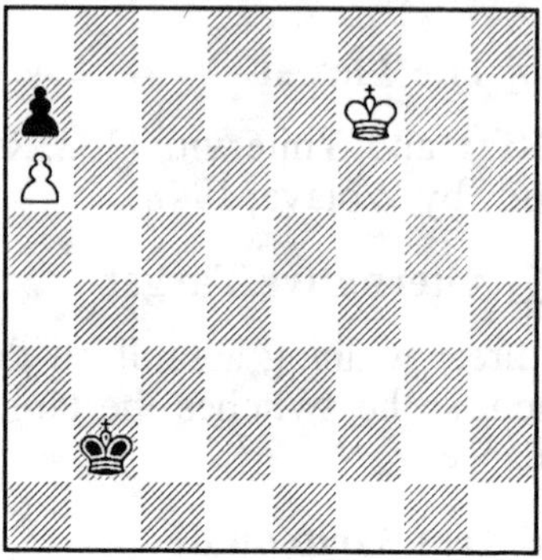

White to move

271.

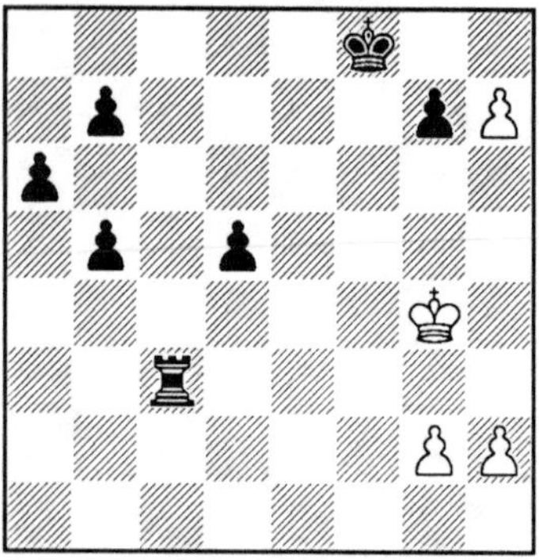

Black to move.
Evaluate the position.

272.

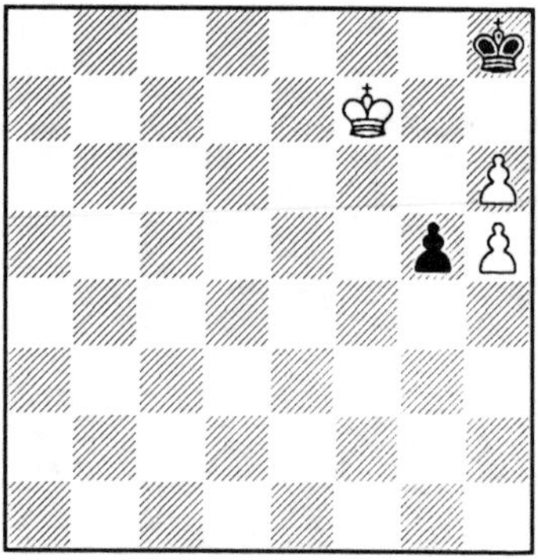

White to move

269. Un-Pin to Pin

White would love to play 1. Bxc6, capturing the Rook and then pinning and winning the Knight on d7. The fly in this ointment, however, is the Rook on g8, which pins the Bishop.

1. Rh8!!, winning a piece after 1. ... Rxh8 2. Bxc6. Black lost after **1. ... Rcg6 2. fxg6 Rxh8 3. Bc6** (the same pin) **3. ... Rg8 4. Bxd7+**. Always look for inventive ways to break troublesome pins. (Stein - Smyslov, 1972)

270. All Roads Don't Lead to a Win

Black's pawn is doomed, and the outcome of the game depends on the ability of the Black King to reach c7 immediately after White's Kxa7. White needs five moves to reach a7, Black — the same five moves to reach c7. However, by choosing a special route, White can prevent his rival's King from reaching c7 on time.

1. Ke6 Kc3 2. Kd5! +-. In the actual game, White played 2. Kd6?, which led to only a draw after 2. ... Kd4 3. Kc6 Ke5 4. Kb7 Kd6 5. Kxa7 Kc7. Blocking Black's King with 2. Kd5 makes him waste a tempo, and lose the game. (Schlage - Auge, 1921)

271. Stop That Pawn!

Black is winning. **1. ... Rc4+ 2. Kh3 Rh4+!!** (the decoy) **3. Kxh4 g5+ 4. Kxg5 Kg7 0-1**. (Lasker, Em. - Loman, 1903)

272. Lose a Tempo, Draw the Game

White's only drawing chance is a stalemate. Let's try the natural sample line: 1. Kg6 g4 2. h7 g3, with the idea of tucking his King away on h6.

Black queens with check. Still, White can draw by the clever **1. Kf6 g4 2. Kg6 g3 3. h7 g2 4. Kh6** and now 4. ... g1(Q) and 4. ... g1(R) both create a stalemate, while underpromoting to a Knight or to a Bishop doesn't leave Black enough power to mate. (study by Kraemer, 1922)

273.

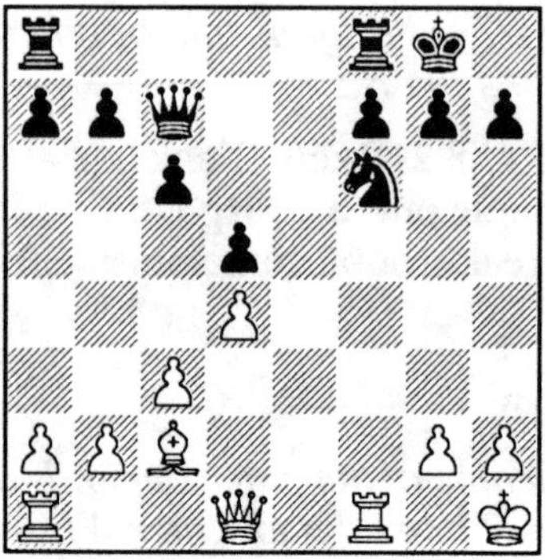

White to move

274.

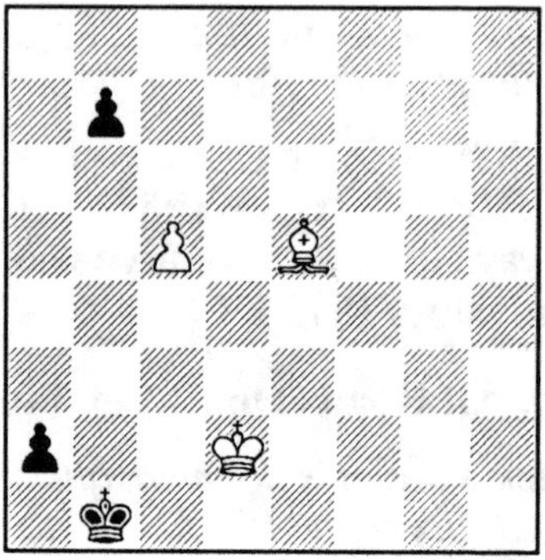

White to move

275.

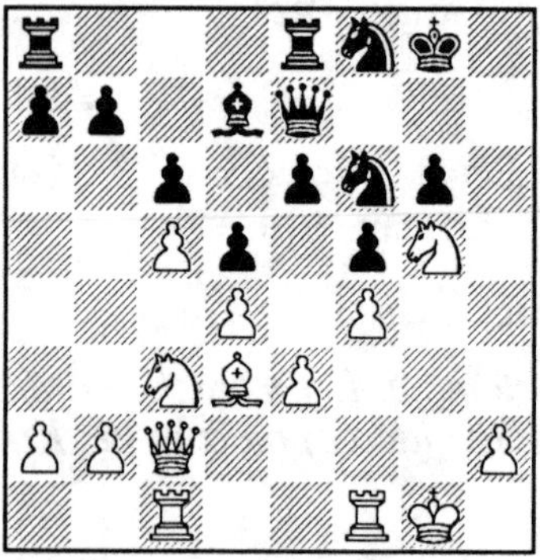

Black to move

276.

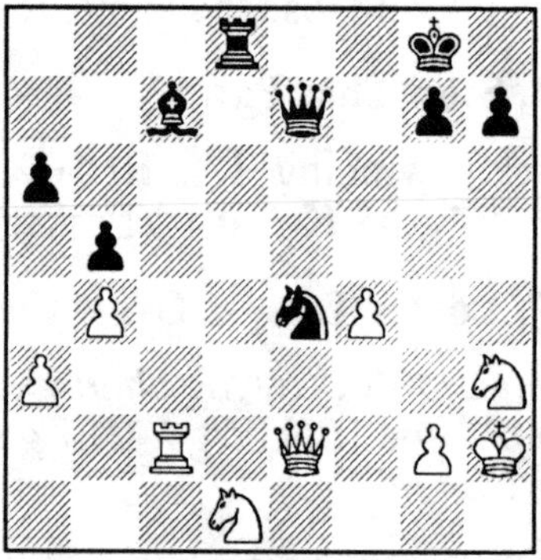

White to move

273. **The Most Common Elimination of the Defender**

1. Rxf6 gxf6 2. Qg4+ (the obvious 2. Qd3 is not so good after 2. ... f5 3. Qxf5 f6, when Black suddenly has his Queen guarding h7!) **2. ... Kh8 3. Qf5**, with mate coming on h7.

274. **Stamma, 1737**

The natural 1. Kd3 leads only to a draw after 1. ... a1(Q) 2. Bxa1 Kxa1 3. Kc4 Kb2 4. Kb5 Kc3 5. Kb6 Kc4 (just in time!). Any other ideas to try?

Yes — **1. Ba1 Kxa1 2. Kc2**. (If you found this move first and saw it through to the win, fine. Equally good if you first tried 2. Kc1, followed it to the draw: 2. ... b5 3. c6 [3. cxb6! 1/2-1/2] b4 4. c7 b3 5. c8(Q) b2+ 6. Kd2! b1(Q) 7. Qc1!, and then turned to 2. Kc2.) **2. ... b5 3. c6 b4 4. c7 b3+ 5. Kxb3 Kb1 6. c8(Q) a1(Q) 7. Qc2#.** (study by Stamma, 1737)

275. **Breaking Down the Fortress At Its Strongest Point**

Is White's grip on e5 ironclad, or can it be broken tactically?

1. ... e5!! 2. dxe5. (Black stands better after 2. Rfe1 exd4 3. exd4 Qxe1+ 4. Rxe1 Rxe1+ 5. Kf2 Re7! [5. ... R8e8? 6. Be2].) **2. ... Ng4 3. Nd1 Nxe5**. White is left with obvious pawn weaknesses. (Przepiorka - Johner, 1925)

276. **Going for the Kill**

1. Ndf2!. In the actual game, White got two Knights for a Rook — a clear edge — with 1. Rxc7, but he should have aimed higher. **1. ... Rd4 2. Qe3! Bb6 3. Rc8+ Kf7 4. Nxe4**. Simple and convincing. If **4. ... Rxe4**, then **5. Qxe4**. (Lasker, Em. - Lasker, Ed., 1924)

277.

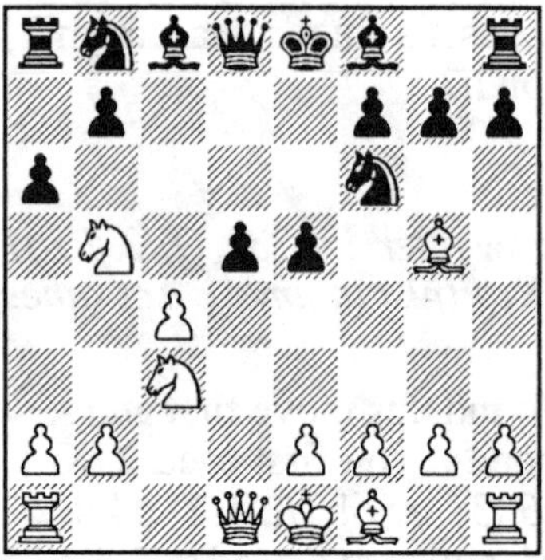

White to move

278.

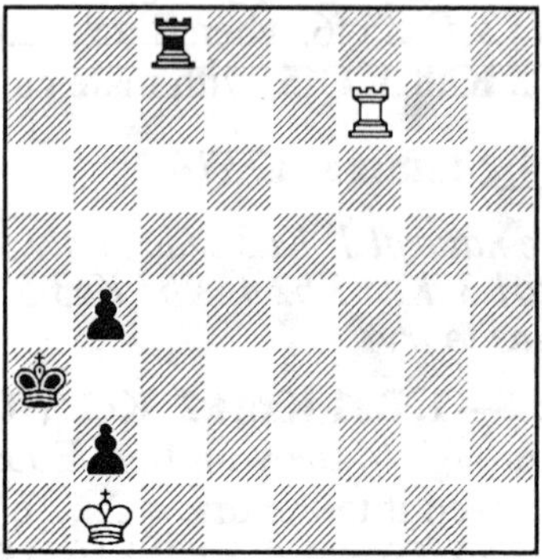

White to move

279.

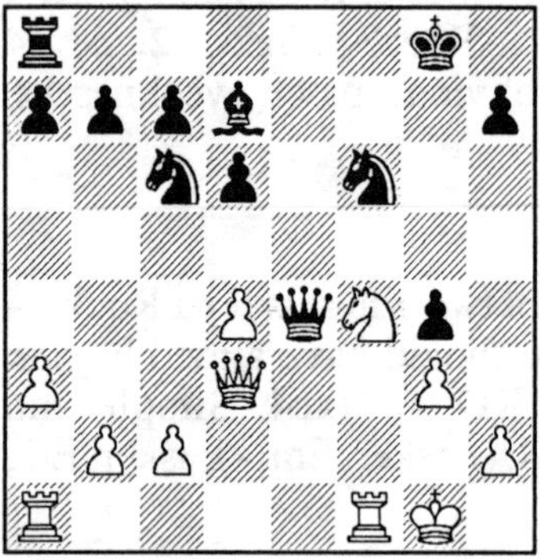

White to move

280.

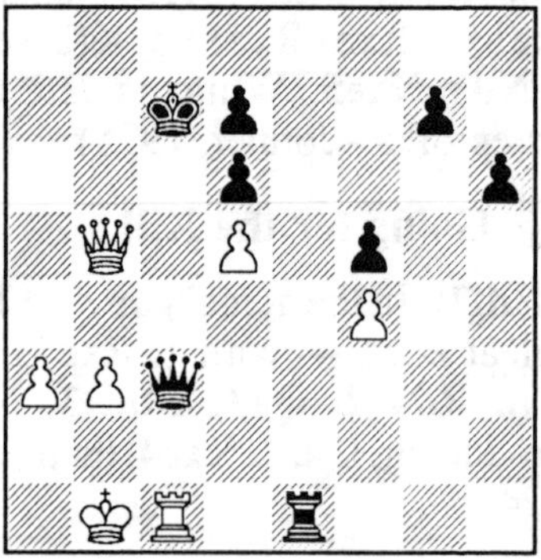

White to move

277. Fatal Flaw

In one of his earliest games, American Grandmaster Reuben Fine crushed his opponent with 1. Nxd5 axb5 2. Nxf6+ gxf6 3. Qxd8+ Kxd8 4. Bxf6+, with a decisive material advantage. Naturally, he didn't mind repeating this pleasant experience and continued 1. Nxd5? — unaware of the fatal flaw in his analysis.

White's best chance was **1. Qa4!**, with an unclear game. After **1. Nxd5 axb5 2. Nxf6+ Qxf6!!** (it's over!) **3. Bxf6 Bb4+ 4. Qd2 Bxd2+ 5. Kxd2 gxf6**. Black, with a material advantage and superior development, won easily. (Fine - Yudovich, 1937)

278. Perpetual Pursuit

Passive defense loses here: 1. Rf1 Rc1+, and Black will queen the remaining pawn. Can White escape, or is he lost, and therefore searching for traps?

1. Ra7+! leads to a forced draw after **1. ... Kb3 2. Rc7 Re8 3. Re7**, etc. Wrong would be 1. Rf3+? Rc3! (not 1. ... b3 2. Rxb3+, winning both pawns or reaching stalemate) 2. Rf1 Rc1+.

279. Zwischenzug

With his last move, 1. ... Qe7-e4, Black, ahead in material, tried to force the trade of Queens. He was in for an unpleasant surprise.

1. Nh5! Qxd3 2. Nxf6+!. A decisive in-between move! (known in chess literature by its German name, *Zwischenzug*). White won a piece and the game. (Duchovny - Fridinsky, 1977)

280. Her Majesty in Chains

1. Qa5+!, winning Black's pinned Queen.

281.

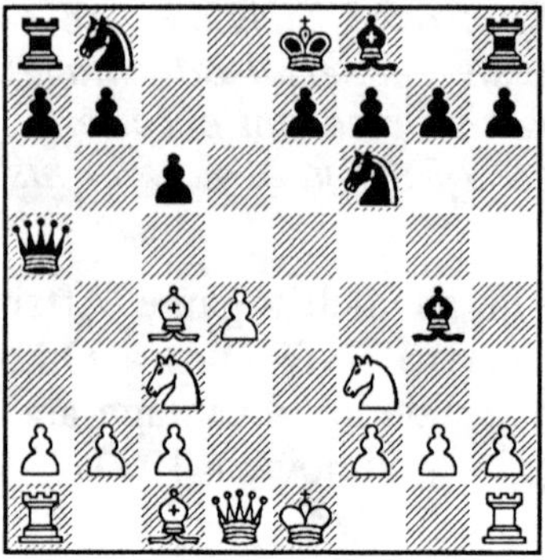

White to move

282.

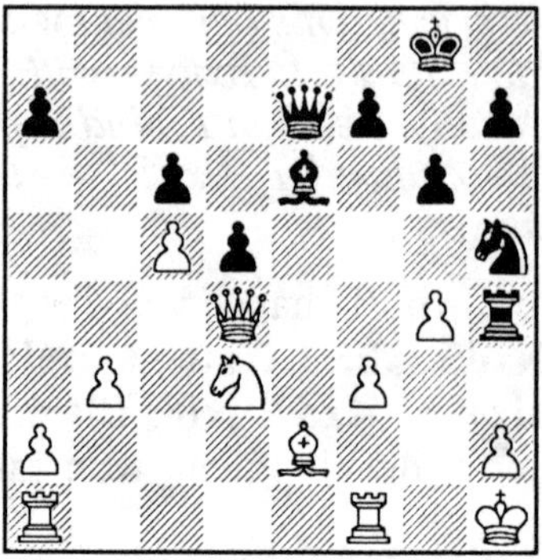

Black to move

283.

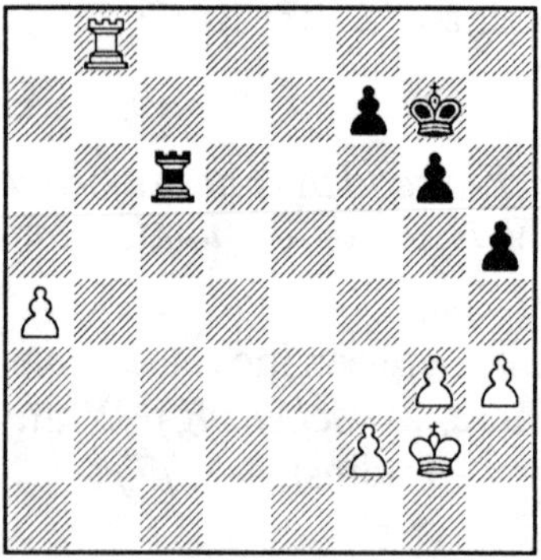

White/Black to move

284.

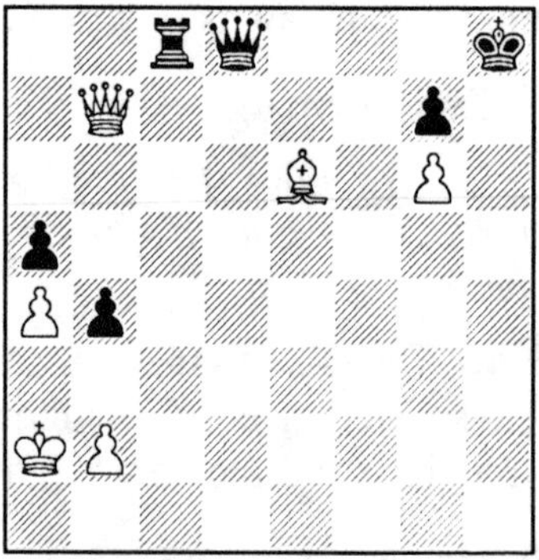

Black to move

281. Exploring Bxf7 Combinations

This position occurs from the *Scandinavian Defense* after **1. e4 d5 2. exd5 Qxd5 3. Nc3 Qa5 4. d4 Nf6 5. Bc4 c6 6. Nf3 Bg4**. White's best move here is **7. h3**, planning to answer **7. ... Bh5** with the aggressive **8. g4 Bg6 9. Ne5** (of course, quieter lines like 8. 0-0 are okay too — and the insertion of the moves h3 and ... Bh5 is likely to benefit White, however slightly).

Wrong is 7. Bxf7+ Kxf7 8. Ne5+ Qxe5+!, and Black ends up getting a piece for just one pawn.

The Scandinavian Defense is a good and solid opening, and can be learned in just a few hours. For a busy person, it's highly recommended.

282. Wise Choice

1. ... Rxh2+! 2. Kxh2 (2. Kg1? Qh4 -+) **2. ... Qh4+, draw.** (Karpov - Kasparov, 1990)

283. Maximize Your Chances!

> A Rook belongs behind the passed pawn,
> whether it's your own or your opponent's.
> — *Dr. Siegbert Tarrasch*

In Rook endings, an extra pawn usually doesn't guarantee a win — it only provides some winning chances. To maximize these chances, remember Tarrasch's dictum (above) and follow it — unless there are strong, concrete reasons not to.

White's best move is **1. Rb1**, followed by **2. Ra1**. For Black, **1. ... Rc3** (just in case, cutting off the White King) and **2. ... Ra3**, with excellent drawing chances.

284. Surprising Escape

1. ... Rc6! and Black holds (2. Qxc6 Qd5+ leads to a stalemate).

285.

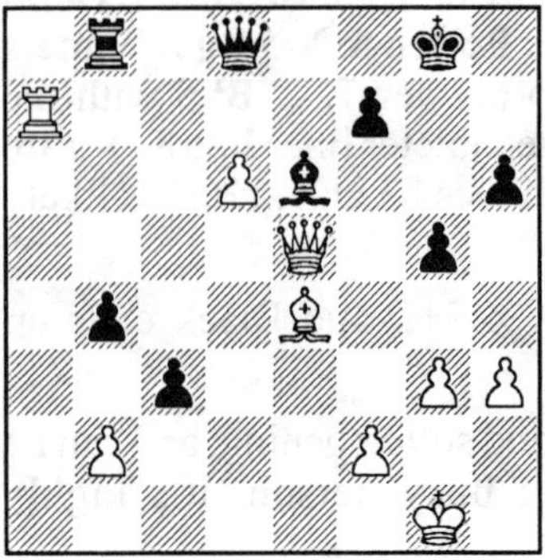

White to move

286.

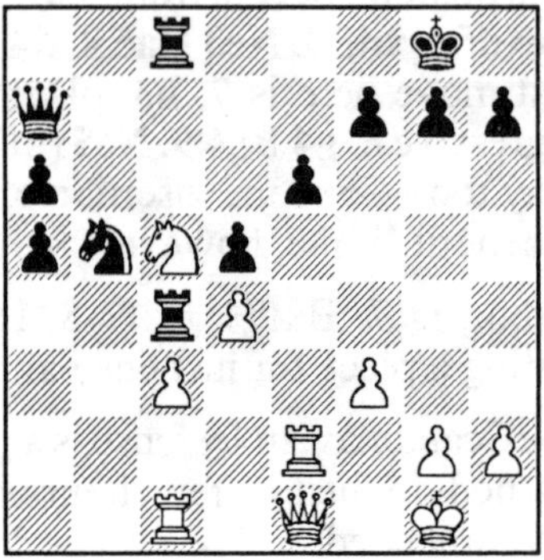

Black to move

287.

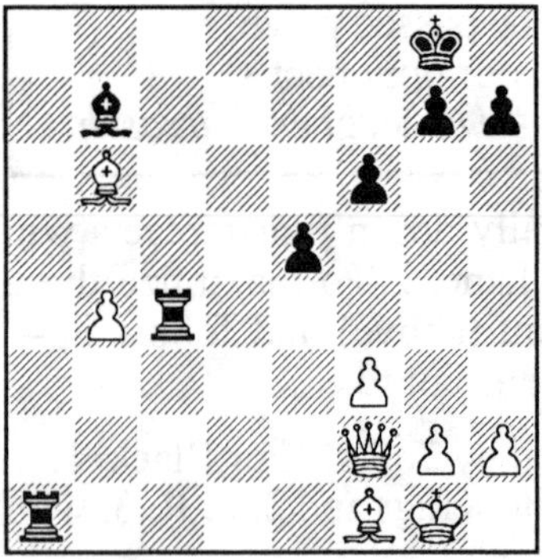

White to move

288.

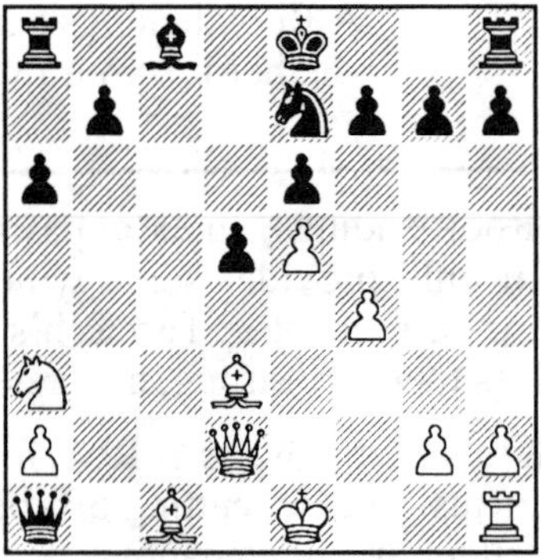

White to move

285. Kasparov's Touch

1. Bh7+! 1-0 (1. ... Kf8 2. Qh8#; 1. ... Kxh7 2. Qxe6). White decoyed the Black King to h7, thus creating a pin, and now uses it to snatch Black's Bishop. Black's seemingly strong fortress is completely ruined. (Kasparov - Browne, 1979)

286. Capablanca's Petite Combination

White's Knight on c5 seems to hinder Black's activities, but the greatest World Champion elegantly finished the game with one of his famous "little combinations."

1. ... Nxd4! 2. cxd4 R8xc5 0-1. If 3. dxc5 Qxc5+ and 4. ... Rxc1, or 3. Rxc4 Rxc4. (Bogoljubov - Capablanca, 1924)

287. Two Rooks, Two Problems

> A man exists, a problem exists.
> No man, no problem.
> —*Joseph Stalin*

White solved his two burning problems with one slicing Queen move.

1. Qa2! 1-0. (Petz - Fernandez, 1989)

288. Poisoned Rook

1. Bb1!, and the Queen will be lost to **2. Bb2 0-1**. (Nezhmetdinov - Konstantinov, 1936)

289.

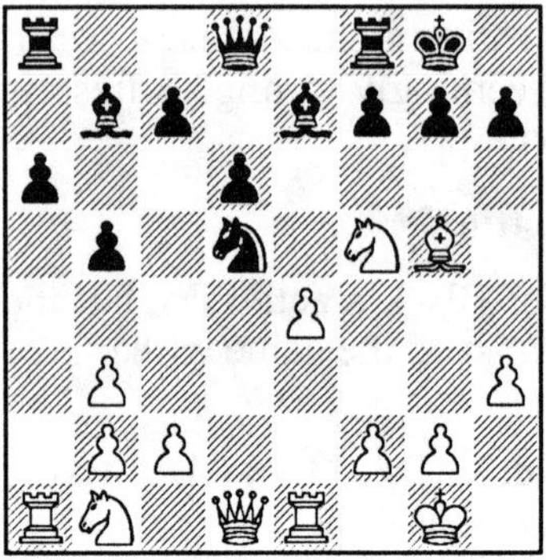

White to move

290.

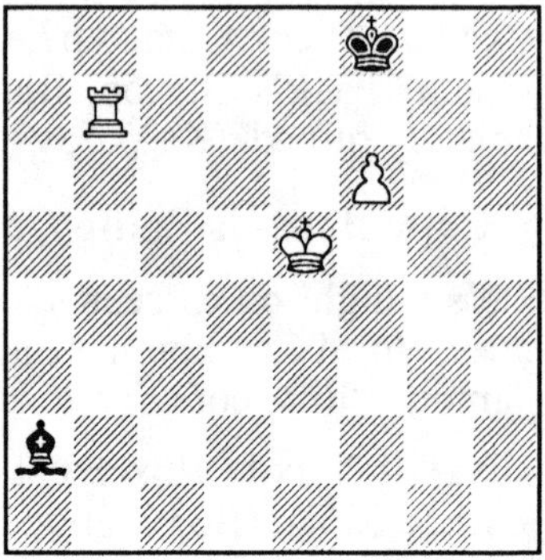

Can White win?

291.

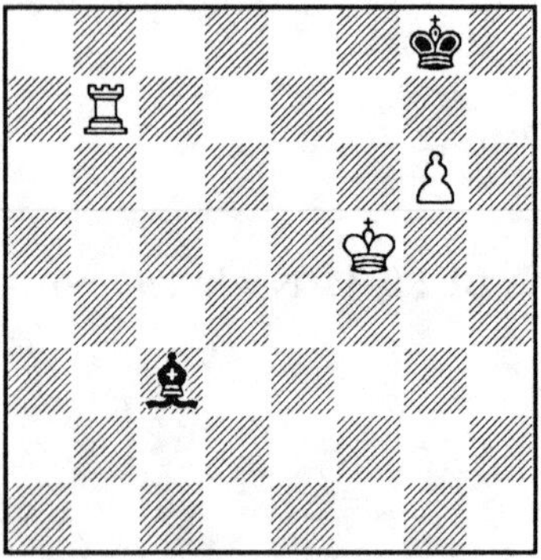

Can White win?

292.

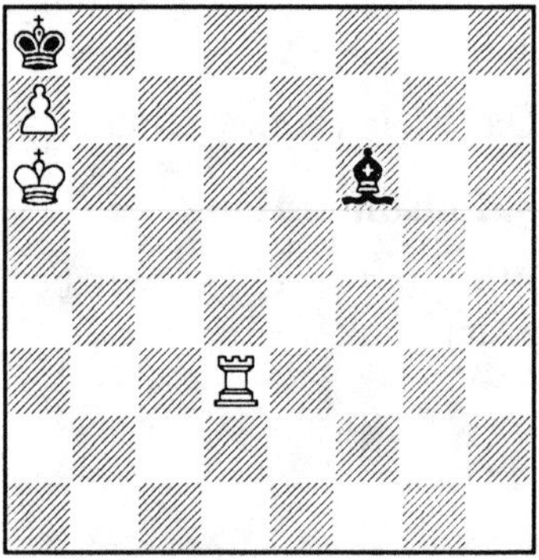

White/Black to move

289. Counting Pieces

> Don't rely solely on counting *captured* men.
> Always count pieces and pawns actually on the board.
> — *Leon Balmazi (from a Russian instructional manual)*

1. Qxd5! Bxd5 2. Nxe7+ Kh8 3. Ng6+ fxg6 4. Bxd8 Raxd8 5. exd5, and White is a piece up. (Henning - Behrens, 1934)

290. This Bishop Holds Off Rook and Pawn!

No, he can't, no matter who's on move. (White's last move, 1. f6?, was a grave error; instead, 1. Kf6 would have won easily. Here, as in King-and-pawn vs. blocking King endings, push your King ahead first!)

After trying to create mating threats — say **1. ... Bc4 2. Kf5 Bd3+** (not 2. ... Ba2? 3. Kg6, and White wins) **3. Ke5 Bc4** (back to square one), White's best bet is to play — confidently — **4. f7!**, hoping for 4. ... Bxf7? 5. Kf6 Be8 6. Rb8 +-. In fact, some grandmasters have resigned in this position! But the not-so-evident **4. ... Kg7** leads to a draw.

291. The Wrong Corner

Move the key players in Diagram 290 one square to the right, and White has a win, albeit not an obvious one.

1. g7! Kh7! 2. Rf7 (with the idea 3. g8(Q)+ and 4. Kg6) **2. ... Bxg7 3. Kg5 Kg8 4. Kg6** and White wins, e.g., **4. ... Bb2 5. Rb7 Be5 6. Re7**, etc. Black's Bishop could try to run earlier by 2. ... Bd4 3. g8(Q)+ Kxg8 4. Kg6 Bg1, but it couldn't hide for long; for example, 5. Rf1 Bh2 6. Rh1 Bg3 7. Rh3 Bf2 8. Ra3 +-.

292. The Right Corner?

White to move wins by **1. Rd7 Be7 2. Rc7**. Black to move draws by 1. ... Bd4, followed by 2. ... Bxa7. White would be able to stalemate Black — but no more!

> A lone Bishop almost always draws against a lone Rook.
> Diagram 291 ("The Wrong Corner") is a rare exception.

293.

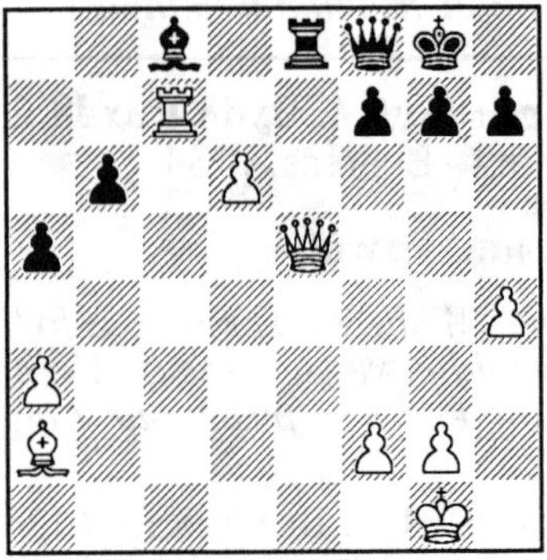

White to move

294.

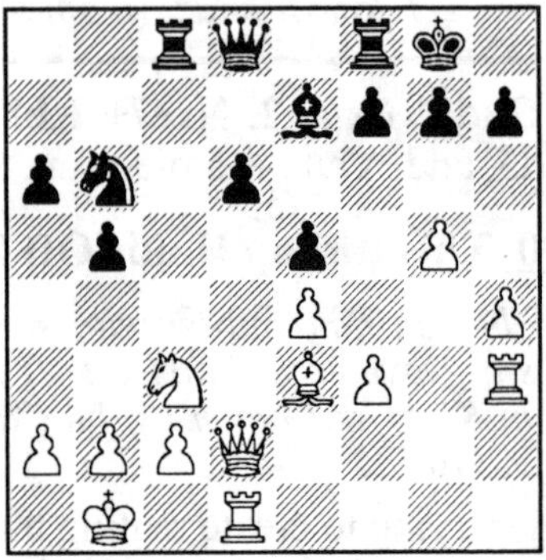

White to move

295.

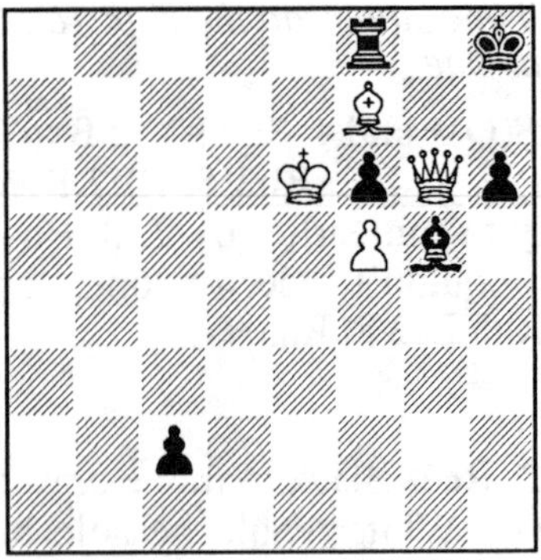

White to move

296.

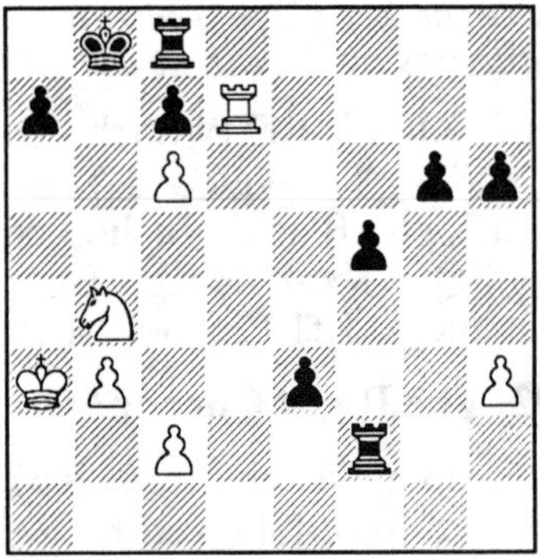

White to move

293. **Cutting the Gordian Knot**

1. Qxe8! (1. Rxf7? Rxe5 2. Rf6+ Be6 -+) **1. ... Qxe8 2. Bxf7+ Qxf7 3. Rxc8+ Qf8 4. d7! 1-0.** (Filip - Urbanek, 1955)

294. **Good Knight, Bad Bishop**

> A Knight in the center on the 5th rank,
> supported by a pawn — if it can't be driven
> away by a pawn, or exchanged — is equal to a Rook.

1. Bxb6! Qxb6 2. Nd5, with a big advantage for White. Often in such positions, the stronger side forces, and wins, the ending. In this game, however, the future 11th World Champion preferred to go for an attack, and won handsomely. (Fischer - Bolbochan, 1962)

295. **Find a Win or Die**

1. Bg8! Rxg8 2. Kf7 Rxg6 3. hxg6 c1(Q) 4. g7+ Kh7 5. g8(Q)#. (from a study by Em. Lasker, 1895)

296. **Deadly Little Threats**

White's outnumbered forces manage to create deadly — and winning — threats.

1. Na6+ Ka8 2. Nxc7+ Kb8 (2. ... Rxc7 3. Rd8+) **3. Na6+ Ka8 4. Rb7!**, and there is no defense against 5. Rb8+ and 6. Nc7#. (Janowsky - NN, 1900)

297.

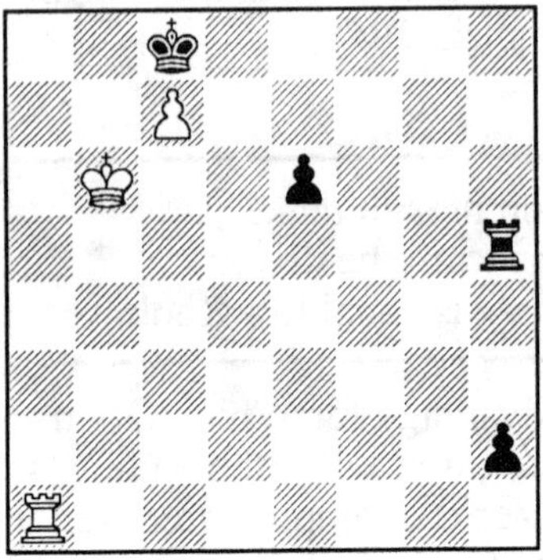

Black to move

298.

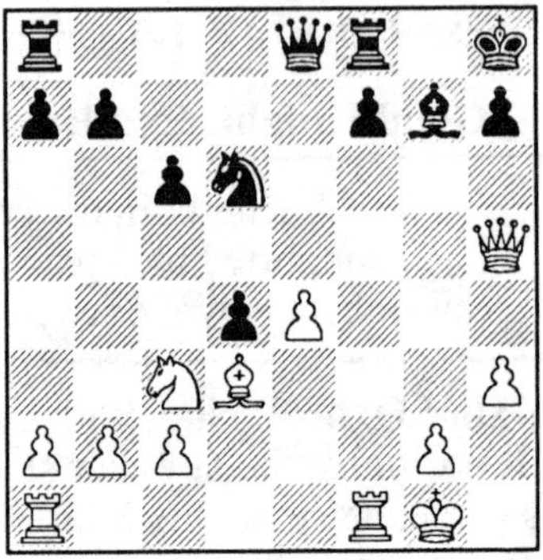

White to move

299.

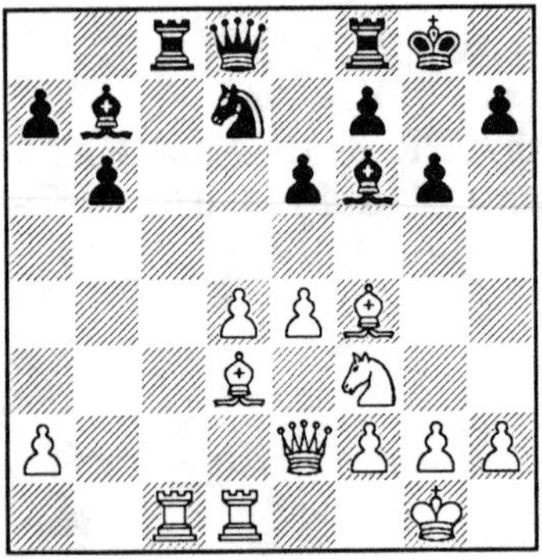

White to move

300.

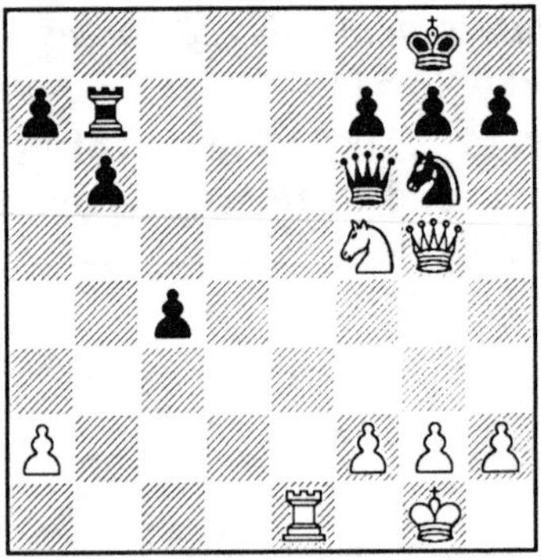

White to move

297. **Sometimes A Queen is Too Much**

1. ... h1(B)! (not 1. ... h1(Q)? 2. Ra8+ Qxa8 stalemate) **2. Rf1 Rh8 3. Rf7 Re8 4. Kc5 e5 5. Kd6 Bb7 0-1**. (Kholmov - Ehlvest, 1983)

298. **Fischer's Iron Grip**

The attractive 1. e5 can be met by 1. ... f5! Even an occasional grandmaster could fall into this trap — but not Bobby Fischer!

1. Rf6! Kg8 2. e5 h6 3. Ne2 1-0. (Fischer - Benko, 1963/64)

299. **Struggle for the File**

> To conquer the file, take control of its back square.
>
> — *Eugene Ruban*

1. Ba6! Bxa6 2. Qxa6 Rxc1 3. Rxc1 Qa8 4. Bd6 Rd8 5. e5! Bg7 6. Rc7. With simple, natural moves White has achieved an overwhelming position. (Geller - Simagin, 1951)

300. **Three Steps to Victory**

1.Re8+ Nf8 2. Nh6+! Qxh6 3. Rxf8+! Kxf8 4. Qd8#. (Alekhine - Friman, 1924)

Index of Games

(Numbers at far right refer to pages.)

Index of Themes

(Numbers refer to positions.)

Executive Editor
Al Lawrence

Author and co-author of eight books on a variety of subjects, Al Lawrence edited and designed *Chess Training Pocket Book* with the goal of making it a pleasure to get the most out of the uniquely instructive ideas of GM Lev Alburt. And to help you win more games!

Lawrence served as Executive Director of the US Chess Federation from 1988 to 1996, a period of innovation and sustained, record-breaking growth. A former public school and college teacher with advanced degrees in instructional techniques, he is especially interested in applying modern teaching theory to chess.

He is president of OutExcel! Corporation, a marketing and publishing firm, where he can be contacted by Email at outexcel@aol.com. He is also Chief Executive Officer of StarFinder, Inc., which develops and patents products that make it easy for amateur stargazers to enjoy observing the night sky. StarFinder's "Night Navigator" has been featured internationally in magazines and on television.

Lawrence is a consulting partner in one of the most popular chess websites—www.chesscafe.com. Chesscafe offers book reviews, photos, chess want ads, and articles by leading chess thinkers from around the world.

Just the Facts : Winning Endgame Knowledge in One Volume
Completes the Course!

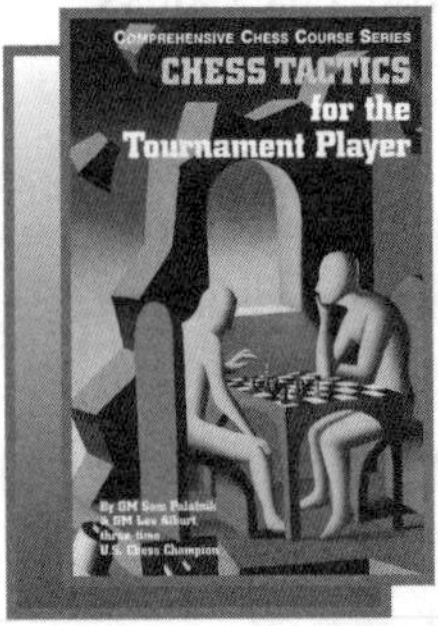

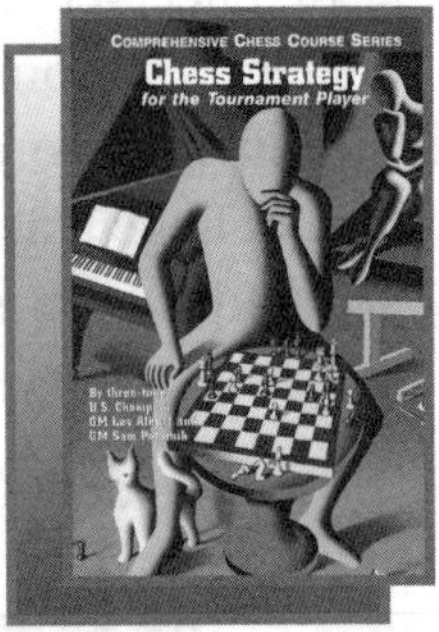

Turn to page 188.

GM Lev Alburt's *Comprehensive Chess Course* Is Now Complete!

It's easy to order any or all
of the seven books in this best-selling
course—even to get
autographed copies!
Just use the order form on the next page.